no ordinary move

a memoir

no ordinary move

Linda Bidabe with Chris Voll

THE PLOUGH PUBLISHING HOUSE

Address all inquiries to: The Plough Publishing House, Route 381 North, Farmington, PA 15437 USA.

In the interest of privacy, the names and/or physical attributes of several people portrayed in this book have been altered.

08 07 06 05 04 03 02 01   10 9 8 7 6 5 4 3 2 1

A catalog record for this book is available from the British Library.

Library of Congress Cataloging-in-Publication Data

Bidabe, Linda, 1945–
  No ordinary move : a memoir / Linda Bidabe with Chris Voll.
    p. cm.
  ISBN 0-87486-915-3 (Hardcover : alk. paper)
  1. Bidabe, Linda, 1945– 2. Teachers of handicapped children–United States–Biography. 3. Handicapped children–Education–United States.
  I. Voll, Chris, 1976– II. Title.
  LC4019 .B53 2001
  371.9'092–dc21   2001002300

Printed in the USA

For Mama and Tanya, my bookends

A bird does not sing
because it has an answer;
it sings because it has a song.

Chinese proverb

gifts

The longest and hardest walk of my life was across a frozen playground to hand someone something I didn't need. It happened on the last day of school in December 1951, the winter I was six. It happened yesterday...

In just a few minutes Miss White will clap her hands and dismiss class, and we'll all scramble into our wraps, shout our good-byes, and traipse out of our three-room schoolhouse into the Kansas cold, and Christmas vacation will begin. I will wait for my older brother, Allen, to extract himself from his knot of buddies, and the two of us will wait for Daddy to pull up in our red Chevy. Then we'll ride the mile home through Lowell's unpaved streets, frozen and spackled smooth in powdered white; past the white backyards of white clapboard houses, past Ball's grocery store and onto our road. Past pastures with snow glossing barbwire fences, glutting into ditches.

The snow under the tires will squeak like loose floorboards when we turn onto the gravel of our driveway. The front walk will be swept and clean. Wood smoke will be lulling around the chimney. At the back of the house, the cows, inert, will be clustered near the barn. The wind off the river will rasp against the freeze-dried bulrushes down in the cow pond. It will bite at my ankles and scrawny wrists when I step from the car, making me dash to reach the house first. In a few minutes —

But first we have to finish our Coca-Cola bottle vases. They are gifts for our parents, and I have painted mine in bright reds and greens and splashes of purple. The colors run down the glass bottle in trails, like wax drippings. It's done, and I think it's pretty, more or less. I take a square of tissue paper and stand the bottle in its center, then scrunch the tissue around it and loop a ribbon at its neck, tying a loose bow. I push the wrapped bottle to the far edge of my desk and lean back to take a discerning look at the overall effect. Squinting, I see my vase perched on our mantelpiece, full of the first yellow and white daffodils of spring, and Mama stepping back to admire the bouquet. I catch her smiling at me. It's not bad, as far as gifts go, I decide — a nice complement to the other things for my parents I've got stashed away in the chest of drawers in my bedroom. All I have to do now is sit and wait for school to be over.

At the back of the classroom the boys are restless. They are big, rowdy boys, third graders, and I watch them quietly, peripherally, so they won't notice. Freedom drifts outside the windows, and release is moments away. The Coca-Cola bottle diversion is wearing as thin as the ice along the banks of Shoal Creek down behind the schoolyard hill. Buster Hopkins, though, is still working. He cradles his vase in both hands, holding it up so the afternoon light from the window behind him can strain through the painted glass. Even from my seat near the front of the room I can tell his bottle is a work of art, a small masterpiece. Buster, shy and quiet, grins gently at it, and begins on the wrapping. He creases his square of tissue paper diagonally in half, then in half again, opens it, and sets the bottle on the crease marks, centered exactly. Gingerly he pulls the sides up, pleating the tissue against the bottle's contours. He fashions his ribbon bow. It takes several attempts before he's satisfied the loops are symmetrical and in balance. Then he picks up scissors, purses his lips, and draws the ribbon ends across the open scissor blade. The ribbon corkscrews into perfect curlicues. The lines on Buster's fore-head relax. He grins again, and it's clear everything has worked out the way he had in mind.

Buster is in the second grade, but he and I have known each other for a while, ever since I learned the reading secret. I hadn't been at school more than a few weeks before Miss White started us first graders on our phonics lessons. The day she put the word "at" on the felt board and then went on to stick a "b" in front of it, a crack opened for me in the heavens and the first rays of comprehension slid through. By the time we finished c-a-t, m-a-t, f-a-t, and h-a-t, a regular hallelujah chorus resounded in my ears. I had been let in! Buster wanted in on that secret in the worst way, too, but the letters never stayed still long enough for him to pin down their sounds. I wanted to help him; it just didn't seem fair that some people might miss out on all that went on inside books. Besides, I thought Buster deserved a chance. He was slow and fat — an easy target for ridicule. Sometimes, for fun, the other boys lured him into the girls' bath-room and then climbed out of the window, leaving Buster to be "discovered" and turned in by a girl who'd been tipped off. Or they'd coax him down the forbidden bank, down to the edge of Shoal Creek, where they'd abandon him and scramble back up to tattle on him. He had no friends. I was not his friend; I was his teacher, on a self-appointed mission. My work of mercy had left me vulnerable. *Linda's Buster's girlfriend! Linda's Buster's girlfriend! Linda and Buster sitting in a tree, k-i-s-s-i-n-g.* But I gritted my teeth (the ones that weren't wiggly) and stuck to helping Buster unravel the mys-teries of Dick, Jane, and Spot. It was tough going, like trying to channel a heifer through a narrow gate, but we made headway.

He fingers the curlicues of ribbon, still smiling to himself. I turn back to face Miss White's desk. There is a crash at the back of the room and a loud groan, and I whip back around. Jimmy Sikes, a smoothly handsome know-it-all in the seat behind Buster's, is glar-ing at the pieces of broken bottle on the floor by his desk. He doesn't glare for long. Teacher, it was Buster! Buster bumped me. He went and shoved me, and my bottle broke. He done it on purpose, Teacher, I know he did.

Jimmy Sikes is glaring at Buster now. Miss White summons Buster to come forward. He shuffles to the front of the room, eyes low. She sighs (hands on hips) as she asks him if he broke Jimmy's bottle. No, he says. Jimmy dropped it. Did anyone else see what happened? Stanley Gipson, another of the big boys who delights in making Buster's life hell, stands up. Yes, Miss. Buster done it, Miss.

Miss White lectures Buster about responsibility and honesty. She tells him there is only one thing for him to do: he must return to his seat and hand over his bottle to Jimmy. From the back of the room, Jimmy snickers. Miss White does not know (or does she?) that Buster's vase is the only gift he has to give his parents. She has not watched (as I have) the lines on Buster's forehead, the purse of his lips; did not see him wince the time his bottle rolled too near the edge of his desk, or notice his contented smile when the last curlicue was laid to rest against the crisp tissue paper. She sees only the shards of glass around Jimmy's desk, and a hapless boy standing before her, guilty as charged. Give Jimmy your bottle, Buster. Now.

And then she claps her hands, like a magician – and we are free. Class Dismissed. Happy Holidays. Merry Christmas. The big boys elbow their way to the front of the line, jousting to be the first out the door. I see Buster hunch into his frayed car coat and walk slump-shouldered out the door behind them, his hands thrust deep into the pockets of his jeans. He has nearly a mile of frozen road to cover before he reaches his family's acres on Lowell's outer edge, and he is heading for home with splinters of glass lancing his heart.

The big boys are out, and the classroom squirms; the rest of us are anxious to leave. I am anxious to do something about the lump in my throat. I clutch my Coca-Cola bottle as I cross the slick play-ground. I can smell the snow in the air. The little blond hairs along my arms snap to attention in the biting cold. Buster, wait. Wait up. He's almost across the playground and doesn't hear me. I don't want anyone to notice me, don't want to yell. But I do. Buster! He turns, brushes a hand across his eyes, snuffles once, stops. For you, Buster, I say, holding out my bottle. Yours was nicer, but you can have this one, if you want. He takes it in both hands. Merry Christmas, Buster, I whisper. I cringe and wait for the expected jeers and laughter from the third grade mafia. But there is nothing, only silence. I hurry back across the playground and reenter the school to grab my coat. It's going to be okay. I can explain it to Mama. She'll understand. She's *got* to understand. Where's Allen? Where's Daddy? Let's get home. It's Christmas.

Half a century later, I have not forgotten that incident nor ever truly recovered from it. Undoubtedly, it was a small thing, transacted between small minds at a small place in a small time. Yet it was large enough to start me thinking, and to change me.

Which is why, when Tanya, my twenty-seven-year-old daughter, gave me an antique Coca-Cola bottle as a gift for Mother's Day 2000, I was caught off guard. I unwrapped it, and started crying. Tanya and I have always shared an understanding that the best gifts mean something. Okay gifts are ones you dart into the mall for, last-minute, and then wait until the party's in full swing before handing over as nonchalantly as possible (with the receipt sneakily tucked inside the card, just in case). A gift that means something, on the other hand, takes thought and work — hunting to find it, maybe, or time invested making it. The best kind of gift need only make sense to the giver and the getter, a sort of secret message coded and decoded, not meant for public knowledge.

Tanya's Coca-Cola bottle was this best kind of gift, and I wasn't ready for it. Today, though, it stands on the tall illuminated shelf in my living room, right next to the gold crocodile nutcracker we lugged back from Australia. They share space with a framed picture of Tanya on the day she won the Stampede Days Rodeo Queen contest in high school, two of her gold medallions from jumping championships, and the tiny leather cowboy boots she wore when she was two. The shelf is weighted with memories. And today I have decided to look back, ready or not.

By the time my superintendent cornered me at a parent-teacher barbecue and demanded answers, things had already gone pretty far. It was the summer of 1986 and I was experimenting with the children in my classroom. Again. There was no hiding it – the results could be seen by anyone walking into our center – and the word was most definitely out. Parents were talking, and some were getting bent out of shape. And now Dr. Kelly F. Blanton, Superintendent of Schools for Kern County, California, wanted an explanation. So I took a deep breath and told him my side of the story.

In more than sixteen years as a teacher in Bakersfield, working with children with disabilities, I had learned a few things myself. It hadn't taken me long in special education to come to the sobering conclusion that we were missing some vital clues, that none of us really knew how to help children with really complex disabilities. Often it felt like we were trying to work a zillion-piece jigsaw puzzle. The pieces were laid out for us, but they were all cardboard side up – which didn't actually make much difference because, most of the time, we were working blindfolded. We were doing a decent job with children who could walk and talk, but we seemed powerless to prevent the nonverbal, non-ambulatory children from withering away. We were supposed to be teachers, but we weren't educating these children; at best, we were running a hospital day care, a place where parents could deposit their children into beanbag chairs on their way to work and return in the afternoon to find them no worse for wear. No one could say we weren't trying. We were. Busting our butts, in fact. Most of the time, though, I felt more like a nurse than a teacher. I drove to school each morning to spend my day feeding, changing, bathing, soothing, holding, suctioning, carrying, lifting, even wearing children with profound disabilities. I was tired. All of us were tired: my colleagues, our students, their parents. Every day we went out and fought our little lopsided skirmishes against relentless enemies with names like hydrocephaly, cerebral palsy, and muscular dystrophy, and at the end of every day we found ourselves shaking our heads, and, often, our fists. Sometimes on the way home I punished my forehead with my knuckles, or with my palm, depending on the traffic. Something had to give, I knew. Something other than my forehead.

That's why I began collecting information and making observations, doing a few studies on the side. Then, together with my colleagues, I began experimenting, trying new ideas. Why not? We had nothing to lose. Still, we often found ourselves caught between the gears of conventional wisdom – the "wisdom" that said most of our students would die before they ever sat, stood, or walked on their own – and the gears did their best to make mincemeat of our enthusiasm for our profession.

I decided I was through with being someone else's hamburger patty, and tried harder.

Success came slowly; sometimes it went unrecognized, the increments were so small. But the parents noticed. We developed a toilet training program, one that worked (*everyone* got excited about that one, believe me), and then a feeding program and a communication program.

By the time Dr. Blanton stopped me at the barbecue we had seen some really exciting developments: students who had spent their entire lives sunk into giant beanbags that conformed to their twisted bodies had developed sitting skills and could remain in normal classroom chairs without needing to be strapped in place. Others had progressed enough to be on their feet and standing, even if they needed the help of special standers designed to hold them upright without requiring their legs to bear weight. And – most incredible of all – we had students who had learned to walk, one laborious step at a time. We held their arms, helped them balance; we rigged walkers for them to provide added stability. We kissed conventional wisdom good-bye and did whatever it took. For the first time in our lives, we were conquering enemy territory on an almost daily basis. The war of attrition was ending.

With a system in place for the students in our care, we were now running a pilot program. People in education pay attention to programs, that much I knew.

Parents pay attention, too. The barbecue thing was a setup. They invited Dr. Blanton and me into an ambush. Why weren't their kids in my program? these parents wanted to know. Why did José deserve a slot in my classroom, when his prognosis was far bleaker than Bobby's? I nearly choked. Hamburger again.

Afterward, when he asked, I told Dr. Blanton I had data that validated what I was doing.

I'm confident, Linda, that you will have that data analyzed and on my desk by eight o'clock tomorrow morning, he told me.

I stayed up all night, but the facts were on Dr. Blanton's desk when he walked into his office the next morning.

And that (more or less) is how I got to tell my Coca-Cola bottle story to the Rotary Club of San Luis Obispo. Dr. Blanton reviewed my report and knew we had a winner; he was that kind of man. How are we going to go about expanding this beyond the pilot program? he wanted to know. We really can't run it anywhere else until it's been documented. You need to write it down.

That's no problem, I assured him, except for just one little four-letter snag. Time.

Applying for a Rotary International Scholarship was Dr. Blanton's brainwave. If I received the grant, it would provide me with the funds to take a year's sabbatical and concentrate on developing the program.

It sounded like a grand idea – until I stopped long enough to consider my chances. Mine would be one of a myriad other presentations, and the competition included some of the nation's top scholars and brightest minds. Moreover, the broad parameters for applying hardly worked in my favor: the only requirement was that the scholarship be used to further goodwill in a foreign country (words to that effect), and that the recipient not be employed during his or her time abroad. But we went ahead and submitted my application, and Dr. Blanton and his wife, Yvonne, drove me west out of Bakersfield to San Luis Obispo, where I was to face a panel of Rotarians and make my presentation. All the while, I considered my chances slimmer than a snowball's in hell.

I gave them my best rendition of *Buster Hopkins and the Coca-Cola Bottle*. They'd asked for it…

When I am done, the only sound in the room is the purr of the air conditioner. I pause, then wrap up: The day I walked across that playground, I was timid and unsure of myself, like Buster. The gift, the sharing, was only important to Buster and me, and only during that one small window in time. But the gift made a difference. I helped him, and looking back, I'm glad I did. There are a lot of Busters out there. I work with them every day. My children aren't dyslexic. They're not targets for bullies. But they know all too well what it's like to be sidelined, to be shunted to the margins and told (even if words are never used) that they will never amount to anything, that they will never make a positive contribution. That they are, in essence, a waste of other people's time, energy, and (the big one) money.

I don't buy that, I tell the Rotarians, not for a minute. If there's one thing I've learned it's that every child in our care can learn, provided we find a way to teach them. Buster needed a Coca-Cola bottle, and I had one to give him. I knew what to do, and I had the resources to help him. For right then, I was his friend. Right now, I need you to be my friends. I'm asking you to come walk across another playground — one where children never run and play, because they can't. One where crying is heard more than laughter; where hopelessness casts its shadow every day. I know some of what my children need — and what I don't know, they're teaching me. What I don't have are the time and means to carry out the research required to put down in writing what I've learned. We've been successful but, as Dr. Blanton says, none of it exists until it's on paper. We need to provide a road map so that our work can be replicated. I know all of you can sit, stand, and walk. You don't need my program, just as I don't need it. But just for today, I'm asking you to be my friends. I need a few more Coca-Cola bottles. I'm asking you to walk toward me. Please.

This time the purr of the air conditioner is joined by the discreet rustle of crumpling Kleenex.

When I'd filled out the scholarship application, I'd listed three travel destinations, as instructed. So when word of my selection arrived from the Rotary, I informed Dr. Blanton that the only place I could possibly find the concentration I was going to need for this undertaking was Sydney, Australia — my first choice. He understood me perfectly. Not long after that, twelve-year-old Tanya and I boarded a plane from Bakersfield to Los Angeles, where we would catch our Qantas flight. We were taking our first bold steps out of the desert.

The crocodile nutcracker came home with us from Australia. I couldn't help it. Like the Coca-Cola bottle, it was Tanya's idea. Tanya loves antiques. Primitives, she calls them. Some thirteen years after our return from Sydney, she and her newlywed husband, Gaines, were prowling the Red River Flea Market in their chosen hometown of Judsonia, Arkansas. They stopped at a collector's booth specializing in Coca-Cola memorabilia. Tanya and the woman running the booth got to talking, as they say, and in the course of conversation my daughter related my Buster Hopkins story. The woman cried. She made Tanya and Gaines wait while she went home and fetched the Coca-Cola bottle, which she then sold to Tanya at a heartfelt discount. Your mom has to have this, she said...

I decided to keep my Mother's Day bottle on the shelf beside the crocodile because you never know when you're going to have a tough nut to crack, or when you'll be needing an empty Coca-Cola bottle. You have to be ready.

Today, I take it down and look at it again. It has Jackson Tenn on it in raised letters. The green-tinted glass is not perfect. There are air bubbles trapped inside. Air from 1917, the year the bottle was made. The year my daddy was born.

The best gifts are the ones you're not ready for.

I'm ready now, I think.

i n t i m a t i o n s

In another life, I follow my childhood dream and become a doctor. I ace my way through med school and go on to have a beautiful career. My patients love me. I am doing this for them, for the love of all humanity, and they rally around me. Together we change things, make things okay. In my other life there are only happy endings, and everyone has a chance to heal.

There is only this life.

Even so, the urge to rescue has always been with me. Certainly by the time my sister Minta arrived July 14, 1952, it had become a part of who I am. I was just two weeks shy of my seventh birthday when Daddy drove Allen and me up to the northeast corner of Kansas and left us with his parents, Grandma Dora and Grandpa Charlie McPherson. We stayed at their farm in Tonganoxie – Tongie to the locals – for two weeks while Mama recouped. Daddy had told us beforehand that we would be getting a baby sister, but I hadn't quite cottoned on to how these things work. I envisioned Minta coming in a box, with wrapping paper and a fancy bow, the way my Terri Lee doll had arrived. I liked the thought of being an older sister, and I liked staying at Grandma and Grandpa's farm. It gave me a new world to explore.

The first visit to Grandpa and Grandma's I remember took place when I was three years old. Mama has photographs from that time and they have taken on memories of their own, to the point where I can no longer be sure what I really recall and what I have fabricated over the years of looking at those grainy sepia prints. Maybe it all happened the way I picture it. Or maybe it didn't.

I know I didn't invent Grandma's crippled rooster. Among her many chickens, this one stood out. It had something wrong with its foot. I could easily catch it, and it accompanied me everywhere around the farm, tucked under my arm. We held long conversations and hated being parted for meals; the rooster was not allowed in the kitchen. I remember sitting outside the house, perched on the mound over the root cellar, the sun in my face. There were chips of limestone scattered in the grass and if I tapped two pieces together, they crumbled into fine yellow powder, like the cornmeal Grandma kept in a kitchen canister. When I sifted the dust through my fingers, the sunlight transformed it to gold before it settled around my feet. I spent hours pulverizing stones. My rooster would scrunch his bad leg up under himself and stay near me, his head bobbing in time with my pounding. If he tried to wander off, I scooped him up again and plunked him into my lap. We were happy then.

The next time we stayed at Grandpa's farm, my rooster was nowhere to be found. No one seemed to know what I was talking about when I asked after him. Only later, when I had grown up enough to know it's never wise to get personal with a chicken, did they tell me that my rooster had been the Sunday dinner centerpiece the last day of our visit.

Like our farm, Grandpa's sat at the end of a road, a graveled lane that cut through the pastures where his Guernsey herd browsed. It ran up the hill past the cow pond and the barn with its corrugated tin roof sagging like an old sow's back, past the well halfway up the hill, and emptied abruptly into the hard dirt dooryard outside the two-story farmhouse.

Grandma and Grandpa McPherson, with Grandpa's sister
Tillie (smiling), outside their Tonganoxie home. The elephant
is behind them, in the living room.

The house: a kitchen and living room downstairs, and upstairs, up those ever-so-tiny, ever-so-steep stairs (a ladder, almost), two bedrooms. Off to the left of the living room, on stilts, was the screened-in porch. Years ago, when Grandpa had first bought the farm, he'd hired his brother-in-law Will, a would-be carpenter, to help him fix up the place. Will was young in years and new to his craft. He went to work on the porch. When he finished, the floorboards sloped away from the house at such an angle, no one could set anything down on the porch table without worrying about it sliding off. But the slope came in handy when, in the summer, the porch was used for baths. Once a week when my daddy was a boy, Grandma heated enough water on her wood stove to half fill the metal washtub. Everyone took a turn getting clean. Grandma poured a little fresh hot water into the tub after each bath. When the family had scrubbed, she tipped the water out onto the porch. It ran off in a slick sheet. The porch was the one improvement Grandpa had contributed to the house, and he was considerably proud of it, in spite of the teasing about the slope, and in spite of the ivy that had run riot, so that stringy tentacles strangled every corner post.

To the right of the house the ground bulged gently above the root cellar. It must have been dug by the man who built the house, otherwise I doubt it would have been there at all; Grandpa had a thing about cellars. The door leading into the cellar was built at an angle into the back of the mound, but I never opened it. There were spiders in the cellar. Big, black spiders that looked after the dark and sometimes scuttled into my dreams, especially my nightmares about Uncle Freddie.

There were spiders in the outhouse, too, set behind the root cellar in back of the house, but I didn't have much choice about going in there. It was a bona fide two-holer. Sometimes when I sat worrying that some hoary spider might attempt to pilfer a piece of my bare behind, I would force myself to ponder the conundrum of the extra hole. Why was it there, gaping like an open maw right beside me?

So far as I knew, no one ever went tandem. Was it in case of emergency? Or for status?

The outhouse – with its stacks of Sears, Roebuck & Co. catalogs and the requisite bag of lime (pour one heaping scoop down hole of choice after each use) – was eternal. Eventually electric lights would replace kerosene lanterns in the house, and a hand pump attached to a rainwater cistern would save numerous trips to the well. But the outhouse remained.

Skirting the yard in front of the house were two chicken coops, one old and decrepit, bleached white by generations of defecating hens, the other newer, built when my daddy was young and the hens had been his responsibility. On his way to school each morning, he'd carried a dozen or more eggs to the Tongie store; the egg money paid his school expenses. Now the store sent a driver to collect the eggs twice a week. These chickens were Grandma's, forty or so white layers and the occasional rooster. At noon each day – no earlier, and no later – she let them out into the sunlit yard to fret and strut. She shooed them in each evening while she still had enough light to sweep the yard clean. Her straw broom whisked whorled patterns in the dust. No one would ever accuse her of having chicken poop on her doorsill.

Grandma always wore an apron while she worked. She sewed her aprons from chicken feed sacks. From the very best sacks she made her dresses. When her clothes wore out, she tore them into strips, got out her carpet needles, and crocheted the strips into oval rugs. The sacks were made of cotton and could be ordered by pattern – pretty floral prints, stripes, geometric designs. Grandma's apron hung around her neck and covered the length of her dress, the bottom hem sweeping the ground when she leaned forward. She spent her days draped in flowers. Grandpa wore overalls all day long, the same pair, every day. They were seldom washed since washing anything involved hauling water. At lunchtime Grandpa would come into the kitchen, take off his overalls and hang them on their special peg behind the door, and sit down at the table in jeans and a long-sleeved shirt. The pungent smell of cow manure, laced with the syrupy smell of warm milk, graced each meal.

Between his cows and her hens, Grandpa and Grandma kept the farm ticking and paid their few bills. It was a balancing act they'd been practicing for years, with varying success.

At our home, I never had much to do with chickens, though I occasionally helped my brother scatter feed in the yard. I stayed out of the henhouse. It was Mama's business. She tended the chickens and collected their eggs for our own use. (At Daddy's insistence, she was required to be home at precisely noon each day, to let the chickens out of their coop for their daily constitutional. Mama never could see how the exact timing made much difference, but Daddy seemed to think it did, so there was no sense arguing.) Grandma, though, enlisted my help the day Allen and I arrived for our two-week stay in Tongie. She took me with her at gathering time. Inside the hen houses, dust motes swooned in air thick with the stench of ammonia and the lesser smells of molding feathers and mildewed wood. I tried holding my breath, with no luck. Grandma showed me how to slide a hand under a nesting hen and find the egg. She swept her right hand beneath the bird, ignoring its crotchety pecks at her wrist, fished out the egg, and placed it carefully in her apron, held up like a sling by her left hand. We moved to the next nest box and Grandma invited me to try it. No way, not with that hen sitting there, its eyes blinking open and shut from the bottom up, taunting me to stick my hand within range of its razor-sharp beak. Grandma pried the hen away, and only then did I reach in – I had to stand on tiptoe to see what I was doing – and pick up the warm, white egg. It filled my cupped hand. I added it to the egg in Grandma's apron. We moved from nest box to nest box, she evicting hens and I gathering their eggs. Near the rear of the coop, one hen stood on the dirt floor ruffling out its feathers and *pwawk-pwawking* nervously. Grandma glanced at it, then at its empty nest box. She untied her apron and took it off,

Someone has to feed Grandma's chickens – it's just too
bad Allen can't handle it by himself.

setting it where the eggs inside its folds would be out of harm's way. I watched Grandma stride over to the ruffled hen and peer into the nest box. Her hand shot forward and snapped back clutching a black snake. Grandma had it by the tail. It writhed furiously, but she whirled it around her head and cracked it like a whip. I heard the snap its body made as it recoiled. Grandma took the snake outside and pounded its head against a post, but it was quite dead by then. I knew the snake was harmless, merely an egg thief — Grandma would never have picked it up had it been poisonous — but my fear of the hen house was now (so far as I was concerned) fully justified. It would not be undone, at least not on that visit to Tongie.

A few mornings after the snake episode, I walked out of the house and discovered an overturned bushel basket sitting off to one side of the yard. Grandma saw me approaching it and came running over to save me from a heart attack. There's a snake under there, she warned, a rattlesnake. It can't hurt you, it's dead, but don't you go touching it, because the fangs might still have their poison in them. Let me show it to you.

I stepped backward as Grandma lifted the basket. The snake, minus head, was twisted around on itself, its underbelly bright in the sunlight. Its head lay a few inches away. Not far enough away, I thought. I had heard that if you didn't put sufficient distance between the head of a snake and its body, it could get back together again and be just as dangerous as it was before, maybe even a bit more. I told Grandma as much. She gave my hand a squeeze, then got a spade and transported the head to the far side of the yard. I felt safer. Grandma came back over to the rest of the snake. She had a kitchen knife in her hand. She slashed off the snake's rattles, shook them playfully, and handed them to me. Unsure, I took them, and looked back at the snake, now missing both ends. When Grandpa gets back, he'll take care of it, Grandma assured me, setting the basket back in place.

For the rest of the morning, I steered clear of that basket and did my best not to think about the snake lying there a few yards away from its own head, but totally unable to do anything about it. Death could be so certain, and a matter of inches.

Grandma's snake killings left me somewhat unglued in other ways too. We were women, Grandma and me, and women just didn't act that way. Mama certainly never killed snakes. Once we'd found a snake in a bucket of eggs at home, and Mama had screamed and called for Allen or Daddy to come and deal with it. Snakes were a man's job. What business, then, did Grandma have doing things like that? I couldn't figure it out. Here were the two strongest women I knew, Mama and Grandma, but they could behave so differently. Maybe, I thought later, maybe that's okay. Maybe it's like families. There had been a time when I thought every family was like ours: a daddy, a mama, a brother (Allen), and a sister (me). I'd had to scrap that theory after we became friends with a family that had two sisters and no brother, and no dog either; they were a cat family. Life, I was beginning to realize, came down to science – you spent a lot of time readjusting hypotheses, or dismissing bogus ideas outright.

Grandma's rattlesnake rattles stayed with me for years, a plaything, or talisman.

The day came for our parents to come and collect us, and none too soon. Allen, by then desperately homesick, went outside early to wait. He sat in the lane, its dust turned to goo from the night's rain, most of the morning. I, on the other hand, skipped out of the farmhouse kitchen in my cotton sundress and sandals, with my doll, Terri Lee, riding my arm. I crossed the yard in front of Grandma's chicken coop, sidestepped my brother, and headed down the lane to Grandpa's barn, where he would be finishing up the milking.

Halfway down the hill the well sat off to the right. It had been dug by hand and lined with large stones. A wooden windlass straddled the well, and a rope with a galvanized tin pail attached to its end was wrapped around the crossbar. Beneath the windlass, a wooden cover kept debris from falling into the well. Grandma was the water carrier. At milking time, she went to the barn to help Grandpa, then fetched water on her way back up the hill. I liked to watch her lift the cover off the well and let the pail and rope free-fall to the water deep in the ground. The splash as the pail hit echoed up the well. There was a thin string tied to the lip of the pail, and when Grandma pulled it, the pail dipped into the water and filled. Then she cranked the rope up again and tipped the water into her hauling pails. She hauled two pails back to the house each trip. Watching her struggle up the lane, I wished I could help her. But there were few pails at Grandpa's farm that I could lift empty, let alone filled with water. Most of the pails had leaked at one time or another, and Grandpa had a cure for pails with leaky bottoms: cement. I knew, too, that even if I were strong enough, Grandpa wouldn't allow me to help. In spite of the wooden cover, he insisted I stay clear of the well altogether; it was too dangerous, he said.

When Allen and I had first arrived, Grandpa had walked with me down the lane and right up to the well. He set aside the cover and held me over the well's edge so I could see down inside it. The cool, damp air turned my face clammy. Grandpa showed me how the windlass worked, and let me help him crank up a full pail of water. He explained away all my curiosity, and spoke in stern tones of the well's dangers. Then he made me practice crossing to the far side of the lane to walk past the well.

Grandpa always worried. There was a certain sadness that seemed to cling to him. It had been a part of him for as long as I could remember, and I had come to accept it, the way I accepted his withered arm. Grandpa was seventeen the day he almost severed his left arm. He and his brothers had gone out hunting, and one of them had propped a shotgun against a barbwire fence while they all

crawled through. The shotgun fell over and went off. The charge
caught Grandpa in his arm, between his elbow and shoulder. After
that, the arm wasn't much use. His wrist hung limp. Though his
hand still worked, he had to use his shoulder muscles to raise his arm
before he could grasp anything. Milking was a chore, but he never
said a word about it. He kept his bad arm covered by the long-
sleeved shirts he always wore, even in July. It was a part of his private sadness, and no one else need interfere.

But it was not so much a cloud of gloom that veiled him as an
aura of penitence. I was first aware of it during the visit when I had
befriended the crippled rooster. We were getting into the car for a
run into town. Mama was driving and Grandpa was in the front
passenger's seat. I climbed in the back – it was a two-door car – and
stood holding on to the back of Grandpa's seat so I could see over
his shoulder and out the windshield. Back then, we never wore
seatbelts, and I always stood up to get the best view. Mama steered
the car out of the yard, swung it into the lane, and started down the
hill. Grandpa had not managed to close his door completely. He
reached out to grab the handle and, tiny thing that I was, I tumbled
right past him and out onto the gravel. I screamed. Mama hit the
brakes, stopped the car, and ran to me. She was panic-stricken.
Grandpa was too. The gravel had burned and scraped me up a bit,
but I was basically okay. Mama took me back to the house to get
patched back together. Her lips were set as she cleaned the blood
and grit from my knees, rubbed Merthiolate into my grated skin,
and slapped on Band-Aids. Grandpa, beside himself, rubbed his
withered arm and looked at the floor. Mama let him have it with both
barrels. My cuts were stinging, more from the Merthiolate than the
abrasions, but I knew I wasn't hurt, just a bit banged up. And here
was Grandpa, who was old and was going to die one day, I knew,
and Mama laying into him for something he wasn't really to blame
for. I wasn't supposed to stand in the car, or lean around the front
seat like that. But Mama had been driving and she was horrified by
the *what ifs* of the situation, made worse because of the hell she

knew she'd catch if Daddy found out. So she turned on poor
Grandpa, who was as remorseful as she was terrified. And I was left
feeling just plain awful – especially when, after all that folderol, I
was not allowed to go with them into town. I felt sorry. Sorry for
myself, but also for Grandpa and the way he'd winced, as though
each of Mama's words had cut his flesh.

That would not be the last time I encountered Grandpa's contri-
tion. A year or so before Minta's birth, we'd paid a visit to Tongie,
and on that occasion I'd made the mistake of asking about Uncle
Freddie.

It would be years before I learned how Grandpa and Grandma
met as young folks in Tongie, where Grandma – Dora Papenhausen
then – taught at the one-room school; how Grandpa (his name was
Charles Emory McPherson, and he came from good Scottish stock),
the winter he first set his sights on that red-haired girl who still
spoke German to her immigrant parents, would roust himself extra
early and trudge to the schoolhouse to set the stove fire blazing so
the room would be warm and ready when Dora and the children
arrived; how they courted and loved and married, and how the dangling promise of farmland for the taking lured them westward.
Grandpa was born to farm. The smell of dirt never left him. He
loaded his young wife and their infant son into a covered wagon and
began the arduous trek to Colorado. There, he and Grandma har-
nessed themselves to a handful of acres and worked them like a pair
of crazed mules. Dirt farming, it was called – the chancy business
of making do and getting by. They were out to beat the odds, to
last out the years necessary to prove their homestead and take title of
the land.

They lived in the log cabin Grandpa built with axe and sledge,
had few neighbors, and stuck to their own affairs. When harvest
came, Grandma arranged her garden in rows of Mason jars. She
lined them three-deep on plank shelves in the root cellars Grandpa
had formed from natural caves near the house. Those dark, under-
ground places were the key to survival – their safeguard against

tornadoes and windstorms, and (on account of the provisions sealed in Grandma's jars) against the hollows in their winter stomachs. Along with the jars were piles of potatoes and carrots, and sauerkraut that farted joylessly in its tubs as it fermented.

Grandpa McPherson turned more than one cave on his homestead into a cellar, cutting down through the sod to gouge security from the hollow ground. When he had a hole dug deep and wide, he spanned it with thick beams, knocking them into place with a sledgehammer. Sunlight slanted through the beams and turned shadows into ribs on the opened earth; the thing took on a carcass look. Then, to finish the job, he laid boards across the beams, and mounded the excavated earth over.

There were the steps, too, of course. Leading down into the cellar through the square-cut door, they linked the dry, hot world above to the dank, cool world beneath. Grandpa set the steps in place before the big beams, before the dirt.

Grandpa's three-year-old son, Freddie, was with him on his last morning of cellar-building. Freddie trotted up and down the cellar steps, exploring the feel of temperature shifting against the skin on his bare arms. Grandpa, packing the dirt into place over the beams with the flat of his shovel, paused and straightened. The work was winding down, and he had done it well. He picked up his sledgehammer, hefting its dead weight, and tamped the head against a beam end. He swung one last time, for good luck. Too hard. The beam shifted – he never knew how – the earth moved, sifted, caved, rumbled, roared – sank down through the ribs, swallowed itself whole. Swallowed Freddie. Grandpa clawed in panic, fisting his way down through the broken soil, tore it back in handfuls, sobbing. By the time he reached Freddie his hands were a bloody pulp, his fingernails ground away. And Freddie was dead.

Grandpa never forgave himself. Never.

When he buried Freddie for the second (and last) time, he laid a piece of himself down in the grave as well. He snuffed out his little flame of self-worth and banked the fires of ambition that had called him west from his boyhood home. He was a man in ruins, with no means to convince himself of the possibility of resurrection. The farm would be sold and he and Grandma – four months pregnant with her second son, Clarence – would return to Tonganoxie, but Freddie was part of them now and wouldn't stay behind.

I didn't know any of that history the day I made my mistake and asked about Freddie. All I knew was that Uncle Freddie was the little boy in the large photograph mounted in the gilded frame above the overstuffed couch in Grandma and Grandpa's living room. His picture was always there, waiting for me every time we visited. But I was never supposed to acknowledge it, not even in whispers – those were Grandma's orders. Some things just were the way they were, and if you planned to survive in the McPherson clan, you learned in a hurry what those things were. Freddie could loom as large as an elephant sitting in the living room, and it made no difference. You tiptoed around the elephant.

Still, whenever I was there, I looked at Freddie. I couldn't help myself: he was hanging right there, staring out at me, and it seemed only polite to sneak a sideways glance at him every now and then, to let him know I cared. But he was so silent, so secret. The time came when I couldn't stand it any longer. I was alone in the living room with Grandpa and seized my chance:

Grandpa, what happened to Uncle Freddie?

Grandpa's face cracked. I felt my hand go to my mouth as I watched him disintegrate. He whimpered like a baby. It was a sound I will never forget. He was trying to tell me something, to make words, but they came out in garbled bubbles, as if he were talking under water. In the end, he gave up and broke down completely. Grandma rushed in to rescue him. She knew. No one had to tell her; one look at Grandpa, drowning, was all she needed.

I forgot, I told her later, lying.

Grandma knew I had not forgotten. Nobody forgets an elephant, ever. I paid royally for my mistake. And Grandpa, because he had blubbered and missed his chance, stayed in the shadows, the rough gray burden of his guilt still massed before him, impassable.

I could understand why Grandpa was anxious about me and the well. He needn't have worried though. Daddy had pulled a snake out of our own well once, and I was terrified of snakes; their only reason for being, as far as I could figure it, was to lie in wait and then slither out and scare you to death.

So now, on the last day of our visit, I crossed the lane to get away from the well. I picked my way through the dewy grass that bordered the road, placing one foot in front of the other tightrope style, because of the ditch. Ditches, I was sure, were where snakes liked to live. I had seen a snake or two in ditches alongside dirt roads in Lowell. The weed that clogged these ditches was known as snake weed. So, naturally, ditches were to be avoided. It made negotiating that bit of lane interesting: I didn't want any snakes jumping out and grabbing me from the ditch, but I didn't want to get too close to Grandpa's well either.

At the bottom of the hill the path to the barn forked off from the lane. The barn, like the well, was on the right. Grandpa had admonished me against ever coming down to the barn on my own; it was too dangerous, he insisted. With Grandpa McPherson, everything was dangerous. I wasn't alone – Terri Lee was with me – but nonetheless I did not veer to the right, choosing instead the narrow path that led off to the left, to the cow pond. I scanned the pond for turtles or other interesting things, but the pond was quiet except for the occasional bullfrog's belch. And then, as I watched, a snake slid away from the pond's bank. Its black body roped sibilantly over the water. The targeted frog never saw it coming. By the time it thought to kick up a fight, its back legs were already disappearing. Appalled, I bore witness to the frog's demise; I alone saw it catch in that snake's oily gullet, making it swell like a bloated bicycle tire. I was disgusted. Turning my back on the pond and the ballooning snake, I picked my way back onto the path – I wasn't about to step on any snakes – and raced for the barn.

Grandpa, intent on his milking, was squatting at a cow's udder as I rushed in. He was raising his bad left arm high to bring his hand into position for another downward pull on the teat when he heard me panting behind him. He got up off his one-legged milking stool and straightened himself, then set to telling me to stay away from the cows, to stay back by the door, to never come down to the barn on my own. I tried to tell him about the murder I'd just witnessed, but he missed my point completely. He just put his big hand on my scrawny shoulder and pointed me toward the house. You'd better go straight up there. Grandma will be worried for you.

On the path outside the barn was a frog, a common green pond frog. I looked down at it and thought, Oh my gosh, that snake is going to eat you too! A brief conference with Terri Lee left me with only one course of action. This was no time for squeamishness: peril lurked at the water's edge, and if there was any hope of a rescue, my usual disdain for creepy-crawlies would have to be shelved. I bent down and picked up the frog between two fingers. Together, Terri Lee and I carried the frog up the hill to the house. Near the door was the empty bushel basket that Grandma had used to cover the decapitated rattlesnake. I placed it in the shade and sat the frog down in it. The frog looked lonely.

Allen was still waiting in the lane. He had his head cocked to one side, listening for engine noises. I brought the bushel basket over to where he was sitting and got him to look at the frog. I explained about the snake and asked him to assist me in executing my evacuation scheme. Allen was a boy and I could count on him for this kind of thing. We spent the rest of the morning building a frog farm. As the collection of frogs inside the basket grew, a feeling of victory, of having accomplished something important, swept over me. I had cheated the snake! By now Allen and I had the bottom of the basket covered with frogs. They were crowding each other, standing on each other's backs and beginning to jump against the basket's wicker sides. I sat Terri Lee down among the frogs and charged her to host them graciously while Allen and I headed back to the pond for yet another load.

We were still collecting frogs when Daddy and Mama pulled in with baby Minta. Allen let out a whoop and ran for the car. I grabbed Terri Lee (the frogs could fend for themselves for a while) and headed after Mama into the house to get a good look at my sister. She was so new, so tiny, all bundled up in a blanket. All mine.

Of course Mama had to hear about how the snake had eaten the frog and how Allen and I had worked to rescue its friends and relations. She listened, even let me take her by the hand and show her the jumping bushel basket outside the door. She was duly impressed, but pragmatic. What are you planning on feeding your frogs? she wanted to know. I hadn't thought about that yet, I told her. What about something for them to drink? Frogs need water, you know. I didn't know. The well had water in it, but I couldn't get any from there; that was a no-no. The frogs and I exchanged glances. Finally I looked up at Mama and said, Maybe I'd better let them go. She agreed that might be the best thing to do, given the options. So before we all climbed in the car and took our baby home to Lowell, Terri Lee and I picked the frogs out of the basket one by one and lined them up. Then we gave them a lecture about staying up near the house, away from the pond and the evil snake, and exhorted them not to hop back down the hill to certain death. I brushed my hands together the way I'd seen grownups do to signal absolution. I had done all I could; no one could say I hadn't tried. But Mama was right: the best long-term arrangement for the frogs didn't include the bushel basket. Sitting down next to Allen in the backseat of the car, I craned my head around to watch out the rear window as Daddy steered into the lane. The frogs were breaking ranks, hopping off in all directions. Mostly downhill. I hugged Terri Lee to my chest, sighed, and rejoined my family.

Mama and me. Oakridge, Tennessee, 1945.

chapter three

dirt

Ethel McPherson was still in the Oak Ridge hospital on August 6, 1945, recovering from my birth seven days before, when Little Boy plummeted from the belly of the B-29 Flying Fortress *Enola Gay* high above Hiroshima and, its parachute lagging like an afterbirth, delivered death to eighty thousand Japanese just like that. The women who shared the maternity ward with my mother were ecstatic: we had dropped this massive bomb (no one could say for sure what it was; "atomic" was still a foreign word then) and the war with Japan was as good as over. We – the people of the United States, the mothers of America – we were winning the war, and Our Boys – our sons, brothers, fathers, husbands, lovers – would be spared; Our Boys would be home soon!

Mama shared their enthusiasm but not their surprise. The principles of atomic fission were not altogether alien to her. In fact, the principles of atomic fission – and the men who conspired to harness them to win the war for the Allies – were solely responsible for her being in Oak Ridge, Tennessee, to begin with.

Back when Mama was a girl, her daddy had been in the business of blowing things up. His name was Roy Horace Whittlesey, and he was a civil engineer. He worked on big projects: bridges, dams, roads. An explosives expert, he'd be there at the beginning to get things leveled and set to go; by the time the diggers and pile drivers and cement mixers showed up, he'd have moved on to a new job, sometimes to a new country. Mama's mama, Kleber Miller Whittlesey (we called her Mimi), tried to keep up with him, bearing his children while the family never stayed still long enough to put down roots. Mimi's first child was a girl, which didn't deter the parents from naming her Joseph Kleber; my Aunt Jo. Next came Mama, Ethel Linda; followed by Minta Katherine; then Horace Miller, my Uncle Whit; and finally Mary Ellen, or Aunt T.

Mama was born in 1921, in Virginia, but the family moved to Mascot, Tennessee, before she was old enough to remember and migrated to Florida by the time she was ready to start elementary school. For three years Roy had work in Florida. When it was over, he left for South America, where there was plenty of construction to be done, and lots of things to blow up.

With Roy gone, Mimi decided to head west. There was vagrant blood in her veins. She gathered her children, loaded their car. Together with another family who possessed a homemade camper and was headed the same direction, they bivouacked their way to Globe, Arizona. There Mimi settled her family in a house right on the edge of an abandoned copper mine full of tarantulas. One night Jo and Mama shared their bed with a king snake.

Arizona lasted a summer, and then Roy was back. He took his family to El Paso, Texas, moved them into a new home, and was off again, this time to Chile to build a bridge. A long, brave bridge, crossing a piece of ocean and linking an island to the mainland. He could already smell the cordite as he kissed his wife good-bye. Mimi, a trained stenographer and expert typist, got a job as a secretary for a tire company so she could keep her children fed.

Roy never saw his bridge finished. The workers had reached the span's midpoint when the Depression hit and all contracts were terminated. Mama's daddy came home with stories of a bridge jutting out into the ocean like an interrupted thought, or a one-sided marriage.

He didn't stay long.

To Mama, a girl of eleven who was often ill, the Depression just seemed to come out of nowhere. The family had been getting by on the money Mimi earned and the paychecks Roy mailed dutifully (there was that to be said for him), but suddenly the money was gone, Roy was out of work, and the bank was after the house. Mimi moved her family back to Tennessee, to Knoxville, where her mother and sisters lived. Roy stayed away. He'd swing through now and again, but never long enough for Mama to ever really know him. The Depression hit them hard, but they had only to look at the worse plight of countless others around them to return to counting blessings.

At Grandmother Miller's invitation, Mama went to live with her; it would free up space for the other children and allow her health to stabilize. The house was clean and cool, its rooms neatly arranged (with a maid on hand to keep things that way). Grandmother Miller was as organized and staunch as her daughter Mimi was whimsical.

Grandmother Miller's birth had cost her mother's life. Her father, a skilled surgeon turned brokenhearted widower, had served the Union Army during the Civil War but had shown a proclivity for doctoring wounded Southern prisoners, and for the trouble he took over them was resented by many of his peers. He entrusted his younger sister with raising his daughter, to whom he eventually deeded his entire estate. It was Grandmother Miller's aunt Annie who saw to it that her niece grew up without once lacking for anything, and who, before the century turned, ensured her anachronous enrollment into college. Her father, by then deceased, would have been proud.

She married into a family of Tennessee plantation owners, but her husband, Early Miller, proved inadequate as a farmer and prodigal in

managing his wife's sizeable inheritance. When it was gone, they retreated to the plot of land in east Tennessee that Grandmother Miller's
father had left to her; land, at least, took effort to spend. They had a
child, a girl, and named her Kleber – our Mimi. A year went by, and
left another girl. Early Miller wanted so badly to be a man. It was a
time of change and consequence. In Detroit, automobile manufacturers were opening new factories nearly daily, and assembly lines
demanded workers. Here was a chance to be part of progress, to influence technology, to break away from the plodding centuries of
windy horses and harrowed fields, and Early couldn't resist. He left
for the Motor City. To get a job, he told his wife. But Grandmother
Miller didn't exactly notch the bedpost to number the days until his
return; she knew better. She took her girls and went to Knoxville,
close to the university, and found work running a boardinghouse.
Early came back periodically, but returned each time to Detroit.
The mark of his visits stayed with Grandmother Miller long after he
had gone, took root and grew inside her.

She delivered five children, each of them girls. The last time,
Early was home when the baby arrived. He looked the baby over,
noted with disgust that it was not a boy, and left for good. Grandmother Miller closed the door behind him. She named her baby
Early.

Of her five girls, four grew to be Southern belles. Mimi did not.
Her face was, well, average. With her gorgeous sisters and their dot-
ing beaus to contend with, she could hardly be blamed for her lack
of self-worth, or for settling for a wayward husband. But at times
her feelings of self-loathing ran amok, and she lashed out at her own
children with put-downs and pointed belittling.

When Mama went to live with Grandmother Miller, she was a
shy girl, wan from her years of illness. Grandmother Miller, sensing
an opportunity, applied herself diligently to the task of boosting
Mama's meager confidence. She pulled Mama up short, sat her
down, told her: Ethel, you're a sharp girl. You could be a straight-A

student – I firmly believe that. I know it takes a lot of work, but I'll bet you can do it.

Mama had never heard anything like that before. She liked the challenge of Grandmother Miller's words, and she didn't want to disappoint her.

According to Mama, Grandmother Miller was the most brilliant woman she ever knew. Self-possessed and able, she had done her best to instill these traits in her daughters. Mimi may have been shortchanged on nest-making abilities, but she inherited ample brains from her mother. When Roy left her and the children to ride out the Depression on their own, she soon concluded that there were no jobs to be had in Tennessee – if men were out of work, what chance did a woman have of finding employment? – so she put her grasp of business matters to the test and established the Mutual Travel Agency. At first it was little more than a glorified carpool: if people had someplace they wanted to go and were willing to pay a car owner to take them there, for a small fee Mimi was the matchmaker. Later, under FDR's New Deal, she took a job with the Works Progress Administration. Gaining confidence as the years went on, she eventually founded a business school for girls, which naturally included classes in stenography and court reporting. Mimi ran it expertly until the war came along and everything was set in motion all over again, to spin full circle and converge on Oak Ridge, Tennessee, where she found herself the personal secretary of General Groves. If Grandmother Miller was the smartest woman Mama ever knew, then no doubt Mimi was the shrewdest.

Mama lived with Grandmother Miller through the Depression, and would have stayed longer had her older sister, Jo, not run off to get married. At Mimi's insistence, Mama returned home. She was sixteen years old and attending high school, but she made it her business to care for her younger siblings and keep the house in tip-top order. By the time Mimi got home from the business school each evening, the floors had been swept and mopped, the dishes washed and put away, the toilet scrubbed, and dinner prepared.

But if Mimi was content to let her daughter handle the household chores, she also insisted she would have gainful employment. Before Mama had finished high school, her mother had arranged a short-term job for her with Mr. Barber, a local architect, whose secretary was on vacation. By the time Mama graduated, Mr. Barber had assured her of a full-time placement. Mama had taken some mechanical drawing classes, and a month or two into her secretarial job Mr. Barber had offered her a chance at the drawing board; a grounds-keeper at a golf course needed a house plan drawn up, and since the job was a freebee Mama's boss figured she could have a shot at it. When she finished, Mr. Barber hired another secretary and kept Mama at the drawing board. Then he helped Mama get a scholarship to St. Louis's Washington University, to study architecture. He died before she enrolled.

In St. Louis, Mama took a job for meager wages with another architect, to gain experience and spending money, but her class schedule didn't allow for many hours at work. Once, her Grandmother Miller sent money. But Mimi never gave her daughter a dime. She never could understand why Mama had left the wonderful job with Mr. Barber's firm. What more could a girl have wanted?

After that, after St. Louis, Mama cashed in on the New Deal too. She was recruited as a cartographer by the Tennessee Valley Authority and went to work in Chattanooga. Her roommate, another TVA girl, knew her way around town better than Mama did. She also knew four boys who worked over at Hercules Powder Company and shared a house – they were new in town, too – and one of them had asked her out. Not wanting to risk it alone, she talked Mama into going along and arranged for one of the other boys to be her date. It had the makings of an entertaining Saturday evening, and the boys would be paying.

She was walking barefooted in the rain. That was the way he always told it, when he wanted to get a smile out of Mama. He was Mac, and he and his buddies were driving home from work Friday night, putting distance between them and the lab at the powder company. Like the others, he was a chemist, in the business of synthesizing explosives for people in the blowing-things-up business. The war was on, and there was a lot of blowing up needing to be done, which meant lots of work for Daddy and his friends. Fresh out of the University of Kansas with a degree in chemistry, he'd landed a job with Hercules Powder, and they'd shipped him to Kankakee, Illinois, to be trained up before sending him on to Chattanooga to make TNT. And then he met Mama. In the rain, walking home from work with her girlfriend. The bare feet were all in his mind, she would forever maintain. The boys slowed the car, pulled up alongside the girls. Mama's roommate recognized them and waved. The car stopped. The girls got in. They made a bayou of the backseat. It was Friday evening and, since no one really felt like waiting until Saturday night to be formal, they all drove south of the city, across the Georgia state line to Lake Winnepesaukah, and swam and laughed into the night, despite the rain. Then Mama and Mac got serious; there was a war on, after all. In a matter of months, they were married. It was April 1943.

Before their first year of marriage was up, Allen arrived. From the beginning he was a horse, with chunky etceteras and the great big bones of a natural survivor. About the same time my brother was born, operations were beginning in earnest at the Clinton Engineering Works in Oak Ridge, twenty miles west of Knoxville. A year earlier General Leslie Groves, Deputy Chief of Construction of the U.S. Army Corps of Engineers (a.k.a. Mimi's boss), had been appointed to direct the country's top-secret effort to develop an atomic weapon — and to see that our scientists beat the Nazis to it. With time as his worst enemy, he had begun the gargantuan endeavor. He coded the operation "The Manhattan Project." In 1942 researchers knew of only two fuels for an atomic bomb: the uranium isotope U-235 and the plutonium isotope Pu-239. So General Groves approved the purchase of fifty-nine thousand acres of wilderness and farmland, okayed the relocation of one thousand farming families, and supervised the development of one of the largest industrial complexes ever conceived on U.S. soil. The Clinton Engineering Works – soon to usurp from the nearby town the less telling name of Oak Ridge – would be responsible for the process of extracting U-235 from its natural source, U-238. And, whether he liked it or not, Wilbur Allen McPherson – Mac – would help. The Defense Department had a proposition for him. He had two choices, he was informed: he could accept a job at the Oak Ridge laboratories as a civilian chemist, or he could decline the invitation and instead be immediately drafted, whereupon he would be posted to the Oak Ridge labs as a private in the employ of the United States Army. Daddy, his civvies covered by his white lab coat, fought his war from within a maze of glass tubing, mastering the techniques of gaseous diffusion and filtration, straining toward U-235.

Afterward, he never talked about the bomb. Not in front of us kids, anyway. He downplayed the fact that he'd helped bring it about. I remember the secrecy – he talked about that – how everything at Oak Ridge was controls and crosschecks and sensors and sideways glances, how no one could leave with so much as a pen without triggering alarms. In the years following the war, as more and more information on atomic science was declassified, the jitters never left him. If, for example, in flipping through a magazine he came across the word "atomic," he would flinch visibly. That was the legacy of Oak Ridge, where everything was hidden, secret, as though it was all something to be ashamed of. He never said so outright, but I think Daddy wished he'd never had to be involved. He had studied nuclear fission in college – it was cutting-edge science – and so going into the job he understood the significance of what they were working to achieve, the destruction they were aiming to create. The men in the Oak Ridge labs weren't supposed to ask questions. They were paid to carry out specific assignments, nothing more. They were also the brightest researchers in the country. There were few real secrets, and no illusions.

If he took any pride in the work he'd been part of, he kept it to himself. There were times, usually on evenings when we were clustered together in the family room, when he'd grow quiet and seem to disappear behind his face for a while. He'd turn to Mama and say, When the kids are grown, when they don't need us, I'd like to adopt an Asian child, maybe a Japanese child. Then he might motion to me and I'd go over to him, and he'd cuddle me in his lap while he ruffled my white hair. You were born six days before the bomb, but you didn't explode. My fizzled-out atomic blond, he'd say. And Daddy would chuckle, and for a while our world would feel warm all over.

With the war over, Daddy had his eye on a job in Kansas City. He'd heard his buddies talk of openings at a new place called the Research Center, and he liked the idea of living so near to Tonganoxie. But by the time we pulled out of Oak Ridge, the Research Center had hired all the chemists it needed. So for five months our family moved in with Grandpa and Grandma McPherson, and Mama tried hard to make do with the austerity of their lifestyle. Daddy, meanwhile, talked about returning to KU and picking up his master's. He drove over to the campus and looked up one of his former professors, and it was from him he first got wind of the job openings at Spencer Chemical, at the fertilizer plant near Pittsburg, Kansas. When Daddy inquired, the folks at Spencer said sure they'd have work for someone with a background in explosives, fertilizers being second cousins to bombs. But Daddy wasn't biting right away, and he held out, hoping to land a job closer to his folks, while the rest of us endured all the amenities of the previous century. In the end, doubtless at Mama's prodding, he accepted Spencer's offer. He and Mama left on their own to find us a place to live.

Daddy bought the flood farm on account of the corn. Corn this full and strong only grows in exceptional soil, he enthused to Mama on their first tour of the eighty acres nesting in the smooth arc of Spring River. The summer of 1946 was a hot one, with only occasional rainfall, excellent corn-growing weather, and Daddy was sold. Then again, Daddy never was much of a shopper. When he and Mama went to town to buy him shoes, for instance, he'd settle on the first pair that fit. He never could see the sense in hunting for something better when what was right under his nose could do the job. The farm at Lowell, Kansas, roughly eight miles from the Spencer Chemical plant, was the first on the real-estate agent's list. It had corn. Exceptionally good corn. Which explains, after a fashion, why Daddy didn't pay much attention to the state the house was in. And it *was* in a state. Even after Mama the Architect undertook major home improvements, it was still less than impressive, what with asbestos siding and tar shingles. But it was our home, and over the years we filled it with memories and came to love its idiosyncrasies.

A toilet headed Mama's list of needed improvements. The house had been plumbed with running water, but apparently an indoor toilet had seemed too extravagant for the original plans. Mama changed that in short order; after five months of Grandpa's two-holer, she needed her indoor toilet. The privy was scrapped, its pit filled.

The newly built bathroom shared the downstairs with the living room and kitchen. The kitchen was remarkable for its sheer size alone. A huge country kitchen with linoleum covering the hardwood floor, it had papered walls with strange watermarks a few feet from the ceiling all the way around the room. Off to one side sat the picnic table on which Mama spread the meals she cooked on the big electric range. We ate seated on picnic benches, which we pulled into position to enjoy the food Mama served in generous portions. My parents may have been strapped for money and furniture when we moved west from Oak Ridge, but tightening belts was never on their agenda, especially not Daddy's.

There was noise in the living room, and warmth. The noise came from the round stove off in the corner, a stumpy old thing that burned coal oil. On cold days the fire in its metal belly raged hot and high, and the stove roared in protest or pleasure, I was never quite sure which. The best thing about the stove was its magic. I discovered if I touched a crayon to its sizzling sides, the crayon pulled a disappearing act, melting like the Wicked Witch of the West, and suddenly would not be in Kansas anymore. Except that it left a stench, which reached the kitchen surprisingly fast, and sent Mama tearing into the living room to demand: Who's been putting crayons on the stove again! Always by then I had retreated up the staircase leading from the living room to the upstairs, to busy myself, ho hum, with a book in my room.

It was Allen's room too. We shared the bedroom across from Mama and Daddy's for the first years at the farm, until Mama finished the biggest improvement to the house: a family room, which doubled as a girls' dorm after my sisters were born. The upstairs bedrooms weren't very big, and they didn't have closets, so storage space was always an issue – another dilemma the family room helped solve. Mama drew up the plans and ordered the materials for the addition. Daddy helped with the construction work, but it was Mama's project all the way. After she erected the stud walls, she hired a contractor to build a fireplace in the room, then fired him for shoddy workmanship, and did the job herself. When Daddy came home in the evenings, his task was to mix mortar and hand up bricks to Mama as she raised the chimney course upon course.

The yard in front of the house was fenced in to make a safe place for Allen and me to play. Beyond the yard was the farm – the world of cows and tractors and corn and Daddy. And beyond the farm was the river.

The curve of Spring River bordered our land to the north and corralled our pastures around to the west. It was a comfortable river, wide enough to be respected, yet narrow enough so that by the time

I was eight I could hurl a stone across it, or almost, I told myself. The riverbanks were cut steep and deep, covered in scrub brush, cocklebur, sumac, and tall grasses. Where the water was widest and shallowest, the rain had tempered the slope of the banks, and in the summer our cows churned up the red silted loam as they lolled their way down to drink.

Spring River was an archer's bow bent around us, protecting and providing for everything within its arc. It was also a weapon formed against us. Most of the year, the river flowed trouble-free, but when big rains fell it worked itself up, swollen and bent out of shape. It stormed its own banks, staggered over the top, and prevailed upon our pastures and cornfields. During floods, there was nothing we could do but herd the cattle up toward the higher ground near the house, and then watch the water.

If the river was the bow, then the road to our farm was the bow-string. The road didn't flow all the way to the river – there was no bridge, and no destination to speak of beyond – but whereas the river took its time skirting around our property, the road honed in on us without flinching. From the crossroads at Thelma and Charlie Ball's grocery store, which marked the entrance to the town of Lowell, the road ran in a straight line for a mile down to our house, passing the Hibbards' farm near midpoint and then the Baumanns', whose fields adjoined ours. It was an unimaginative road, utilitarian, direct, sensible. It was we who gave it purpose. Consequently the gravel petered out a short way past our yard, in front of what we called the old Dobkin's place, a tumbledown two-room shack that nobody lived in anymore.

The road and the river gave us our bearings. They were our points of reference, and they kept us in check. Yin and yang. When the river ran engorged and, rampaging, threatened to engulf us all, the road could bear us to safety, provided we timed our retreat right. We lived between their tension. Arrows in their quiver.

This is where I spent my girlhood, the testing ground where I came of age. There were blissful summers spent playing by the culvert that ran under the road halfway between our house and the Baumanns' and channeled runoff away from the wheat fields. Janice Baumann was a couple years younger than I, but that didn't stop us from passing endless hours together. When we tired of playing store, we'd sneak down the road, beyond my home, out to the old Dobkin's place and stand blinking in its dingy doorway until our eyes adjusted and we screwed up enough courage to swat away cobwebs and conduct our illicit exploration.

I grew up fond of the *idea* of farm life. The gentle animals, the wholesome food, the pure air, the romping in the fields and dabbling by the river – these things still make glorious sense to me in concept. In fact, I am a natural farm girl in every respect except one: I loathe dirt. My family knows this, which is why they call me every year to ask if I'm coming out to help with the potato planting. It's an old joke, but it still gets a laugh. By now we're all old enough to accept that Linda doesn't do dirt. Period.

Of course, I didn't always have a choice in the matter.

Each spring, when the time came to plant seed potatoes, I braced myself. The seed potatoes were purchased in town and stored in the dark of the barn until Daddy said it was time to plant. When we brought them outside into the light, they were frightening to look at, with sallow tentacles that reached out like the arms of baby squid. Worse, we had to cut them into pieces, one eye per chunk. Starchy slime got everywhere. We lugged these butchered potatoes to the garden by the bucketful. Daddy plowed trenches to prepare the soil for planting. Mama, Allen, and I were supposed to drop the potato chunks into place at intervals, so Daddy could come along later and give them proper burial. I was not about to get slime on my hands or dress or anywhere else, so I took tongs from the kitchen and used them to lower each chunk into place. Yuck.

During the summer months, wheat, corn, and alfalfa grew in the fields of every farm along our road, and the air droned with honey bees ranging from their hives to return with legs weighed down by amber pollen grains. They filled their sacs with nectar from the clusters of brilliant orange-scarlet trumpet creepers that bloomed along fence rows and in hedges. Those sweet, lazy days, the stuff of idylls, were made for childhood, for noting the changing colors of the landscape and watching the harvest ripen as you played.

For the men, of course, summer meant long sweaty hours in the humid fields, anxious glances at the sky, the lurking threat of tornadoes, and the worry of mildew getting into the cut alfalfa or rain interrupting the wheat harvest. It meant a stiff back and sore backside from endless joggling on the metal seat of an International Harvester, its white paint rubbed clean off by years of jeans' bottoms, and hands cracked open and callused over from repairing antiquated and refractory machinery. And when the sun had begun its downward slope through the muggy days of July, the men would band together and go from farm to farm, harvesting. It was our privilege as children to clamber into the back of the truck that drove alongside the combine as it gobbled up whole fields of wheat and showered grain and grasshoppers and the remains of summer into a heap around us, and we would scoop handfuls of grain into our mouths and chew it to a gummy paste, tasting the sweetness. Dust covered us and dried out our noses. It turned the skin of our arms gray, our sweat leaving tiny craters where it erupted through pores. Dust devils skittered like dervishes across the fresh-cut fields, lifting wheat chaff and spinning it down the unbuttoned collars of the men on the tractors. In the shade near the farm's house, the women spread rich tables of food and drink. They ferried thermoses of iced tea and Kool-Aid to the workers in the fields. They fueled the harvest. Everyone worked side by side, each family relying on the help of the next, and all intent on pulling together before winter overtook us.

While the community could be counted on to help with the field harvest, the vegetable garden was family business. All summer long we tended the crops: lettuces, cabbages, carrots, radishes, onions, potatoes, sweet corn, popcorn, peas, watermelons. Even as a toddler, I would tag at my mother's heels as she went from row to row, watering and fertilizing and weeding. When I was older, Allen and I waited eagerly for the corn tassels to brown and the ears to fill out. Ripe corn meant cash. We sold our corn to local grocery stores and took orders from people in Lowell, and Daddy paid us a dime for every dozen ears we picked. He overpaid us something awful, on purpose. Allen and I got up early, put on long-sleeved flannel shirts, and went out into the dewy corn patch to earn our bicycles. We snapped the ears off the stalks and piled them between the rows, returning later with gunnysacks to haul them back to the house.

That was the good part of corn season. Of course, once the corn matured, the window of time for picking was narrow. Daddy always planted part of the patch late, so some corn would ripen later, but there were still a few short weeks during which corn ran our lives. What we couldn't sell we brought to the house, and Allen and I sat in the yard amid piles of shucks and silk and stripped clean ear after ear. Mama boiled the corn in huge pots on the stove, then after it cooled she worked at a cutting board hacking off bowlfuls of yellow kernels. I stood on a stool to reach the countertop and scooped the kernels into Mason jars for canning. Later, by the time I started school, Daddy bought a couple chest freezers. We stopped canning corn and froze it instead. It took as much work to put up, but the taste was better. For my part, I always thought the cows got the better end of the deal. Allen and I carted all the shucks and cobs to them, and they butted their way to the feeder to get their due.

The field corn harvest came later, after the first frost. By then the corn had dried on the stalk, and the plants' green leaves had withered and blanched. We would rise early on a cold October morning

and layer on sweatshirts. It was my job to roust the little white tractor from the shed, coaxing it into action after Daddy or Allen
hitched the trailer to it.

I had learned to drive the International when I was eight or nine
years old. It was Mama's idea. She showed me how to stand on the
hitch and boost myself up over the back of the seat. She pointed out
the clutch and gave me a rundown on how the gears worked. Then
she herself stood on the hitch and coached me from there. I got the
thing going and was doing fine until we approached a barbwire
fence. Okay, step on the brake, Mama said. I tried, but I wasn't
heavy enough to make it go down. The tractor plowed through the
fence and ripped out several fence posts before I managed to rein it
in. Mama and I had to own up to Daddy, who was none too pleased
about any of it. But after that I learned how to haul up on the steering wheel and lunge at the brake pedal to engage it properly, and
Daddy figured I might as well put my driving skills to use. From
then on, it was my job to drive the trailer around. When Allen and
Daddy bailed the alfalfa fields, I circled with the tractor while they
bucked the bails onto the trailer. Alfalfa dust stuck to my skin and
rasped in my lungs, and sometimes I muttered under my breath
about Mama's brainwave.

Harvesting field corn was different, but no more enjoyable.
Daddy and Allen rode on the trailer as I brought the tractor out to
the field in the thin sunrise. They put on gloves. Their right-hand
gloves had a sharp metal hook sewn into the palm. My job was to
inch the tractor forward in low gear while Daddy and Allen,
stooped into their work, each took a row and ripped off the ears.
They raked the hooked glove across the ear, tore away the husks,
and pitched the stripped ear onto the trailer. The cornstalks snapped
in the brittle air. My breath hung in clouds. Despite my gloves, my
hands stiffened, my fingers curled around the steering wheel as
though in rigor mortis. Just when I thought for sure I was going to
die from frostbite, Daddy would declare the load full, and we'd

head for the barn and shovel the corn into the corncrib, and blood would flow through me once more.

Like the field corn, we left the popcorn standing until it dried. Of all the corn harvests, popcorn was the most redemptive: it meant winter evenings in front of the fireplace, *Little House on the Prairie* style. We stuffed the shucked ears in our gunnysacks and stored them in the corncrib in the barn. There was a machine with a hand crank and gears that we fed the ears between. It shelled the tough little kernels into a hopper. The ears it didn't strip clean, we took to the family room and used our thumbs to ply free the remaining kernels, dropping them into bowls clamped between our knees. After the first evening of shelling, my thumbs blistered. By the end of the week, I had calluses to rival the permanent ones on Daddy's fingertips. But it was worth the work.

On winter evenings when the wind blew smoke back down the chimney and blustered against the sides of the house, we sat around the fire in the family room and ate salted and buttered popcorn before bedtime. The hulls caught in my gums and gave me something comforting to worry on as I lay in bed and tried to fall asleep with the wind rattling the windows.

We popped hegari too. A sorghum favorite of Kansas cattle farmers (they pronounced its name "high gear"), it ripened early and ensured fodder for the winter months. We always kept a bit back from the cows, popping the tiny chalk-white seeds as a special treat.

Regardless of the season, our bellies were always full. Daddy saw to that. He had been hungry for enough of his life, and there was no way any one of us was going to suffer. It wasn't often he talked about his childhood, but as I grew older I pieced together scraps from his stories. They made a sad picture. Daddy, born in Tongie in 1917, was Dora McPherson's baby. Clarence, his older brother, had the misfortune of being next in line after Freddie. My Grandpa Charlie McPherson kept his distance from Clarence. Perhaps Clarence shared too many of his deceased brother's characteristics, or perhaps the torment of blame paralyzed Grandpa. Or perhaps Freddie's death had taught him that life was haphazard, a crapshoot, the difference between one hammer-blow more or less; and that the best way forward was for a man to strangle all emotion and shield himself from the risk of love and to teach his offspring to do the same. Grandpa swatted Daddy with a belt plenty of times, but Clarence took most of the abuse.

Daddy didn't talk about those times. Occasionally he'd pull out a good memory and dust it off, so that for at least a few moments the past took on a warm glow. He remembered horses. The horses that ran Grandpa's farm before any tractor ever tracked its fields. Big white draft horses, with feathers that fluffed out around mammoth bell-shaped feet. Sometimes Daddy and Clarence rode to school on the back of one of them. They jumped off in front of the school, and the horse walked home on its own. Daddy said the horse even knew when to pick them up, but I was never too sure about that.

When Daddy talked about these huge horses, I felt small. I had seen Grandpa's horses (he always kept a pair), and they were as big as our house, or pretty near to it. And I shared Daddy's marveling at how anything that monstrous could be so gentle and timid.

The McPhersons were poor, but proud nonetheless. When Daddy started at the tiny one-room school in Tongie, he carried his satchel under his arm and walked alongside his brother. Both boys wore short pants, with black leggings under them. Daddy's leggings were so old and threadbare, his knees wore holes in them. Clarence's weren't in any better shape. The two of them would walk down the hill away from the farm and out of sight, and then scoot off behind a bush and dig their ink bottles out of their satchels. They'd dip a forefinger in the black ink and smear it over their knees to hide their shame and save face.

But there was no way Daddy could disguise his red hair. It made him a sitting target, and over the years the harsh teasing and cat-calling built up a residue of shame inside him. The shame he felt at being poor and wearing worn-out clothes and having red hair was too great to be offset by his acuity inside the classroom. Schoolwork was never a problem for him. In fact, Daddy was downright brilliant. Of course nobody ever acknowledged his gifts. No one ever told him, Good job, or anything like that. There was scant pride in being brainy, and only shame in poverty.

The Depression as good as missed the McPhersons; they were so poor anyway, what did Wall Street mean to them? The farm had always provided them with enough to eat, even if it was monotonous fare. After the Depression, though, the wind started blowing. Daddy was in the eighth grade. The wind didn't quit until he was through with high school. From 1931 until 1935, the Dust Bowl plagued the Midwest, its winds choking families with the heisted soil of their own farms, forcing them to abandon their acres and hit the road. Tonganoxie was spared the biggest of the winds but not the drought, not the pangs of hunger. One winter the McPhersons survived on potatoes.

Small wonder that Daddy didn't hang around after high school. He went west to Montana and worked as a farmhand for a couple years, but decided he wasn't cut out for ranch work. He'd always been an excellent student, and though his parents didn't see the need for further education, his mother's unwed sister Matilda knew Daddy had potential.

He returned from Montana and with her help enrolled at the University of Kansas for his four years of chemistry. One day something blew up in the lab and a flying piece of glass gashed his left eyeball from top to center, opening it up completely. He was rushed to the eye institute in Kansas City, where deft surgeons miraculously saved his eyeball, but for the rest of his life he would be troubled by massive scar tissue and impaired vision. A job as a short-order cook put him through college and provided the rent for his basement apartment. With the money he had left, he bought food. In his senior year the

recruiters from Hercules Powder Company came with their job of-
fers. Real jobs that paid real money. Daddy signed on, vowing never
to be hungry again.

For Lowell's standards, then, we were in good shape. The budget
was tight – Daddy's salary from Spencer wasn't terrific, and most of
the time Mama wasn't a wage-earner – but compared to our farming neighbors, we were well off. Unlike most of them, we had chosen to be farmers. Or rather, Daddy had chosen for us. It had to do
with his love of dirt. In spite of the hardships of his growing-up
years, he loved farming, wanted to farm, wanted those cows. Mama
would have much preferred a home in the city, but Daddy wouldn't
hear of it. Farming was his first love; his job at the chemical company was far secondary to it. More important, he wanted good food
for his family. His line never changed: you can go out and buy food,
but it's never as good as what you can raise at home.

Daddy found security in eating. He expected each meal to be a
masterpiece. Whatever was in season, we ate. It was up to Mama to
find ways of being inventive, three times a day, seven days a week.
And to make dessert. A meal, according to Daddy, wasn't complete
without it. Pies, puddings, meringues, cakes, cobblers, fruit salads –
he devoured them all. The rest of us had to fall in line and do the
same. No matter that I was a naturally scrawny little thing whose
metabolism had no use for the overdose of calories. No matter that I
simply didn't have space in my stomach for all the food Daddy
pushed across the table and onto my plate. He sat directly opposite
me, and if I didn't eat enough for his liking or didn't heap my plate
to his standards, he would reach across the table and slap me in the
face. Not to eat was to be ungrateful, and he wasn't going to stand
for it. I was skinny. He had been skinny, too, because of hunger, and
hunger was not going to have its way with any child of his. Daddy
was through with poverty, through with being ashamed, and who
did Linda think she was rubbing it in his face all over again.

For breakfast, Mama fixed him oatmeal, a plate of fried eggs, a liberal rasher of bacon, toast, fresh fruit, and a mug of dark coffee. When he finished eating, he prepared breakfast for his favorite hounds. Daddy always kept three or four dogs around the farm, of which one or two were his chosen pets. They got special treatment. Every morning he performed the same routine: he poured dry dog food into their dishes, put a fried egg on each, added a piece of cheese, and placed a strip of crispy bacon on top. Daddy's dogs took breakfast in the kitchen. When he was a young teenager, he had a lop-eared, quizzical-faced spaniel named Midget (I'd seen pictures in the old albums Mama kept), but he came home from school one day to find his dog gone. He spent weeks looking for her, calling her name for hours on end as he trudged the Tongie hills. Grandma and Grandpa McPherson finally had to tell him the truth. Midget was dead, from a bullet through her head. There had been a rumor of rabies in the neighborhood, and Grandpa McPherson wasn't leaving anything to chance. Daddy found the place where Midget was buried, and cursed his father. Now that he was his own man, he chose the dogs he loved. They were his, and his alone. There was a fenced-in place near the center of Daddy's heart where he kept his dogs, and no one else was ever allowed to share that space.

In later years I would come to realize that Daddy's dogs understood him better than any of us ever could. They seemed to sense when it was safe to approach him for a scratch behind the ears, when best to make themselves scarce. The rest of us weren't that fortunate. One day he could be so congenial, so caring, so dedicated. But something always happened. It could be anything: a broken plowshare, a misplaced object, dirt on the family room floor. He'd go into a black mood that might last a week or more. In my early thoughts I could never reason out how such trivial things could trigger such results; there was something almost awe-inspiring about it. When a black mood was upon him, Daddy went about his daily tasks in brooding silence, except that he might lash out at any given moment, for any, or no, reason at all. The rest of us were powerless. We tried as much as we dared to steer him back – I even made a game of it, testing my courage by asking him to read me a story, to do anything to bring his mind back to us – but we understood our inability to change a thing. Instead, our primary focus was on staying clear of him so as not to rile him further. We cringed and waited, because we knew he was going to find a reason to lash out. Anything that went wrong, there was hell to pay. Mama, Allen, and I, we became pros at walking on eggshells. But the strain took its toll, especially on Mama. She bore the brunt. Prevention was her only means of defense, and she would try to make sure none of us did anything that would cause trouble. She tried to make everything okay. Her method was pragmatic: if you broke something, you repaired it yourself. If you didn't know how, you found out. Regardless, you'd damn well take care of it fast, before Daddy heard about it.

The black moods lifted just as arbitrarily as they set in. One morning Daddy would get out of bed and the world would be bright and new again. He would be back with us, and I for my part would try to keep him for as long as I could, acting on my best behavior, handling everything I touched with great care so nothing in our lives would break apart. Until the next time something happened.

My sister Minta arrived in time for my seventh birthday. From the moment Mama slid out of the car at Grandpa and Grandma's with the baby in her arms, I was hooked. That baby belonged to me. She was my sister, and I was going to make it my business to take care of her for always and always. The way I figured it, I was her second mommy.

It was 1952, and that September I began second grade. During the day I tried to concentrate on my studies, but each afternoon I gave my full attention to Minta. Mama was great. She taught me to

Daddy, all dressed up, with Midget and Grandma,
before the rabies scare.

bathe my little sister, how to change her diaper, how to fix a bottle and feed her. Poor Terri Lee was relegated to a cushion on my bed; I had the real thing now, and my doll would just have to come to terms with that.

Being seven was so much better than being six. Besides having a baby sister who needed me, I was so grown up in so many other ways. I could read and write, add and subtract – that was first-grade stuff – and now I was taking it to a whole new level. Lesta Lea Garber and I, best friends since the year before, made a point of memorizing the spelling of our weekly vocabulary lists both for-wards and backwards. This was no mere intellectual pursuit. Such feats were often rewarded with an extra five minutes of recess for our entire class – which boosted our popularity ratings – or with personal perks, like being allowed to wash dishes in the school's kitchen while the lesson continued without us. That's how every-thing got started with Mr. Brown.

Lesta Lea and I were in the kitchen. We had been instructed to wash dishes very, very quietly, and we were calling on every reserve of restraint we possessed to suppress the giggles that seemed natu-rally to well up at such moments. Both of us were concentrating on the sudsy dishwater, not daring to risk a look at each other, which is why we didn't notice the door to the boiler room at the opposite end of the kitchen open and Mr. Brown, the school's interim janitor, step through it. He cleared his throat a safe distance away from us. I turned around to see him smiling, holding out an open book in his hands. It was a Dick and Jane reader. He pointed to a word. What's it say? he asked. I went over and looked, helped him sound out the word. Tight lines scrunched the skin of his forehead as he concen-trated. Then he seemed to have a breakthrough, the word falling into place for him. Oh, okay, okay, he said, running his finger once more across the word. He turned around and headed back for the boiler room, reading aloud as he went.

Lesta Lea and I looked at each other. Here was Mr. Brown, a kind, wonderful man who seemed to get a kick out of kids and genuinely enjoyed his job puttering around the school but whom we never paid much attention to, and he was reading about Dick, Jane, and Spot. He had asked us for help, because we knew something he didn't.

I walked over to the boiler room and stuck my head through the door. If you need any more help, just ask me, I told Mr. Brown. He grinned. Want to hear me read this book? he asked. I beckoned for Lesta Lea to come join me. The two of us tucked our dresses under us and sat in the boiler room like such little ladies while Mr. Brown waded in. *Go, Dick, go!* His eyes were shining as he looked up. I can read, he said. He said it to himself, as a statement of fact. I *can* read. I saw the look in his eyes and knew he shared the mystery with me.

From then on, I helped Mr. Brown. I brought him more difficult books and sat with him while he read them to me, prompting him when he bogged down, sharing his delight as his speed and comprehension increased.

Each time I ventured to the boiler room, there was an element of risk involved. I didn't care. I was on a roll, and I wasn't going to let anyone's funny ideas about black people stop me. After all, it wasn't Mr. Brown's fault that he happened to be a black man from the deep South, or that he didn't have an education. He couldn't be blamed for those things. But I knew better than to mention my teaching enterprise at home. Like it or not, Mr. Brown was black, and thus off limits. Daddy had been raised in a different time and place, so it was best for me to stay quiet and lay low about the whole thing.

Mr. Brown wasn't the only one who needed me. Now that I was established as the best reading teacher in the whole world, I felt the pressure of my obligations mounting. There was Buster Hopkins, a third grader now, still struggling to make the letters stand still. It was common practice at Lowell Grade School for the older kids to help the younger ones along; that's the way it works when you have eight grades and only three rooms. But no little kid ever, ever helped a big kid do anything. At the same time, no big kids ever seemed interested in even coming within ten feet of Buster. I decided to continue the teaching efforts I'd started the previous year, before the Coca-Cola bottle incident. After that December day when I'd done my errand of mercy out on the icy playground, not one kid at school ever teased me about Buster again. The taunting stopped, and I was free to adopt Buster as my primary pupil.

Of course, I wasn't very successful. Reading frustrated Buster, baffled him endlessly. Buster was a marked boy. He might as well have had a tag pinned to his shirt: RETARDED. In those days the idea of learning disabilities (dyslexia and the like) was completely foreign. If Buster couldn't read, it was because his brain was deficient – that was the automatic assumption. Eventually, Buster beat the odds. He learned to read. (Whether I was any real help to him I'll never know.) But I imagine it took him longer to get over the harassment he endured because of his disability. Even at a school as small as ours, a child could feel terribly lonely.

When Daddy caught wind of my attempts to help Buster, he snorted. Daddy had kept quiet the year before when the Coca-Cola vase that should have sat on our mantelpiece never made it home, but now his oldest daughter was putting him to the test once more. Buster was a red flag waving smack in Daddy's face, with POVERTY stenciled on it in big bold letters. Keep going, and you'll end up married to Buster, with fourteen dumb redheaded kids. You want that? he scoffed. Daddy was always saying I'd finish up with red hair (never mind that mine was unquestionably blond), or that I'd grow big white puffy eyebrows like his; it was as though he wanted me to share his insecurities. But Buster agitated him and made him sharpen his jabs at me. Buster was too much of a threat, a nightmare revisited.

There was the potato issue, for example. Sometimes Buster brought a baked potato to school. He kept it deep in a front pocket of his coat, and in the winter at least one of his hands stayed a little warm on the walk to school. The potato was his lunch. He ate it in bites, like an apple. Daddy knew about Buster's potato (everyone in Lowell knew about everything; it was a small town), and it irked him greatly. He remembered too well the winters of his own child-hood during the drought, when there was nothing to eat except po-tato soup, and few potatoes at that. For years afterward, he refused to touch potato soup. If Buster Hopkins was eating potatoes just to get by, it was too bad, but Daddy's girl didn't need to be involved. No sir.

The pie-box supper that Halloween didn't help anything either. Pie-box suppers were hot stuff in the Midwest of my girlhood, our idea of high cuisine. For our school, they meant a chance to raise some funds and to include the community in our activities. This year, we were combining our Halloween party with the supper, and everybody in Lowell would be coming. With our mothers' help, each of us girls decorated a cardboard pie box, created a supper for two, and arranged it delicately inside the box. On the big night, these were displayed on long tables set up in the front of the largest of the three classrooms, from which the desks had been cleared away. The menfolk inspected them solemnly. Then the pie boxes were auctioned off, and the highest bidder won not only the supper but also the privilege of sharing the company of the female who prepared it.

My pie-box dinner would go for big bucks, I felt sure. I had car-ried out an inspection of my own and had objectively concluded that mine was far superior to any other in both content and design. Mama's artistic talents had come through again. Lacy frills and rib-bons conspired with a cream-topped blackberry pie and crispy fried chicken to create an effect so beguiling, no man would withstand its allure. The money my dinner raked in for the school would translate into brownie points for me. My entire family was on hand to witness my glory. Mama was holding baby Minta and chatting with a group of other mothers. Daddy and Allen, in freshly pressed shirts, were eyeing the pie boxes, weighing the pros and cons of each. They had money to spend. It was going to be a terrific evening, I just knew.

The bidding started, and everyone chuckled as little bitsy girls wound up eating across from grizzly old men. I waited anxiously for my pie box to be presented at the podium. Finally it was brought forward, and I thought I sensed a wave of reverent awe sweep through the crowd: we were in the presence of beauty.

The bidding began at a nickel. A dime. Twelve cents. Maybe more, I don't remember. Because about then Buster called out his bid. Someone raised him a few pennies, and he bid again. No one answered, and the auctioneer called his going once, going twice and *sold my pie-box supper to Buster Hopkins!* Terror-stricken, I looked around for my mother. I wanted to hide behind her skirts, I wanted to run far away, to go home, to throw up. Buster Hopkins had bought my pie-box supper, *and my father was there*. The horror, the horror! I felt my brain go numb with paralysis. Tears welled up in my eyes as I watched Buster, radiant, walk forward and take my dinner in both his hands. I was watching a living nightmare more horrible than any I could have ever imagined. My pie box was *important*. It was going to make money and find favor among the gods of Lowell school. And here it was, sold to Buster for nothing, right in front of my father's eyes. It was all so terribly horrible. Still, I fought for control. I had to do something. I had to reclaim my ambushed dignity. Falling apart would be counterproductive, I reasoned; it would only serve to validate Daddy's ridicule. I would not succumb. I would not cry, would not do any of the things I so badly wanted to do. Instead, I would meet this like a woman, and no one would know my disappointment. I would never let on, I resolved as I walked toward the table near the center of the room where Buster was already spreading out the dinner I had worked so hard to prepare. Good evening, Buster, I said. Thank you for buying my supper. Won't you please sit down?

Buster Hopkins had saved pennies and nickels and dimes for this for an eternity. In those days people rarely, if ever, ate out; there certainly were no restaurants in Lowell. Not that Buster's family would have ever been able to afford such a treat. Buster ate whatever his family could scrape together, and he never went anywhere. For him the pie-box supper was a miracle, the kind of rare event to feed his dreams for years. So every coin that made it into his hands, he stashed away. He hadn't known it was my pie box he was after, and I sure hadn't known he'd set his heart on it either. If I had, I would have hidden it until after he'd bid on someone else's. Buster knew only what was obvious to everyone, that mine was the best-looking one in the lot, and so he decided he would have it. The men doing the bidding seemed to grasp intuitively how much that pie box meant to Buster, and they backed off and let him walk away with it. For that moment, they understood what was important, and it had nothing to do with raising money for the school.

He ate with his head bent over his plate, determined not to let so much as a scrap fall wasted. Occasionally he glanced up at me between stuffed mouthfuls and chanced a shy smile. For my part, I was a perfect lady. My appetite was gone, and there was nobody to slap me for not eating, so instead I concentrated on making conversation with Buster as I imagined other more sophisticated couples might be doing.

He never guessed my embarrassment, and I'm quite sure our supper was the fine-dining experience he'd visualized all along.

Afterward, I made sure I was the last one to get in the car for the ride home. It was a short drive, hardly more than a mile, but I remember it well. Daddy, of course, was at the wheel, with Mama next to him. Allen and baby Minta and I shared the backseat. As soon as we hit the road away from the school, Daddy started in. He craned his head around so he could see me and wheedled, Well, Linda — But that was as far as he got. Mama whipped around and squared her shoulders to him. Mac, she said, I want to tell you something. I'm saying this in front of the children, because I want them to hear it too. If you ever tease Linda about Buster again, if you ever bring up his name or tease her about red hair again, then I will leave you. I'll take the kids, and I *will* leave you, and you will not be seeing us again.

She meant every word, and Daddy knew it. The rest of the ride was silent. I have no idea what conversations went on later that night between Mama and Daddy, but I do know that Mama took care of the problem. Because Daddy never teased me again.

chapter four

planted by water

And so we lived, our lives governed by physics, by Newtonian laws of push and pull, of opposite and equal reactions. With Daddy, force always resulted from interaction — it was simple science. But there were unaccountable lulls, too, moments when the forces slackened and grew silent. Then, good things happened. Like getting another sister.

Mary was born in March 1954. I was in the third grade. Mama had told me we were going to have another baby (I'd had my suspicions), and just like that, there she was: a creamy bundle of baldness, spits, and gurgles. Now I had double the mothering to do. My purpose in life was rapidly crystallizing as I plied myself to the demands of big-sisterhood. I was useful, necessary, needed, and it felt wonderful.

Daddy loved his babies too. With them, he was soft. His callused hands moved gently when he bent to scoop Mary from her crib, and he held her close to whisper funny nothings into her wafer-thin ears. Minta, two years older than Mary, toddled to his chair with a book for him to read. She nestled in his lap, her wide eyes drinking in the book's pictures while, night after night, he repeated her favorite Green Goblin story.

I had been his baby once, and Allen, too, and no doubt he had been the same with us, had cuddled us, or crawled around the family room floor on his hands and knees with one of us clinging to his back, opossum-style, the way he did now with Minta. But for Allen and me those were bygone days. We were old enough now to be responsible, and responsibility was a mantra Daddy repeated more often than the Green Goblin. Our baby sisters might not be culpable for anything yet, but for us older two nothing "just happened" anymore, nothing was "by accident." Not where Daddy was concerned. There was always – always – someone to blame. A wrench slipping off a nut and landing on his hand, a gate inadvertently left open, a septic tank overflowing, a shovel lying in the yard – such things did not just happen. They were not accidents.

Times were different then. Discipline was fast and sometimes painful. Children came to school with bruises, and no one said anything. We kids looked at each other and knew what the bruises meant, but we pretended we didn't, and eventually the bruises went away and didn't mean anything anymore. I never had bruises; Daddy wasn't like that. Instead, as punishment for whatever crimes he found me guilty of, I had to bear his black moods, and subsequent "lessons," which invariably ended with *don't you ever let me catch you doing that again.* He was my daddy; in his mind, I'm sure, he was doing what every good parent should: training his offspring for life. And life, as Daddy saw it, was a harsh and unyielding force that trampled the weak and feeble-hearted and tested every survivor's mettle. His parenting reflected this outlook.

With many of his animals it was different. For them, as for his babies, he had more patience, perhaps because he saw them as victims over whom he held an advantage. There was the paraplegic steer, for instance. Soon after its birth, even before its testicles had been done away with, Daddy noticed its back legs were useless. It could gather its forelegs under itself and wobble onto them, but its back legs could not follow suit and stuck out crazily any which way;

Children of the flood farm. 1954.

when it tried to rise, it looked more like a great squatting dog than a soon-to-be-disinherited bull. Daddy found something comical in this steer's efforts to make its rear end behave, and rather than put a bullet through its head he took it into his own to rig up a wire contraption near the barn, a sort of sling harness strung between posts that buoyed the steer up from beneath and enabled it to stand, albeit awkwardly, on all four legs. With time, the animal gained strength and managed its first faltering steps, aided by the supportive harness. Eventually it learned to walk unassisted but with the gait of a peg-legged, hung-over sailor. Daddy named the steer Drunken Hinds and welcomed it to the herd.

Besides cows, which we kept for milk and meat, we raised pigs. We were into recycling long before it was in vogue. What vegetables and leftovers we didn't eat, our hogs did, and converted into delicious hams. We had a boar and two or three breeding sows, ponderous females with tubby bellies and loaded teats. Most of the time the sows wallowed behind the barn in mud up to their axles, their range of movement restricted by barbwire fencing. But sometimes they escaped.

Daddy was cutting weeds with a sickle one morning, working his way through a section of long grass near the barn. He swung methodically, matting down the swath with his boots as he went, the way his Daddy had taught him many years before. Suddenly his sickle sliced flesh and bit in. A sow had gotten loose and was taking advantage of the weeds' shade when Daddy's sickle prescribed an arc that took in her rump. Caught napping and by no means prepared to render up her bacon without a fight, the sow squealed and struck out for the barn. Daddy, equally vexed, dropped his sickle and trotted after her in heated pursuit, uttering oaths with each right footfall and yelling for Mama at every left. I heard the yelling and came around the back of the house in time to see Mama, a dishcloth still in her hand, running toward the barn. I think she and I had reached the same conclusion: Daddy was hurt. But, as we soon discovered, it was his feelings that had been wounded and no one was in any real peril, with the exception, perhaps, of the unfortunate sow. Daddy cornered her against a fence and managed to straddle her and wrestle her to the ground. It took all his strength and every expletive he could summon, but he held her down while Mama ran back to the house for a carpet needle and twine. Daddy kept that sow pinned between his legs while Mama threaded the wheat-colored twine through the eye of the curved needle and started stitching shut the ten-inch gash in the sow's behind. There was little blood, just oozing fat, grainy and tremulous, leaking from the wound. Mama pushed it back under the surface with her fingers, and dug in the needle. The sow's skin was tough, and Mama had to twist and work the needle with all her strength to get it through. It dug into her palm, and she sent me into the barn to fetch a pair of pliers. With the pliers to take the strain of the needle, the stitching went faster, but the sow still squealed at every jab and Daddy cursed at each squeal. But they got it done together, Daddy and Mama. They always did. That's the way our family was: each of us took our share of gashes, and we did our share of pained squealing and heard our share of obscenities. But we were never left to bleed, and Daddy, who was not without cuts of his own, always ended up working side by side with Mama to stitch everything back together again.

I am growing up. I know I am growing up because Daddy is talking to me about his work, and Daddy never talks to me about his work. He leaves the house after the morning chores and gets back in time for the evening session. What he does in between is a mystery. I know he's worked up to a job at Spencer's new pilot plant, where they're into product research and development, but what that means I have no idea. So when he decides to talk, I marvel and pay close attention. They've started making pellet fertilizers, Daddy says. After months of calculations and work and trial and error, they've got a machine to do it. Daddy helped create the machine. He describes a big rotating drum with holes in it, with another partial drum turning the opposite direction inside, like a mouse running on a wheel. There is a shower nozzle that sprays a film of liquid fertilizer onto the big drum. It drips through the holes, and then blowers dry it just enough so that when the partial inner drum rolls across it, the fertilizer forms perfect little balls. Daddy uses words like nitrates and prilling tower. The way he explains it, the machine makes perfect sense to me. I visualize its workings and see the pearls of fertilizer my Daddy's intelligence has brought about. He talks the whole thing through, and I listen and feel amazed at my comprehension but more than that I don't want him to stop talking because right now I feel so close to my daddy I could get up and give him a big hug throw my arms around his neck maybe even say – but of course I won't do that because I am growing up.

In early spring, as the snow melted and the skies sagged with the weight of rain clouds, my little sisters tagged after me around the farm. Minta was four years old now, and Mary two. They held my hands everywhere we went and swamped me with incessant questions. We went nowhere, however, without our galoshes. Those were the rules. In Kansas, during the rainy season, you've got to have your feet covered. Galoshes, though, are hard to keep track of, and ours had a way of going missing. Dogs ate them. The ground swallowed them. Or they just plain disappeared with no explanation. They were the bane of Mama's shopping runs across the state line into Joplin, Missouri, the nearest big town and the only place around where you could buy galoshes. She was forever having to buy a new pair for one or the other of us, and bemoaning the fact that she couldn't simply buy a single galosh but had to splurge for a complete pair. Of course, lost galoshes were strictly a matter for Mama, and even then we only confessed our losses to her when absolutely necessary. We knew she would chew us out roundly for our negligence, but it was far safer to face her frenzy than gamble on

Daddy's reaction. There was no telling how he'd handle it, and Mama knew that as well as we did. In spite of her dedication to him, she always ended up in cahoots with us, partners in subterfuge.

I felt bad about Mama always having to cover for us, and I determined never to let galoshes get the better of me again. So when I took the little girls out to the cow pastures to play under the budding catalpa trees down near the river, I walked a step behind them and kept an eye on their feet. Linda the galoshes monitor. We skirted around the edge of the fields, where the ground squished the least. The rain had gone on for several weeks, and there were still vast puddles in the low places. There was no avoiding the mud. It clogged the soles of our galoshes, worked its way up the instep, squirmed over the lip at the ankles, and slid up our socks. The cuffs of our jeans grew black and heavy. But our galoshes stayed on our feet throughout the afternoon as we played.

When it was time to return to the house I decided we'd take a shortcut, straight across the pasture. We started out, Minta and Mary in front of me, and got halfway across the spongy field when my sisters stopped moving. Suddenly they were shrinking, sinking as I watched. And then I realized my feet were stuck, too, and mud was sucking around my ankles, trying to pull me down. I yanked my right foot upward. It popped free – abandoning shoe and galosh. Balancing on my left foot, which sank deeper under my full weight, I leaned down and fished in the goop for my shoe, simultaneously yelling at my sisters not to struggle; it would only make things worse, I told them as I lost my balance and pitched forward, my socked right foot disappearing again in fresh mud as my left foot made its break, leaving its galoshed shoe in the lurch. I was on my hands and knees, in mud to my elbows, but I now had enough personal surface area in contact with the quagmire to keep me from going under. I groveled back around and plunged my hands down into the fast-closing holes my feet had left. Success: two shoes, two galoshes. I stuck my black hands deep into my shoes, planted them in front of me, and began crawling back in a half circle to face my sisters. Their faces registered horror, whether at their harrowing plight or at my demented appearance I was unsure. Hold still, I told them again, needlessly; they were by now both up to their bottoms in mud and were going nowhere but down. I started with Mary, the youngest. I popped her free, and dug for her galoshes. I was getting good at this. She was already sinking again when I came up with her shoes. I told her to put them on her hands and to start crawling forward and not to stop, and to stop crying. Then I fished out Minta. She was heavier and I had to lie down next to her, ice-rescue fashion, and have her pull herself by my arms before we could get the suction to break. We saved her shoes and galoshes, and then, hands inside our shoes, we all blundered on. Minta got stuck. I pried her loose. Mary bogged down. I cajoled her onward. And then we were through the mud and the ground squished happily again. I knew we were going to make it. We had six shoes and six galoshes between us, and I was proud. Until I thought about what I was going to tell Mama to explain our muddy clothes.

Several days passed before we ventured back across the fields, and it took the prospect of seeing a dead cow in the river to convince me to take the risk again. I had overheard Daddy telling Mama about the cow, and even though I knew the riverbank was out of bounds for the little girls, I decided to take them for a look. It was something to do.

The river was running high and threatening a flood. At the place we called Clay Banks, where the ground tapered to the river's edge and the cows gathered to drink, the water churned a few feet below the grass on which we stood. The herd was nowhere in sight. The dead cow was on its side in the water, snagged in the scrub that grew against the bank. The cow was gray and bloated, swollen like the river. Its head was submerged. The huge ribcage lifted and fell with the current, as though the carcass was breathing water. I stared at the dead cow a long time.

Minta, bored, wanted to move on. She kicked her right foot hard in the direction of the cow. And everything ground into slow motion:

The galosh flies from her shoe, spins end over end, rainbows high above the body of the cow, seems to hang regretfully for a moment before falling, smacking into the surface of the racing water that whisks it away like a slick brown conveyor belt. I tear off my shoes and jump in after it. A glass bottle explodes inside my head as I go under, sending shards through my brain. I come up gasping, and find I can't breathe. The water is a boa constrictor – fire – steak knives – electric – piranhas. Liquid ice.

Too stunned to swim, I focus on staying alive. I can see my sisters on the bank. Their mouths are working up and down, like gulping fish. I try to kick my way toward them, to move my body out of the current, but my legs are far away, so far away…and then it isn't so cold after all; there's just this glowing feeling that spreads from my insides out and fills my head, and actually the water is too warm for comfort really much too warm no wonder my fingers are blazing and my feet – my feet touch mud, and the bank is there, and I grab onto the grass hanging down from the bank, and Minta and Mary are on the bank, screaming, and I pull myself to the edge and somehow, somehow, I am out of the river and lying on my back with Minta and Mary beside me, still screaming.

Back at the house, Mama yells too. You almost died! What were you thinking? Those galoshes aren't worth it. What *were* you thinking? You almost *died!*

And all I can say as I shiver and drip and cry is I'm sorry, Mama. I'm so, so sorry. Mama.

In spring we lived with one eye on the river and the other on the sky. When the river rose out of its banks and filled our fields, it was time to watch for tornadoes. Ever since I was little and Daddy had taken me outside and pointed at the funny snake winding high above our heads, I had thrilled at the sight of tornado funnels as they passed over our farm. I knew that so long as they stayed up in the sky — cobras in their baskets — they couldn't hurt us.

Unlike many homes in Lowell, ours had no basement. As I grew older and became aware of the damage tornadoes were capable of inflicting, I worried that we had no place to go in the event one should touch down on our farm. The old Dobkin's place had a storm cellar down under the weeds beside the shack, but it was caving in and unsafe, and too far away. Daddy said that if a tornado came our way, we should all run outside and lie in the ditch that lay between our house and the south grain fields.

One March morning when I was eleven years old, Daddy left home and drove into Lowell to check on Grandma and Grandpa McPherson, who had come down from Tongie not long before; Grandpa, too old to farm, had packed up his and Grandma's belongings, sold their land, and moved to a tidy white bungalow a mile and a half from our house. The sky was dark and roiling with thick storm clouds when Daddy left home, the weather of a typical spring day in southeast Kansas. He hadn't been gone more than half an hour when Allen walked to the screen door and was about to head out when he stopped, gestured wildly, and yelled, Mama, look!

Mama and I looked. There, in front of a coal-black bank of clouds sweeping in a phalanx over the south field, was a tornado — coming right at us. Lightning slashed through the clouds behind it, and everything was flashbulb luminous. This was no sky-dancing snake, no happy funnel spinning like cotton candy. This was a freight train, huge and black, driven by the undead. It whistle-moaned *whoo-whoo-whoo-whoo* and bore down on us *chugga-chugga-chugga-chugga* as Mama screamed, To the ditch! I grabbed Minta, Allen scooped up Mary, and all of us raced outside. A fence stood between us and the ditch. I climbed it while Allen hoisted the two little girls to the other side and helped Mama over. He jumped the fence and we all lay down in the ditch, Allen on top of Mary and I on top of Minta. The train came on, louder and louder. The world shook. We dug our toes into the ground and grabbed fistfuls of grass. We did not look up.

And then, silence. A complete and fearsome silence. No killdeer cries, no squirrel chatter. Only a void. And the smell of rotten leaves, of mildewed earth, a damp smell. The Angel of Death had passed over us.

I remember feeling surprised to be alive as I got unsteadily to my feet and pulled Minta up. All of us ran to the end of the fence row to get back to the house; I couldn't have trusted my knees to hold out for a climb over the fence. We were still fifty paces from the house when the wind caught us. In the wake of every tornado, there is a space of dead air, sucked lifeless by the force of the cyclone, and then the storm follows after. The wind hit us in the back and pitched us forward. I gripped Minta's hand and prayed I'd be strong enough to hold on to her. Terror made the distance to our door seem greater than it was, but we reached the house safely and pushed the door shut behind us. Minta and Mary were crying, mostly because they'd wanted to see the tornado and Allen and I had been on top of them and they'd missed their chance. Mama, Allen, and I could hardly believe the house was still standing. The tornado hadn't even scratched it. When the wind slacked off enough for us to venture outside again, we found our yard littered with tree limbs, odd scraps of plastic, chunks of plywood, roofing shingles – booty the tornado had scavenged before it got to us. Away from the house, down toward the river, a stand of trees had been savaged, their roots ripped from the ground, their branches mangled. A few trunks had been corkscrewed clean off in a fury of bark and splinters. The tornado had hopscotched over our house, dropped down to molest the trees, then skittered off over the river, heading northward.

Daddy came home. He did not believe us – What tornado? – until he walked outside and saw the trees. Those great trees, gone. Whoa! I guess we did have a tornado, he whistled. We just nodded.

North of Lowell and across the river lies the town of Riverton. The road from Lowell bridges the river and the Empire District Electric Company's hydroelectric dam, dissects the flat land surrounding Riverton, then interrupts Route 66 at the town's main intersection.

A half mile short of the highway is Riverton High School, where in 1957 I entered the seventh grade. No more three-room school house and bag lunches – this was the big time. I was twelve years old, and confident in my ability to conquer whatever challenges the capacious corridors, cafeteria, and classrooms held. It wasn't just my age that gave me confidence. Allen had gone before me; he was in eighth grade when I entered junior high, and his jovial personality had won him instant acceptance and made him a leader. I knew he'd always stick up for me if things got out of hand.

But this was my show, and I was ready. Away from the cramped spaces of Lowell Grade School, I exhaled, and excelled. Or tried to, at least. The thing was, I hadn't figured on becoming a teenager. I had looked forward eagerly to the freedom of middle school – but I'd forgotten that I'd be bringing myself along with me. And right then, myself wasn't someone I liked all that much.

In sixth grade, I'd been one of the smallest in my class. Little itty-bitty Linda. Over the next two years, though, I grew like a bean stalk, so that by the end of eighth grade I was right up there with the tallest giants in the school. And still I weighed, oh, about zero pounds. To make things worse, I had huge feet. Designed for walking on water – that kind of huge. Every time I looked down, there they were, sticking way out in front of me. In the sanctuary of my bedroom, I measured my feet and my height each day, and prayed I would wake one morning to find myself "settled down" to a reasonable height. It didn't seem too much to ask. I didn't need to be petite or anything – five foot two would be fine, thank you very much. My best friend, Sue, was the perfect size, the perfect girl: small, cute, coordinated, popular, and smart. I wanted to be like Sue.

I kept right on growing instead.

In seventh grade, I went steady seven times. ID bracelets were in – the surest way to know who was hitched to whom. Chris was a guy I really liked, and I finally settled on him. We traded bracelets. But all the while we went together, I was growing up and he was growing out. By eighth grade I was a good head taller than Chris, and still rake thin. He, however, grew in the other direction. We were like Olive Oyl and Popeye – definitely not an okay match in junior-high terms. Chris and I exchanged bracelets for the second time, and we were done.

I felt like a victim of circumstances. Nobody ever asked me how tall I wanted to be. Nobody asked Chris how wide he wanted to be. Mama tried to make it better. She kept telling me that some day I would be wonderfully happy about my height. While other people struggled to stick to diets, I would be able to carry any weight I had. It didn't help. Daddy still said I didn't eat enough, and I began to think he was right. I tried everything. I ate and ate and ate, but I was afraid that eating would only extend my height and not add mass to my boobs (my projected spot). I thought about answering the wimp ads I saw in magazines, but I was never brave enough to try them. They were for boys. So I just kept praying for that miracle.

In spite of my height/weight ratio woes, I knew enough to realize I was lucky in other ways. I might not be ecstatic about the whole puberty thing, but in the classroom at least, I found I could stop obsessing long enough to enjoy my studies. Academic achievement was one thing I could take pride in. Finally.

With forty-odd students to each year, Riverton High seemed vast; yet at the same time, the school had an undeniable order to it. Through the ranks of button-shirted, slicked-haired boys and pleat-skirted, saddle-shoed girls an invisible line ran right down the middle. One side of the line was cast in shadow, the other in lime-light. Your future depended on where you stood in relation to the line. From our first days in junior high we were being earmarked like so many cattle, tagged for our likelihood to succeed or fail in the academic environment. Those early decisions opened or barred our access to college prep courses later in high school. This culling process went on supposedly unbeknownst to us. But we knew, all right; we knew who was in the slow class and who was in the faster class, and based our perceptions of each other's worth accordingly. The division split us into two groups roughly equal in number.

No doubt it made perfect sense to the school's administration: put the slow kids in one class and the fast kids in another, so everyone's needs can be met. Fair enough. What, it seemed to me, the administration had overlooked was that the universe does not dole out ignorance and intelligence in equal measure. It's not a fifty-fifty split. Of course there were students with learning disabilities who certainly needed and benefited from remedial help. But there were others who, because they had been allotted a place on the dark side of the line (it came down to a toss-up, in many cases), got remedial education whether they needed it or not. There seemed to be little regard for the continuum of learning – you were either smart, or not. How smart, or how not, wasn't a factor. So students on the dark side were plowed under with drill-and-grill exercises, while those on the lighter side were salted with creativity and peppered with challenge. On the one side self-esteem was buried, while on the other it was lifted and fanned.

No one ever bothered explaining why we better-heeled kids ended up on the brighter side of the line, regardless, while the kids who bused to school with cow dung clinging to their soles and mends in their coats often found themselves in the shadows. Maybe there was nothing to explain. Maybe that's just how it was.

Sue was in most of my classes. I was glad to have my best friend with me. She was the only girl in a large, wonderful family, which made her extra-special to them. But she still knew how to carry her own weight, and she helped me find my feet too. Sue's family didn't have money. They lived in a log cabin long before cabins became a popular commodity. Usually Sue slept in a bed with her grandmother, but whenever I came over for the night (which was as often as I was allowed), we shared a pallet on the floor. It occurred to me that Sue easily might have ended up on the dark side of the line had the balance been shifted even a little. Maybe I might have too. But we hadn't, so it didn't matter.

At least, I thought it didn't. In eighth grade, I had a schedule conflict between English class and an elective I wanted to try. I went to talk it over with our principal. I'll just be in the other English class, I told him. He hesitated. That's not a good idea, Linda. You'll be ahead of the others, he said. My antennae went up. Somehow, that wasn't right. That's okay, I said. I don't mind. It's only for a year. He hemmed. Hawed. But in the end he said I could try it. It's your decision, Linda.

I lasted about three weeks. In the "other" English class, we were force-fed nouns and verbs as though the solution to world hunger depended on our ability to spot the difference between the two. It was third grade stuff. I abducted and, with great humility, went back to the principal and asked to return to my original class. I moved back into the light. Back where we had a teacher with a vision, someone eager to stretch our minds and make us think.

Later, in high school, the darker side rose up and elected me to a class office. They remembered. I had chosen to be part of them, if only for a few weeks.

Riverton High was a house of learning, but ignorance was rife within its walls too. Especially when it came to sex. In theory we knew nothing about it. We were, after all, America's golden children, born in the blossom time of our nation's prosperity, when liberty and justice and chastity belts held sway. We giggled at Elvis and swooned over James Dean, but we stuck to our slide rules and grammars so that the world would stay safe and white and shiny and clean. Until one of us got PG.

Whenever the PG talk went around, the girl in question was invariably from the shadows. We whispered it in the girls' room, discussed it in the parking lot, pondered it after hours. Always it was PG — pregnant was too ugly for any of us to manage, as distasteful a word as abortion or divorce or Communist. So when fourteen-year-old Norma Mae got PG and tried to fix her problem by funneling Malathion into her bellybutton, we shielded our mouths with our hands and passed the word around in short order. Some girls were just *that way*, we rationalized, never grasping that the real miscreant was ignorance. And so it went: when the fall from grace came, the fated one slunk away silently before her belly swelled smooth and ripe and indiscreet; and we, our clucking abating, returned to the sunshine with the tang of disassociation on our tongues.

When our literature curriculum mandated that we read *The Grapes of Wrath*, I had no idea of the impact the book would have on me. But Steinbeck's classic jarred my consciousness like a hand in the night shaking me by the shoulder. I woke up and realized he was writing about a part of my world, describing events my family had lived through and survived, recounting a chapter of history a piece of which had played out right in our backyard.

Route 66, the "Mother Road" that begins in Chicago and ends in California, and in the withering days of the Dust Bowl bore the brunt of the exodus from the ravaged heartland, runs for thirteen miles in Kansas and slices off the state's bottom right corner. This "Main Street of America" passes through Joplin, Missouri, crosses into Kansas at the old mining town of Galena, cuts Riverton straight down the middle, runs west to Baxter Springs, Kansas's oldest cow town, then dips south into Oklahoma and jogs west, on out across the wheat belt.

Okie families like Steinbeck's Joadses, who could only watch impotently as their farm literally blew away before their eyes, made the westward pilgrimage along Route 66 to a mecca called California, a place where the sun shone and peaches and citrus hung in lush orchards, where soil was rich and work plentiful – at least if the handbills that circulated throughout the drought-stricken Midwest were to be believed. Which they weren't.

My daddy's parents had sweated out those dry years, fortunate to be far enough from the maelstrom that their fields did not take to the skies, yet with knots in the pits of their stomachs nonetheless as their crops wilted and the brittle ground cracked open. Grandpa and Grandma McPherson, Clarence, and Daddy had survived on potatoes and willpower. They had been lucky, I thought, as I read my way into the heart of Steinbeck's novel. Grandpa and Grandma could very well have ended up like the Joad family – displaced persons improvising their escape aboard an overloaded jalopy – and where would that have left us?

But what really set me on edge as I read was the realization, for the first time in my life, of just how mean-spirited people could be. I began to see *The Grapes of Wrath* not so much as an historical novel to be read and pondered and summarized in an essay, but as a journalist's portrayal of bigotry; of the ill-conceived lines of division people draw between what they know and what they don't understand; of the psychosis of fear; of the invincible ties that bind men and women together and rally families; of the fierce strength of mother-love; of the awesome determination that drives men to overcome and to harness the anger that stems from injustice. In short, I was being exposed to facets – and facts – of life that I had never considered. My mind was going through a smelting process, and when it was over I found myself newly malleable even as my resolve hardened.

My junior and senior years, I danced away my afternoons. It was swing your partner, sashay down, and do-si-do. It was allemande lefts and star promenades. It was *chicken in the bread pan kickin' out dough* and *turkey in the straw, turkey in the hay.* I was in love with square dancing, and the Spring River Valley 4-H was the perfect place for me. We were good. So good. We won contests, and performed at local banquets and functions. We put our own spin on tradition, even danced to "Mack the Knife," with our caller's commands replacing the lyrics.

I belonged in square dancing. It had taken me a while to figure that out. When I first joined 4-H, I was a nine-year-old girl wanting to get in on the fun my brother was having; Allen had joined two years before. I was perfectly okay with being a girl – that wasn't the issue. Clearly, girls have the advantage. When we get in trouble, we can cry and some big strong man always comes to bail us out. At least, that's how I figured it was supposed to work. Little did I know... I wanted to be in 4-H simply because I didn't want to miss out. It took a few weeks of pouting, punctuated by some serious temper tantrums, before Mama and Daddy caved in. I was sent off with an admonishment on the responsibilities of belonging to an organization. In exchange for my promise to be a grown-up, my parents allowed me to pledge my head, heart, hands, and health.

I intended to join in with what the boys were doing – until I found out what, exactly, that was. Cows, complete with cow poop.

Rabbits. I'll do rabbits instead, I decided. Rabbits made cute little round balls, not pies. Daddy got me several hutches. I was only going to start with two rabbits, and didn't understand why one hutch wouldn't suffice. You'll learn soon enough, Daddy told me. Daisy Mae and her buck, Li'l Abner, wasted no time. When I had ticked twenty-nine days off my calendar and Daisy Mae had grown fat, I put a wooden box and a small pile of straw in her hutch so she could make a nest. She pulled fur from her dewlap to line the box. Next thing I knew, she had eight tiny blind, bald babies squirming around in her fur nest. I didn't touch them, though, not until they started to grow fur; Daisy Mae might reject them if they smelled like me.

Spring River Valley 4-H square dancers. We were
good. So good.

Daisy Mae and Li'l Abner made lots of babies. I named them all. Mama saved empty one-pound coffee cans for me to use as watering dishes. Before long, I had twenty cans to remove from my row of cages, clean, fill, and put back once a day. And without fail, the moment I finished washing and filling every can, our evil geese materialized out of nowhere, like a plague of locusts. Great, long-necked locusts that honked and hissed and came for me with their ravenous beaks clacking. They attached themselves to my heels, until I had no choice but to run for it. Bite, bite, bite, honk, honk, honk. Then they waddled through my coffee cans, knocked them all over and splattered them full of mud. Where were snakes when you needed them?

The evening before my bunnies were to be butchered, I left home. I knew it had to be done, but I couldn't stand to be there; I felt my complicity too keenly. Instead, I spent the night at a girlfriend's house, Sue's usually, and stayed clear of our farm until Allen's knife-wielding was over. One time, I crept back home to find Daisy Mae gone from her cage. I asked Allen where she was. His look of shock gave me the answer. He had mistaken her for one of her offspring, and my poor little Daisy Mae had gotten the bonk-slice-skin treatment. Undone, I went to the 4-H people and told them I *really* liked sewing and cooking. And square dancing. Especially square dancing.

All that learning, all that activity – and yet my greatest, and hardest, lessons during my teen years came not from the classroom or the clubhouse, but from our home on the flood farm.

I was a sophomore when construction began on our new house. Daddy and Mama had first set out to build an addition onto the house that had come with the farm, which was feeling the strain of four growing children. Mama had drawn up the plans, and they'd gone as far as pouring the foundations when they reconsidered. The old house, they decided, was too difficult to heat in winter, and too

big a hassle in spring, when flood waters might swirl over the doorsill and silt up the downstairs rooms, leaving us with weeks of cleaning and a dank smell that never quite seemed to work its way out of
the walls. It was time, they concluded, for a fresh start.

The new house, a standard rectangle, was constructed to Mama's
specifications. The downstairs was built of concrete blocks and fea-
tured a storage and tool room, with a wood-fired furnace built into a
brick chimney against the interior wall; a work room for Mama's
home repairs; a modest bedroom for Allen; and – most important
of all – a reinforced concrete bunker of a room that doubled as a
storm shelter and a storage space for our potatoes. The downstairs
rear wall, facing west away from the river, was built just as solidly.
When it was finished, a bulldozer pushed a mountain of excavated
earth against it, ceiling-high. Daddy joked about giving Mama back
at least one of her Tennessee hills. The excavation created a crater a
hundred feet across about the same distance from the house. When
the job was finished, the farm had its first hill, and the three bedrooms, living room, and kitchen on the second floor of the new
house had ground-level access but were still a full story's height
above the flood plain. It was a work of genius, of salvation, made all
the more miraculous by the fact that we now had a pond just yards
from our front door. And I loved to swim – despite my near-
drowning while trying to rescue Minta's galosh from the river.

Under normal circumstances I was an excellent swimmer. Long-
limbed and lightweight, I was built for it. Daddy had begun to teach
me to swim as soon as I was old enough to dog-paddle. He was himself an exceptional swimmer, having trained and worked as a life-
guard at a public beach during his college years. He taught me to
respect the water but not to fear it. With the river so much a part of
our lives, Daddy knew the importance of teaching us to swim well.

By the time I graduated from high school, I was queen of the
river, swimming easily against its strong current and diving beneath
its brown surface for sheer enjoyment. I was also a volunteer assistant

to Mary Alice, the woman in charge of the Baxter Springs public swimming pool. It was she who recommended me for aquatic school. Mary Alice needed someone to run the Red Cross swimming program at the pool, and even though I was only seventeen she talked the pool authorities into bending their policy and letting me attend. I was excited. Here was an opportunity to have fun and make money at the same time – that is, if I made it through the required two weeks of aquatic school. Mary Alice believed I would and arranged for the town of Baxter Springs to cover my training fee. I understood there was no guarantee I'd last out the course, and knew that even if I did, I didn't stand to make much money at the pool, not at my age. But I didn't care. This would be my first real job, outside of picking corn for Daddy.

It would also be my first time away from home for more than the usual night or two I and my friends spent at summer camp. Thinking about it made me feel very adult and mature, and very small and quivery all at the same time. Mama must have sensed my fears. She did all she could to make sure I had everything I needed – the proper clothing, the right swimsuit – so I would not be embarrassed or stick out as a country bumpkin.

Mama, with Minta and Mary in tow (as always), drove me to the aquatic school – it was several hours from home – gave me a hug, and wished me luck. Then I was on my own for two whole weeks. I was the youngest candidate in the program, and scared stiff of failure.

It was two weeks of torture. For one thing, I was still a beanpole, and aquatic training demanded physical strength that I simply didn't possess. For another, I burned to a crisp. I was blond, and this was long before anyone came up with sunscreen. After three days in the intense sun my skin peeled in ashy scales, my lips puffed and split, and my body shivered with fever.

Still, I refused to quit; I would have killed myself first. I stuck out my upper lip (actually, it did that on its own) and got on with doing what I had to do. Which was a lot of canoeing, a lot of rowing around the lake in flat-bottom prams, and a tremendous amount of swimming. And, by glory, I made it. At the end of those two weeks, I was certified as a Water Safety Instructor for the Red Cross, and I was ready to get on with the job of teaching the beginner swimmers at the Baxter Springs pool.

In retrospect, it amazes me that not once during those two weeks did anyone broach the topic of how to go about training a person to swim. The entire purpose for being in the program was to receive WSI certification, and yet not one word, not one demonstration, was offered to help us make the transition from proficient swimmers to useful teachers. We knew the mechanics – that much we proved – but how to share that information with others seemed to be of no particular interest to our aquatic school instructors. I would just have to learn as I went along, and hope my students caught on. In the years to come, I would find myself in similar predicaments time and again. As lame as it sounds, that's the way things were done, and there was little use getting upset about it.

Later that same summer Mama and Daddy did the unthinkable: they went away for a week. Mama's high school in Tennessee was having a reunion, and she and Daddy decided to step out of character, just this once, and go. They took the two little girls with them. Allen, like so many other college boys trying to earn a buck, was harvesting wheat in the western part of the state, so I was the only one left at home. Not that I minded. My parents trusted me, and I had my job at the swimming pool to keep me occupied during the day, and the animals to tend to when I got home in the evening.

Nature shows no mercy to the vulnerable. Two days after my parents left, the rain began. It pelted against the windows and filled the gutters along the eaves so that they spilled over and made ditches of Mama's flowerbeds. Morning dawned gray and drenched, and still the rain fell. On the fourth day of rain, I woke despondent. Once again, there would be no work for me at the pool. I snatched some breakfast, pulled on my raincoat and galoshes, and headed out across the pooling fields to the river. The cows were huddled together in the meager shelter of the scrub along the far pasture. I kept an eye on them as I hunted for a long, strong stick with which to test the rate of the river's rise the way I'd seen my daddy do whenever big rains fell. The cows were my chief concern: under no circumstances could they come to harm.

When the river is on its best behavior, it curves majestically around our property and sweeps past us and out toward Baxter Springs. But when rankled by rains, Spring River takes it out on us by cutting the corner, flooding the northeast field first and then channeling into the heart of our farm along a natural sunken swath. This kitty-corner maneuver effectively cuts off a large triangle of the pasture nearest the river. The higher the water climbs, the smaller this raised triangle grows and the wider the channel becomes. If enough rain falls, of course, our pastures disappear altogether, and the fate of the house comes into question.

As it was, the river had already begun to channel through the fields. Most of the herd had of their own volition waded through the water and were for the moment safe on the higher ground on the house-side of the channel. Seven cows, though, were stranded on the triangle of pasture. What would happen to them if they stayed there was obvious: the river was rising faster now, and it wouldn't be long before it wiped out the triangle and carried off the cows.

Terrified, I followed the only course of action that seemed open to me. I crossed the channel and began to swim the cows out, one at a time, whooping and hollering and waving to make myself more of a threat than the fifty feet of moving water that separated them from the rest of the herd. The water came up to my shoulders, and I had to stay right with each cow to keep her headed in the right direction. Once across, I shooed her off toward the herd, then swam back to the remaining cows. With five cows down, two to go, I was near exhaustion. But I wasn't giving up. Those cows were not going to drown, I promised myself as I swam the ever-widening channel for the tenth time. The next cow, though, proved recalcitrant. I chased her into the water and urged her halfway across before she decided to turn back. I headed her off, screaming, and she lumbered into the water once more, only to retreat again. She seemed to prefer her chances on the triangle. I followed her back out of the water, my legs shaking. I crumpled and sat down. You've got to think, Linda, I told myself. Use your head. She's a cow, you're a girl; by rights, you should be smarter. My brain felt as jellified as my legs, but I hit on a plan, got to my feet, and drove the monstrous old brute down into the tip of the triangle, to where her swim would be the longest. There, I ran at her, wielding a big stick, and scared her into the current. This time, though, I stayed out of the water and goaded her on from its edge. Each time she tried to return to my side of the channel, I diverted her back into the stream. By the time she'd struggled her way to where I'd wanted her to cross in the first place, her strength was giving out, and when her feet touched ground on the opposite side she turned toward me with a look that said, Oh, thank goodness! Then she heaved herself off to join the other ladies.

For my part, I heaved a sigh of relief, booed the last remaining cow into the water (she didn't have much fight in her), and made the crossing for the last time. I was limp from exhaustion, and soaked through, but the cows were safe.

As I sloshed my way back to the house, I noticed that the International had been left out in one of the lower fields. It would have to be moved to higher ground. I went over and climbed up on the seat and got the engine going. The tractor was only a two-wheel drive, and when I put it in gear the wheels spun in place, the ground was already so saturated. I went to the barn and fetched a couple planks and stuck them under the back wheels so that they angled up, like water skis prior to takeoff. They didn't help; the ground was too wet. The wheels sank in up to the axle. I had no choice but to leave the tractor in the rain and go back to the house and wring out my clothes.

All that afternoon and evening I fretted over the tractor, worried that the water might somehow destroy the engine, or worse, that the river might rise beyond all reason and carry it away.

And then the rain abated and Mama and Daddy came home and I acted as though everything had been hunky-dory. Later that day I took Mama aside and told her I'd had to swim the cows. Oh, horrors, Linda! You could have drowned. What were you *thinking?* No cow is worth that... Mama looked at me, amazed; and I felt foolish, but proud of myself nonetheless. Standing there in front of Mama, I didn't know what to say. Daddy took care of that. He came back from his tour of the farm, stomped into the kitchen, and threw a purple temper tantrum. He had discovered the tractor.

And just like that, as smoothly as actors taking their places after an intermission, each of us resumed our usual role, and the show went on. As it always would.

chapter five

shore leave

Many people go to college. I tumbled this simple thought over and over, like a sheet in a washing machine, as Mama and I drove due north twenty-five miles to Pittsburg, where I was to begin classes at Pittsburg State. There was nothing extraordinary about what I was doing – many people go to college; no one expected less of me, I was merely next in line in our family's tradition of education. These thoughts helped take the edge off my nervousness as we approached downtown Pittsburg and entered the college campus. I was going to be just fine. I'd brought my brains with me, and they hadn't failed me yet. Many people go to college.

But I hadn't reckoned on so many of them going to *my* college. So many people, each with a face I didn't know. Mama, this place is big!

This was my first time on campus – I hadn't made it to freshman orientation week because of my job at the swimming pool – and I was starting to feel just a little overwhelmed. Mama stayed right with me, though, and together we stood in all the necessary lines, signed the necessary forms, shook the necessary hands. I was now a registered freshman, and ready to check in at my dorm (no boys in sight, of course) and meet my roommates, Gwen and Patricia. Mama hugged me good-bye and drove home, and for a moment I felt as alone as I had when she left me at the aquatic school. Only for a moment, though; and then I dove in headfirst and immersed myself in college life, determined to soak up as much as I could over the four years ahead.

The first order of business was to bring my wardrobe up to speed. Away went the pleated skirts and saddle shoes, and in their place I adopted the cutoff denim jeans of my more worldly-wise peers. Over long-sleeved shirts with button-down collars I wore baggy sweatshirts, with the neck carefully cut out and the sleeves lopped off above the elbows. White canvas Keds completed the ensemble. Miniskirts and a pair of go-go boots (leather, glossy white, calf-high, zippered) rounded out my collection. It was, I figured, high time I got in on the sixties.

I started college in September 1963. America was rocking to an uneasy beat. Kennedy was in his third year in the White House, and many people – especially young people – were taking seriously his inaugural declaration. All across the country, my peers were joining forces to tear at the veneer of decorum that had been the hallmark of the previous decade, showing their readiness, as JFK had said, to "assure the survival and success of liberty." It was time to challenge the status quo, to do away with old-boy politics, and to destroy the barriers erected by the bigotry of the color line. Earlier that summer, in August, the Reverend Martin Luther King had stood in the shadows of Washington's Lincoln Memorial and, before one of the largest gatherings ever assembled around the reflecting pool, called a nation back to its original creed – and forward to a bold dream of a new, harmonious America. Also in 1963, Betty Friedan's *The Feminine Mystique* hit bookstands – and nightstands – landing smack-dab in the middle of the intensifying furor over women's "place" in society. And halfway around the world, in a little country called Vietnam, trouble was brewing.

But in Pittsburg, Kansas, nothing seemed amiss. Blacks and whites attended classes and dormed together harmoniously enough, though the nighttime party scene was more exclusive. Television news of racial strife and political chicanery seemed to come from some very far-off place.

In high school my graduating class of thirty-eight had only one black student, James Moore. He had been our hero: soft-spoken and shy, yet the only one of us brave enough to stand up front at our noontime assemblies and sing – and could he ever sing! We would stomp our feet and shriek and cheer. James was a jazz musician, a football, basketball, baseball, track, and weight-lifting star, and he belonged to us. We'd bused to Colorado for our two-week senior trip instead of Florida, because we didn't want to take any chances; nobody was going to mess with James.

Pittsburg wasn't much different from Riverton. We were still tucked away in *Ozzie and Harriet* land. For us the golden years had yet to lose their luster. We lived secure in the knowledge that our country was safe in the hands of a wonderful Irish-Catholic redhead who, by the way, looked great without a shirt. The storm mounted around us, roiled the nation's big cities. Pittsburg, it seemed, was in the dead center, in the trauma-free eye. Yet even here strains of the fomenting music reached us. By the year's end it had taken on the bass roar of war.

November 22, 1963. I am walking across campus to my dorm. A girl comes out of the dorm and heads toward me. Her face, I notice immediately, is ashen, the color of the concrete sidewalk. President Kennedy has just been shot, she blurts. No, I say. What is it with college kids and their sick sense of humor? Yes, she says, it's true. A nick in the shoulder, I think.

I race up to my room. A couple of girls are there already, and the radio's on, crackling. The reporters repeat themselves over and over: President Kennedy has been shot in Dallas — we have no updates — we have no reports. Until: President Kennedy is dead.

I don't want to believe it. No one shoots the man who has red hair, just like my daddy. The man who has freckles, like Daddy and me both, but who (unlike us) never seems to be ashamed. No one kills my president.

In our dorm room, we cry for a man we never met but to whom we gave our hearts. Across campus, students and faculty join in mourning. Classes are cancelled, sports events postponed, flags lowered. In dorm lounges, we cluster in front of television sets for hour after hour. John-John and Jackie break our hearts all over again as in silence we watch the national drama close in a long, somber procession to Arlington. It's not fair, I think, as the riderless horse carries its empty saddle with a pair of boots stuck backward in the stirrups through the streets of the capital. This isn't how this story should end. This isn't how any story should end.

It wasn't the first time I'd fallen apart over death. Back in 1957 Mama had taken Allen and me to Joplin to see *Old Yeller*. I sat through it helplessly, watching the big, good-natured dog contract hydrophobia and be summarily executed by the very child who loved him most. I cried through the credits, and by the time we got home I was inconsolable, devastated. I sat in the living room, bawling and baying beyond control, awash in a flood of grief for every departed animal I had ever loved. I cried for our beloved boxer, Lorna Doone of Lodi, the dog I thought was my sister. The dog I'd accidentally trampled with a horse. She'd lived through that, despite the hoofprints on her back, only to crawl home one evening with her belly in tatters from gunshot. She died in our kitchen. I knew how it felt when things died. I knew what it was like for Old Yeller. It's fiction, Linda, Mama told me gently. It's a story, celluloid. It didn't really happen. Someone dreamed the whole thing up. She was right,

of course, but her reasoning was totally lost on me. In my woebe-
gone state, I needed more than logic. Mama understood, and tried a
different tack. She handed me a pencil and a sheet of lined paper. It's
a story, okay? If you don't like the ending, you write a better one. A
story can end any way you want it to. Go ahead and change it.

I spent days with Old Yeller's life in the balance. Though twelve,
I understood that every drama needs a certain amount of tragedy,
but there was no way I was willing to let Old Yeller die. I wrote
ending after ending. But no matter what I tried, they all lacked
punch, and I knew it. Maybe Old Yeller's creator, Fred Gipson, was
on to something. I didn't like how his story ended, but now that I'd
calmed down, I could see how it made things interesting. It was best,
I decided, not to tamper with it. There was, after all, some satisfac-
tion to be gained from grieving Old Yeller's death on my own.

Kennedy's assassination was different, though. The cowering
bodies in the back of the black convertible, the close-ups of blood
and roses on the car's floor – these images did not originate on some
Hollywood lot. No deft work in the cutting room could make this
scene go away. Pencil and paper were useless. There was no rewrit-
ing this ending. Only grief, borne by millions.

As trite as it sounds to compare a president's death to a Disney
picture, there are parallels between the lessons both taught me.
Mama made me analyze something I would otherwise have simply
taken for granted. She did not humiliate me for my childish sorrow.
Instead, she equipped me with the necessary tools – pad and pencil,
and a gentle prod – to work things through on my own. What could
I change? What couldn't I? She helped me poke a little hole in the
veil between fact and fiction. She led me a step down the path to
maturity – something she would never have achieved had she simply told me to pull myself together. Kennedy's murder helped me
grow up, too, but in a different way. After all the elegies and the
stirrings of patriotic solidarity, I was left with a sense of uncertainty
that I could not shake. Though nothing swayed my belief in the

infallibility of our nation or its cause, I felt the fragility of life, my own included. I faced the fact of mortality, and took a few more steps along the path.

Years later, as a classroom teacher struggling to figure out a way to help children with profound disabilities, I would find myself still clinging to the lessons Old Yeller and Kennedy had taught me. I hunted for the line between fact and fiction. In the saga of special education, there were some things I could not rewrite – degenerative diseases couldn't be scripted away. Some things were unchangeable fact. But other things could be challenged, and needed to be. *You have to crawl before you walk... Children who aren't walking by the age of seven will never walk... Contractures can only be helped by surgery...* Says who? I thought. It's just a matter of picking battles. Of taking steps.

Winter gave way to spring. The semester ended, and Mama came to take me home. As the days warmed into summer, I began my second season as a water safety instructor at Baxter Springs. With close to two hundred students of widely varying abilities, I had my hands full. But I had the help of two gifted senior lifesaving students, Larry O'Neal and Mickey Freeburg. We formed a team, instructing our minions of advanced, intermediate, and beginner swimmers, and teaching a Red Cross junior lifesaving class as well. We were going great guns and, spurred on by our success, planned to put on a water show. It was to be the most extravagant water show ever, we decided. So "Alice in Waterland" became the focus of our summer, and I spent weeks of evenings at home sewing costumes for every single one of our little swimmers.

Mary was eight years old that summer, and she came with me to the pool every day. Often we stopped on the way to town and picked up her friend Vicki Baert. The two of them had a grand time swimming and playing while I supervised the pool and worked with my students, rehearsing for our big production.

One August morning not long after my birthday, Larry, Mickey, and I had divided the students into three groups. I was in the pool, overseeing the beginners, and the junior lifesavers were assisting me with taking the little kids out of their depth for the first time. We were all concentrating hard and paying close attention, watching to see that everyone was safe. Mary and Vicki had swum to the deepest end of the pool and were thrilled to have the high dive and springboard to themselves; they were well out of the way of my charges, so I let them be, turning to glance at them once in a while.

To this day I do not know what first drew my attention to my sister. Perhaps it was Vicki's wild scream. She was standing on the high dive waving her hands hysterically and pointing to Mary, who was lying spread-eagled on the wet concrete beside the pool. I stayed calm and called to Mickey and Larry to get everyone out of the water. I grabbed the edge of the pool, pulled myself out, and started walking around the pool to see what the trouble was. As I got closer to Mary, it dawned on me that something was terribly wrong, and I felt my feet move faster and faster. By the time the pool was evacuated and Mickey and Larry had come over to see how they could help, I was kneeling alongside my sister, my face next to hers, asking, Mary, Mary, what happened? She was moaning, I don't know.

Are you hurt?

Mary didn't say anything, just groaned.

Where?

I looked at her arms, limp and crooked, and knew they were broken. A dislocated finger on her right hand stuck straight backward, and a jagged knuckle jutted out through the skin.

Tell me, Mary – where does it hurt the most?

My knee, my knee!

Oh, my God, how can her knees hurt worse than her arms? I thought. I didn't want to move her until I knew the extent of her injuries, but slowly and carefully I lifted her right leg a few inches off the concrete so I could get a look at her knee. It was a dark purple nightmare.

Not that one, Linda, the other one.

Get an ambulance now, I said to Mickey. He ran for the phone. If the knee I had seen, already so swollen and purple and mangled, was in better shape than her other one, then Mary was in a bad way and I wasn't going to move her any further.

Someone got a beach towel and I put it over her to keep her warm, scared she'd go into shock. Mickey came back from calling the ambulance. He and Larry stayed right with me, executing our emergency procedures perfectly, monitoring Mary's breathing and pulse and joining me in trying to comfort her. Are my arms broken? she wanted to know. I looked down at them again, at the waves bending in both of them, and couldn't bring myself to tell her the truth, afraid she'd be frightened and move and make things worse. I think one of them might be, I fudged. She looked up at me, tears spilling from the corners of her eyes. Will Daddy be mad? she asked, biting her lip to try to stop her voice from quavering. I didn't know what to say then, so I just told her to stay quiet, to lie still, not to move; that everything would be okay.

When the ambulance finally arrived from Baxter Springs Hospital, the medics couldn't wheel the gurney around the springboard, to Mary's right, and had to collapse it to get to her. I waited until they were at Mary's side, then gave them a rundown of her condition as I had evaluated it: She's got two broken arms, a dislocated and broken finger, there's something wrong with her knees, and I have no idea about her back or neck.

All five of us – Mickey and Larry and me and the two ambulance men – helped transfer Mary onto the gurney. I watched the four others hoist Mary back over the spring board, yelling at them each time they jarred the gurney. Mary was my sister. I would have had no qualms drowning those two medics if they'd made a mistake. By the time we were loading Mary into the ambulance a crowd of students and their parents had formed; no doubt they'd been there all along. Mickey and Larry promised to take care of everything at the pool, and I climbed into the back of the ambulance and rode to the hospital with my sister.

Sometimes small towns are a blessing. As it happened, Mama was in Baxter Springs shopping, and one of the ladies who was in the crowd at the pool had just seen her. She went back to the store, found Mama, and told her, Go to the hospital quick, one of your kids has been hurt, I don't know which one. Mama found a telephone and called home to tell Daddy. Allen answered – Daddy wasn't around – so Mama told him to get in the truck and drive to the hospital, fast.

Meanwhile I was holding on to one of Mary's broken arms while a doctor jerked on her finger to get it back into place. Mary was in agony. The side of her face that had hit the concrete was a hideous mass of purple, her eye swollen shut. I love you, Mama, she cried.

When Mama came into the emergency room I'd never been so glad to see anyone in my whole life. At the same time, I wished I'd never been born. But Mama read the look on my face and, despite the tremble in her voice, said, Let me tell you, Linda, it will be okay.

I couldn't take it anymore. A nurse showed me to the waiting room. Mama stayed with Mary to hold her while the doctor set her arms in casts and went to work on her battered, broken knees.

Later Allen arrived and the three of us stayed by Mary's bedside until she'd drifted into something resembling sleep. Then we drove home.

Dinner began silently that night, but Daddy, being Daddy, had to find a reason for this tragedy. Allen had thrown a load of hay off the truck so it wouldn't slow him up as he raced into town. Daddy's fury began with that, and Allen, by all accounts a grown man, made it worse by justifying his actions. Then it was my turn.

This was your fault, Linda. This was *your fault*, Linda! Weren't you even watching your little sister? Don't you care? You were in charge, and you nearly killed Mary. *This was your fault, Linda…*

I wanted to die. I wanted to crawl away into a dark, dark place and die. If Mary hadn't needed me to take care of her, I don't know what I would have done; the accident, I truly believed, was totally and completely my fault. Children can die in accidents – I knew that from Grandpa and Uncle Freddie – and from Daddy I knew an accident never *just happens*. Someone is always to blame; someone always could have prevented it. It was all my fault.

It took Mary several days to recover enough strength so that she could come home. With her arms in casts across her chest and her eyes gleaming out from huge black bruises, she looked like a mummified raccoon. Mary knew it, and didn't want anyone to see her. I, however, appointed myself to be her personal slave. I helped her in and out of her clothes, spooned her meals into her mouth, brushed her teeth, held her arms above the water while I bathed her, washed her hair. I was at her beck and call. At night I insisted she share my bed with me; otherwise I would never have been able to sleep. All this was my penance, and it saved me from total despair.

Six weeks later Mary's casts were due to come off. It was nearly time for school to begin again, and she was eager to be done with the whole ordeal. But when the doctor removed the casts, he discovered a problem: the way the bones were setting, it didn't look as though Mary's forearms would grow evenly; the inside bones would grow while the outside ones would remain stunted, which would twist her arms until they splayed away from her body. The only way to correct this was to twist the arms in the other direction and reset them. New casts, for at least another month.

With her arms curled and twisted at strange angles from her body, Mary was hard to lie next to in bed. She was always a wild little terrier, thrashing around in her sleep, but the casts made her as dangerous as a pit bull. They jabbed into my ribcage every time she turned. Mary, I told her one evening, you're doing so well. Why don't you try sleeping in your own bed tonight – it's your chance to start being a big girl.

She fell for it. But halfway through that first night with my bed to myself, I woke to hear the scrape of a piece of paper sliding under my door. I swung out of bed, turned on the lamp, and retrieved the note. MY HARM HURTS. It was Mary's writing, scratched painstakingly, misspelling and all.

Mary slept in my bed with me until her casts came off. Whatever was good for her was good for me.

Apart from his outburst at the dinner table the night of Mary's accident, Daddy never mentioned it to me again. Once he had locked in on someone to blame and had expended his initial rant, his anger subsided. Mary, though, felt the long-term effects of his fears. Daddy made it a rule that Mary could never have her feet more than twelve inches off the ground. He made Mary feel terrible. She understood the implication: You're so clumsy, you shouldn't try to do anything.

It wasn't really that Daddy didn't want us to do anything, only that doing things meant risk, and risk meant the potential for something to go wrong, for something to fail. Doing things meant someone might get hurt, which would mean someone was to blame, which would bring on guilt and gut-wrenching fear. These two things had haunted Daddy's childhood and lashed out at him. Now his love for his children left him paralyzed by a fear so deep he could hardly bring himself to think about it.

When the time came for me to leave home and return to college for my sophomore year, I breathed a sigh of relief, even as a twinge of guilt flickered through me.

I felt safe at college, no longer intimidated by its size. Pittsburg was built around the university and offered plentiful distractions, yet I stayed centered on my studies, and on having a good time when my

My feminine mystique. Pittsburg State, 1966.

workload allowed. Despite my love of the sciences and my desire to study medicine, I declared English and Art as my double major. I made safe (and affordable) choices. For adventure, I contented myself with *The Hobbit*. Tolkien's fantastic novels were hot stuff, second only to the latest Beatles single. Near cultish in our obsession, my friends and I finished *The Hobbit* and moved on to *The Lord of the Rings* trilogy and *The Silmarillion*. Anyone who hadn't at least read *The Hobbit* was, in our books, woefully out of touch and not to be taken seriously. In a gray time, we relished the black-and-white contrasts, the distinct forces of good and evil, that Tolkien so marvelously portrayed in his allegorical tales. My circle of friends was not wide, but those included in it were of the best sort – fun-loving and caring. Often we went dancing together, or sat in each other's rooms spinning the newest vinyl from The Doors, The Carpenters, The Beatles, or Peter, Paul & Mary.

And there was Jeff Foster. He and his brother were musicians with the most popular band on campus. I pined for Jeff throughout my four years of college, but he and I seemed cursed to be best friends. He enjoyed having me around, and we went everywhere together, but my pining for him was equaled only by his pining for someone else. Eventually Jeff began seeing Jill, his "someone else," but he still invited me to hang out with them, welcoming me on some of their dates (how Jill tolerated my presence I never understood). When they married, it broke my heart – as I had known it would. From the day I had realized I would never be the love of Jeff's life, I had understood that he would one day break my heart. Still, it had seemed a small price to pay for the friendship, warmth, and security he offered. Jeff was the first man I felt truly comfortable around. He set me at ease, made me relax, allowed me to be myself. I didn't have the words for it then, but know now I was drawn to Jeff for his open, non-threatening behavior. He kept me happy and safe through four potentially hazardous years, and left me wiser for it.

In the early 1960s, American presidents were still good guys who kept us safe from the bad guys. As I saw it, they would never have risen to the office had they been less than commendable. Sure, some presidents had done a better – or worse – job of governing than others, but by and large they were a good lot, and whatever they said I supported. So when Lyndon Johnson, president by default, ushered the Gulf of Tonkin Resolution through Congress in the summer of 1964 and secured backing for military action in Vietnam, I naturally figured he knew what he was doing. I got involved in ROTC (and was nominated to represent my dorm for the ROTC Queen contest one year) and did my part for the Red, White, and Blue.

South Pacific was more laughs, less pomp. I got involved in campus theater because I wanted to do something with my art. Painting flats and backdrops and designing sets gave me an outlet – at least the canvases were vast. After a few productions, I tried acting, playing safe bit parts. I danced in *Dark of the Moon*, and had a complete lark. Gary Busey starred in that production, before he was Gary Busey. Events like that gave me an excuse to arrange for Mama to come get me from school, take me home, and then for me to drive back up to school with my sisters. They'd stay with me for the production, spend the night in my dorm, and I'd return them to Mama the next morning. I may have been twenty-five miles from home and in a different world, but that never once stopped me reaching back for my sisters' hands, wanting them to share my life with me, even if we were separated by distance and years.

The summer of my sophomore year, though, I decided not to go home. Instead, I went north to Kansas City, got a job lifeguarding, and stayed with Gwen, my college roommate. I had my own car by then, a Chevy Corvair that Mama and Daddy had bought for me. It wasn't new, but it did okay, except that the engine, mounted in the rear like a VW Beetle, went through a lot of fan belts.

I liked the pace of the city and liked my job at the pool (the money was better than Baxter Springs had been), but I did miss my sisters. So I arranged for them to spend a weekend with me, and drove home to pick them up. They would be part of my life for at least three days that summer.

I'm sure we had a fine weekend together – I just don't remember a single detail of it. The ride home was a different story...

We are driving south on Highway 69 – a straight shot from Kansas City to Lowell – and we've been on the road for about an hour. It's Sunday, mid-afternoon, and I have the car in low gear, the wipers boogying frantically as I navigate through a typical Kansas thunderstorm. And then, right on cue, the fan belt breaks. The Corvair's air-cooled engine flounders, begins to overheat. I pull onto the shoulder of the highway and shut it off. This is not happening, I think. But it is, and we have little choice but to get out, all three of us, and start walking in the rain, like Hemingway characters.

We walk the better part of a mile, drenched through, before we come to any signs of human habitation. And these are few enough. There is one sign. It reads JINGO, KANSAS. If it hadn't, we might have walked through the town without ever knowing we'd been there. Jingo is an intersection, not a town. Not even a traffic light. But there is what looks like a gas station on the corner, and I head for it. The man who answers my knock says they don't have any fan belts. He says they closed down a long time ago, but that Bill, across town, might be able to help us. Could I call him from here? I ask. The man looks just a little put out, but says he reckons that would be okay. We traipse in, my sisters and I, and stand dripping inside the doorway. There is a woman in the house. She and the man are getting ready to go someplace. They are both dressed in black, the woman in a dress that sweeps to her ankles, around which she's fastened dainty white lace anklets. She is lacing up a pair of polished black shoes. Both the man and the woman are fussing with their clothes the way people do when they want you to know they're in a hurry. I'm sorry for the trouble, I say. We won't be long.

The telephone is ancient, like the one at Grandma and Grandpa's in Tongie. I look at it, nonplused. The man sees the puzzled expression on my face. Give one good ring, he says. That'll get you the operator. I pick up the handset, hold it to my ear, and give a good turn to the crank on the side of the phone. *Rrrriiinng.* Who do you want? a woman's voice says. I tell her I want Bill. Well, the voice says, I don't know. I can try his garage, but I doubt he'll be there. I could well imagine they'd be closed right about now. His mom's awful sick, you know. She's real bad, in the hospital, and Bill's been spending a lot of time out there. For all I know he might be th — She warms to her theme, launching into an expanded and annotated history of Bill's family. I pull the handset away from my ear and study it, as though it might offer an explanation for the voice steam-rolling down its wires. Well, I'll try the garage first, I hear the voice say. If he's not there, we'll try the hospital, and they at least should know his whereabouts. I try to thank her, but she runs right over my words, flattens me. The phone clicks, takes her voice with it. I wait. I notice the wallpaper. It's a pastel pattern of frilly flowers and fluttery butterflies. In between the flowers and the butterflies are the words Jesus Christ. Jesus Christ wallpaper. I have never seen anything like this in my life. I take in more of the room. There are some shelves on the walls, and each is loaded with what appear to be crosses and other religious paraphernalia. Jesus Christ wallpaper. Icons. A man and a woman dressed in black, in a hole of a town that still has crank phones and an operator with a bad case of verbal diarrhea. I am beginning to think I should grab my sisters and make a dash out of here, back to reality, but I find myself praying to the wallpaper instead. Then the phone clicks again, and the woman's voice informs me she's located Bill. She puts him on the line. Bill sounds nice, especially when he says he's pretty sure he has the fan belt we need. We just have to sit tight, and he'll be right over with his truck to pick us up.

Bill's going to pick us up, I tell the man and the woman, thanking them for the use of their phone. That's good, they say. Across the street from their onetime gas station is a church. The rain has slackened, and people are walking into the church for the evening service. Everyone in black. I can tell the man and woman want to go join them, but they don't. We can wait outside, I offer. They ignore this. They wait with us for Bill and don't leave the house until he arrives and we get in his truck.

Bill is as nice as his voice. He drives us the mile back to my car and goes to work. Only, I can't find my keys. I've left them at the house with the Jesus Christ wallpaper. I don't want to believe it, but I have no choice. So Bill takes us back to town, and I have to walk up the steps of that church full of people in black. There is an aisle down the middle. On one side sit the men, their feet flat on the floor, their backs straight, their eyes forward. On the other sit the women, equally rigid. I take a few cautious steps through the open door and down the aisle. Heads turn. The man from the onetime gas station sees me, gets up. We step to the door. I am a nervous wreck, I feel so ashamed, but I manage to explain the problem. He does his best not to scowl. The service has started already, he informs me. I repeat my apology. We'll have to hurry, he says, and ushers me out of the church, down the steps, and across the street.

Bill drives us back to my car again, this time with the keys, and he fixes the fan belt. He charges me the price of the belt; that's all the money he'll accept. I thank him as best I know how. When we drive past the Jingo sign, I slow down. What a place, I think. I shake my head slowly as we pass the church, as though to sort out my thoughts, and drive on with my eyes open wider than they had been that morning.

When I began college, the girls' dorms were located to one side of campus and the boys' clear on the opposite boundary, as divided as

the men and women of the Jingo church. We had dorm hours, a cur-
few, and it was death if you were late. By my senior year, the great
divide had been breached. Boys' and girls' dorms sat alongside each
other. Coed housing was still around the corner, but changes had
begun. And at a school as quiet as ours, such changes did not go
unperceived. Bob Dylan was right about the times, even in
Pittsburg, Kansas.

Yet right through 1967, my senior year, the campus stayed
quiet – except for the incessant playing of Procul Harum's "A
Whiter Shade of Pale," a mega-hit destined to become the number-
one song in the world by early summer. Woodstock was still two
years off, but it would take longer than that for the hippie generation
to make inroads into our insulated cultural environment. Over four-
hundred thousand US troops were now in Vietnam, but we would
never have known it had it not been for the televised nightly news-
casts and their obsession with body counts. There was some worry
among the boys over being A-1 and draft eligible, but no one played
it up much. We were too busy skipping the light fandango and trying to puzzle out Keith Reid's layered lyrics to get excited about
Vietnam. Besides, kids who were sent there generally weren't college types, at least not yet. As for me, I had the feeling that if I just
laid low, as I had when the tornado passed over us in the ditch, everything that threatened to make my life unsafe would blow over.

Of course, my perspective on national and world events was
about as limited as my view of the tornado had been. I was aware of
a general spinning going on around me, but nothing during those
college years shook my heart and soul. Kennedy's death was the one
exception. Just as I crammed late into the night prior to midterms so
I could cough up the right answers – without ever thinking to question the data in front of me – so too I did not look beyond the immediate messages beamed at me from the set. I readily accepted as
truth just about any story our governing leaders presented. After all,
presidents and their colleagues were good guys.

Only later, after graduation, did I discover the viewpoint I had been missing. The realization brought me up short: I had been filling in all the right boxes, but I had no concept of what any of it really meant. Away from the sanctuary of the heartland, I glimpsed a little of the harshness of racism, the reality of poverty, the ugliness of war – and I was left to wonder how I had missed it during those decisive college years.

What turned out to be the biggest decision I made in college started as a no-brainer. The school hosted a job fair my senior year, and I went to look into my options. The first interviewer to catch my attention was a man representing the high school at Tehachapi, California. I liked the sound of the name – Te-*hach*-a-pee: it reminded me of a squelched sneeze – and I was immediately intrigued at the thought of moving to the West Coast. This would be a bold move, a leap into the unknown, a break with everything familiar. The start of something new. The perfect job. But I had to get through the interview first. I sat down, smiled, and handed the man my transcript. He looked it over, frowned, then handed it back to me. My grades worried him, he said. Had I over-committed? I glanced down at the transcript to make sure I understood: as far as I could see, the numbers were nothing to worry about. I had one of the top grade point averages of my graduating class. I'm sorry, I said, not getting it. Your grades, he explained patiently, they're a little high. He went on for a while, to be sure I understood him: People with GPAs like mine usually don't get along well with others; they are, as a rule of thumb, ambitious and spend considerable amounts of energy in trying to better their lot; in short, they do not thrive within the constrained environment of a rural school, even one drenched in California sunshine.

I didn't buy it. I was perfect for the job, I told him, and ready to pack my bags and get to work. He must have sensed the sincerity in my tone, because the upshot of the interview, despite the litany of caveats, was an invitation to teach English at Tehachapi.

Before I would be eligible to teach, though, I first had to pick up a handful of post-grad credits – a prerequisite in those days. I had a fan club in my well-to-do great-aunt and uncle, Teddy and Frank Engert (she was a sister of my grandmother Mimi), and they lobbied to have me return to the family's Knoxville roots and do my summer's worth of work at the University of Tennessee while living with them. I remembered the happiness of the few visits we'd made to the Engerts when I was a child, and was glad to go. So that summer, while Secretary of Defense Robert McNamara was lecturing a Senate subcommittee on the ineffectiveness of America's bombing campaign and Martin Luther King was speaking out against the war in Vietnam and urging a convergence of the civil rights and peace movements, I tooled around Knoxville in Uncle Frank's white Porsche convertible.

When Grandmother Miller married the son of plantation owners, she married into Southern tradition. Until the Emancipation Proclamation and the Civil War changed everything, the Millers lived their unfettered life and sipped their mint juleps and drawled their languid vowels. The war freed their slaves, turned them into servants. The Millers had been kind masters and, for those who chose to stay on, guaranteed food in the belly and a dry place to sleep, even if wages were meager. A century later, Teddy and Frank were linked to the Miller legacy by little more than her maiden name. They lived in style, in a colonnaded Southern mansion not unlike their ancestors', but they'd had to work for it.

Ever since I was a little girl, I had loved our visits to Teddy and Frank, not just because I liked these two good-natured old people, but because of their cook, Callie. She spoiled me rotten. The kitchen was her domain, and no one entered without her permission. I had her permission. She would grab me around my skinny waist with her warm, worn, black hands and hoist me up onto the counter, and I would sit for hours on end watching her prepare apple pies or stir huge pots of steaming vegetables on the giant stove. Callie was always at home around her range, and I loved to sit near its warmth, breathing in the delicious smells or toying with a floury lump of pastry. Callie had been with the Engerts forever. They were her family, and she was part of theirs. It had always been that way, as far as I knew. She was part of the tradition.

Callie had retired by the time I came to UT for summer school, but Frank and Teddy and her unmarried sister, Minta, welcomed me as part of the family. Berfie took a little more convincing. He was a pedigreed bulldog, a gift from my daddy, who at the time was into raising bulldogs. Berfie's real name was Bereford, to rhyme with Hereford (as a hobby, Frank kept a small herd of prime stock, lorded over by Fancy Pants, a well-hung prize bull), but Berfie suited him better. He was, after all, the Engerts' little taffy-and-cream baby, and they pampered him shamelessly. He had a bedroom to himself, furnished to his tastes, and a monogrammed gold brush, comb, and mirror set employed by his doters for tending to his coiffure. He took his meals in the dining room along with the rest of us, sampling only the very best in gourmet doggie foods. From what I could tell, the only things he lacked were a monocle and a subscription to the *Wall Street Journal*.

If staying with Teddy and Frank was an education in how the other half lives, that summer at UT was equally informative in an entirely different way, beyond providing me with the post-grad art credits I needed to begin my teaching career. The UT campus was a whole lot bigger than Pittsburg State, the students much more in tune with the sixties. There was the House of Colors, for instance. More or less a flophouse within walking distance from campus, it was *the* place to hang out if you were into the hippie scene. The place where things *happened*. Outside, the two-story building was sided with vertical slats, each one painted a different color by a different group of people. The effect was psychedelic. Inside, pot smoke hung in the air. Doorways draped with strings of beads and shells led to rooms where longhaired men and loose-haired women lounged in happy harmony, grooving to guitar riffs and dragging on jays.

I had heard of pot, but I'd never seen it before, or smelled it. I knew they smoked pot at the House of Colors. No one was dropping acid or anything – or if they were, I knew nothing about it. Still, marijuana was illegal, and I just didn't do illegal things. In all honesty, I was terrified of it. Every once in a while, though, I would go along with friends from school when they hit the House of Colors, but each time I felt uneasy, scared of what would happen if I were discovered there. The regulars unsettled me. I had no way of relating to them. I was as out of sync with them as I had been with those high school classmates of mine who were having sex when I was still totally naïve about how it worked. I'm just a late bloomer, I decided.

My eyes continued to be opened almost in spite of me. My friends in the art department, hippies to a fault, decided to attend a meeting of the local chapter of the John Birch Society, and casually invited me to go with them. We were a mixed group, blacks and whites, and I had no idea where we were going or what we were going to do when we got there, though I pretended otherwise. So I went along and sat in on the meeting. Imagine my surprise when the fellow doing the talking started spouting putrid filth about "keeping America safe" from black people (he called them something else) and the meeting erupted in cheers. What were we *doing* there? I wondered. But my friends seemed calm, if alert. They had come in silent protest. So this is what a sit-in is, I thought to myself, the lights slowly coming on inside my head. There had never been any protests or marches around Pittsburg; the civil rights movement sort of missed us out. But my next thought appalled me: What if Teddy and Frank find out! Teddy and Frank had been so wonderful to me. But they were very Deep South, very cautious. They were citizens in good social standing, affluent and respected, and it simply would not do for me to make waves.

At summer's end Frank decided I needed a going-away present. He took me down to the dealership and helped me buy my first brand-new car: a four-door, medium blue Chevy II. Frank made the bulk of the down payment himself; Mama and Daddy chipped in, too – a wonderful surprise. They had paid four years of tuition for me, as well as twenty-five dollars a month for my room, and I had honestly never expected more. I had saved on my own, money I'd earned from lifeguarding and from the minimum-wage jobs I'd had at Pittsburg State (I was dorm receptionist for a while, and occasionally modeled, clothed, for an art class), but most of what I'd made had gone toward school expenses, to supplement the money my parents gave me. But Frank and I did the math and figured I'd be able to handle the rest of the car payments once I got going with my teaching job in California.

I finished up at UT, took leave of Teddy, Frank, and Aunt Minta (and Berfie, of course), got in my Chevy, and returned home to Kansas with that wonderful new-car smell tickling the insides of my nose.

I didn't bother unpacking my bags. As I got everything ready for my trip to California, Mama kept poking her head into my room and asking, Are you sure you don't want me to go with you, Linda? And each time I answered, No, Mama, I can do this. I can do this.

Maybe a faint tremor in my voice gave me away, or maybe she just couldn't reconcile herself to the fact that I was leaving, but in the end Mama once again insisted on accompanying me on the next leg of my journey. We loaded the car for our drive halfway across the country to California. I said good-bye to Daddy and Allen and to Mary and Minta, now so grown up at fifteen and sixteen, and then Mama and I pulled away from the house and onto the gravel road to Lowell, past our cow pastures and the Baumanns' farm, turning left at Ball's grocery store and crossing the bridges to Riverton, where we joined the westbound traffic on the Mother Road until it metamorphosed into the Interstate.

Oklahoma, Texas, New Mexico, Arizona. Wheat fields gave way to ranch towns, then desert dust; humidity yielded to dry heat. I imagined Mama and I were two Okie women escaping west out of the Dust Bowl – we were, after all, taking the same route. I marveled at the distances between towns, and imagined the jalopies wheezing from one remote gas station to the next. As we crossed mile after mile of desert, I drank in the intense color of the landscape. Before, I'd always assumed those calendar pictures of flowerpot-red mesas were photographically enhanced. Now I knew better. We stayed a night in Tucumcari, New Mexico, at a small inn. The owners treated us like long-lost relatives. They were too young to have been running the inn during the Dust Bowl years, but I imagined their kin saving more than one desperate family during that time; that's the kind of people they were. When we finally reached Needles, the heat was so intense, it hurt to breathe. I thought of the many Okie families who had been refused entrance to California here. Compared with their worries, what were my fears about my future? As we crossed into the Golden State, I felt like a wimp.

We drove through the Mojave Desert, where tumbleweed rolled beside the highway and cacti stood like stick figures alongside red rocks. Tehachapi, I had been told by my interviewer, was situated in the mountains to the southeast of the great San Joaquin Valley. I had visions of the Great Smokies of Tennessee – rugged, forested peaks that commanded respect and silence. So when we began our climb through the yellow hills, which reddened as we gained altitude, I waited for the mountains to materialize. They did not. We climbed through the Tehachapi Pass (elevation 3793 ft.) and found the town nestled twenty miles on, snug in the curves of the yellow hills. A sign read TEHACHAPI — LAND OF FOUR SEASONS. Surely there's more than that to brag about, I thought, peering out at the wind-rounded rocks clustered like sheep among the tufted grasses in the fields on either side of the road. This was not the California of my Pittsburg dreams. This was something off the set of a John Wayne movie, and I was about to let myself be collared into a role as an extra. This is terrible, I thought as we slowed to cross the train tracks that slice through the town on their way to the valley. At least they'll give me a straight line to follow when I decide to shoulder my duffel and trudge out of here, I consoled myself.

We did a quick reconnoiter of the town, driving past greasy spoons with painted signs advertising biscuits and gravy, corrugated tin workshops where farm implements awaited repair, boxcar sidings and oil tanks, white-painted dwellings with children's bicycles flopped against chain-link fences. Behind us, a train whistle sounded. It gave way to a low rumble. I turned to see a line of freight cars moving slowly across the street behind us. The train obliterated the mountain backdrop. The rumble continued as we moved on down the street.

We found the high school, its front steps facing the road that sloped up the gradual hill. Constructed around an open square, the school's buildings were low-lying and stuccoed white. At the rear of the school were basketball and tennis courts and the football field. It took only a few minutes to drive slowly around the block with the high school at its center. The school might be small, yet seeing it put me at ease: though completely different in design and setting, it reminded me of Riverton High and the safety of its memories.

There was a motel on the edge of town. We checked in for the night. The next morning, we went apartment hunting. Rumor had it, the townies informed us with pride, that an apartment complex was in the works for two years down the road. I wasn't going to hold my breath waiting. I was scheduled to start my teaching career in less than a week, and I had nowhere to live, no furniture to my name, and no idea how to go about setting myself up. Mama, trooper that she is, came through again, and before long I had my hands on the keys for the one available apartment in town.

The place came with some useful (if well-used) furniture, including a sofa that looked suspiciously like the bench seat off an old car. It had no arms and the fabric was worn thin, down to threads in some places. It was also booby-trapped. One of the seat springs had come dislodged and had poked its way up near the surface. The spring lurked below the fabric, like the spiders in Grandpa's bona fide two-holer. If I sat down too quickly or without thinking, it lunged upward and jabbed at my unsuspecting bottom.

Mama and I buy groceries. We go to the bank and open an account in my name. She stays with me a week. Then I drive her to the airport to catch a flight home. I feel ashamed for not having wanted her to accompany me in the first place. *Mama, the bravest, brightest, strongest woman I have ever known.* You'll do fine, she reassures me, and I know she means it, despite the cliché. Everything's going to be fine. *She has shepherded me through the desert, kept me safe thus far.* I'll do my best, Mama. Tell Daddy and Allen and the girls I love them. *She put Band-Aids on my knees when I skinned them on the gravel road.* Do you need anything else? *She knows I love her, doesn't she?* I don't think so, I'm all set. *Am I? Shouldn't I be going with her, going home where I belong? What am I doing? Who is going to...* Hug me, Mama. Just hug me. *I'm her little girl, always. Even though she's smaller than me now, shrinking. But still strong. We are still strong.* Thank you – for everything.

Good-bye, Mama.

the miller's daughter

The Monday after Labor Day I reported for duty. I parked in the teachers' lot, gathered my things from the car and, clutching them protectively, made for the main door, conscious of eyes watching me. As I opened the glass door to walk into Tehachapi High for my first day on the job, I caught sight of my reflection and did a double take. I look like them, I couldn't help thinking. Like the kids I'm supposed to be teaching. Can I really be so young?

By the time I found my classroom my nerves were a mess. I knew my stuff – that wasn't my worry. We'd studied curriculum development at Pittsburg, and the curriculum for Tehachapi High was obviously well-constructed. As for classroom experience, I'd done my requisite stint of student teaching, in Kansas City, so I'd at least stood in front of a roomful of teenagers before. But compared with this, all that was mere play-acting. This – this was *different*. This was a job. My first real job. My future. Everything I'd worked toward. Would I manage? Would that thin young girl in the glass door, with her nervous eyes and blond hair and an armful of notebooks and planners, would she be woman enough to make this work? Would she?

My students set my mind to rest in short order. Ecstatic at having a teacher young enough to understand their juvenile points of view, they flocked around me and welcomed me as the ally they'd never had. As for me, I soon felt more comfortable around them than around other members of the faculty, the youngest of whom was twice my age. It was hard for me to feel accepted as an equal by colleagues old enough to be my parents, or grandparents. At the same time, however, I found myself having to juggle the students' enthusiasm over my presence on campus with my need to stay in sync with the other teachers – no small feat. There were constantly students at my door wanting my attention, wanting me to help them out of a bind, and, sometimes, wanting me for their lackey, to run interference for items on their personal agendas.

There was also the lunch monitor to be reckoned with. Built like a sumo wrestler, she had found her power niche and was hell-bent on maintaining order in her lunch-line ranks. Teachers, I had been instructed, were to cut to the front of the line. The time we saved was to be used for lesson planning. My first day, I hesitantly walked toward the front of the line. (Midwestern girls are raised to stand in queues. We don't fight, crowd, or break the rules. Ever.) I smiled a flitty smile at the students I passed, and tiptoed on. That is, until Mrs. Monitor's radar caught me. She zoomed down on me like a mud snake homing in on a frog. What do you think you are doing! she bellowed. Get to the back of the line. I waited for my ears to quit ringing, but they didn't. I'm a teacher, I said. I was told to come to the front of the li – She didn't believe me. The students behind me verified that I was, indeed, a teacher. But their giggles didn't lend credence to the situation. Finally, she stomped over to one of the older teachers. Yes, indeedy, he sighed. She's a teacher. Judging by his tone, what he meant to say was, What is this world coming to? I brought my own lunch a lot after that.

Both the students and the school administrators put me through my paces. I was assigned to teach a full load of English and art classes, with about twenty-five students in each. I taught kids from all four grades, many of whom were functioning below acceptable reading and writing standards. As the newest teacher on staff, it fell to me to work with these slower learners and attempt to bring them up to speed, while my more experienced colleagues taught the students whose potential seemed greater.

They were a great bunch, the kids in my English and art classes, polite and good-natured, if somewhat mischievous. Outside of sports – by far the biggest focus of our high school – there wasn't much for a kid to do around Tehachapi in the late years of the sixties, and sometimes they got bored. In other parts of the state, the swan song for the hippie era had already begun, to be replaced by the jittery tempo of the disco generation. But up in our mountains (such as they were) students came to school decked in the replete regalia of the times: bell-bottomed pants, boots, mini-skirts, and tie-dyed sundries. The students got away with it, but my college wardrobe no longer passed muster; as a teacher, I was obliged to subdue my tastes and adopt dyed-to-match skirt and sweater outfits and other dowdy getups deemed more in keeping with my position. My choices were limited, and not only by the staff dress code. Money was tight. I was a first-year teacher on a one-year contract, and if I expected better, I was going to have to earn it.

As a teacher, I was required to help out at extracurricular events, which usually meant sports. Football was everything, basketball not far behind. Tehachapi High took pride in its Warriors and their storied history of gridiron conquest. Next to God, the football coach was the most important being in the universe, and woe betide if our team failed to rank among the top contenders for the league crown. Or if teachers didn't show up for the Friday night games. I was there, always. Taking tickets. Cheering as loudly as the kids. *Go, Warriors!*

Monday morning, though, I was back in the classroom, back at it, trying to find the key – to make learning fun enough for my students so they'd catch on. For as much as they genuinely seemed to like me, with many there was little I could do to inspire them. They just were not interested in learning anything, and it broke my heart. One of my English classes, in particular, was made up almost exclusively of non-readers. I tried to spark some enthusiasm by focusing on creative writing exercises, hoping to stir up some pride, which might lead to comprehension. No such luck. My art classes weren't much better. I wanted my students to be able to explore art, to work with media and enjoy the feeling of creating something from nothing, but usually by the time we got started on a project, the period was over, and I was left with a huge mess to clean up. Besides, at least one of my art classes was filled with senior jocks looking for easy credits to meet graduation requirements. Before too many weeks had gone by, I had the nagging sensation that I was being set up, and not just by the students.

I felt clueless, left to my own devices. Classroom control and motivation were not subjects we'd addressed at Pittsburg or during my student teaching at Kansas City. Now here I was, far from the relative safety of the university, facing the reality that I wasn't a big cheese anymore, didn't have lots and lots of choices, simply didn't really know what I was doing. The staff I worked with were wonderful people, all of them, but they couldn't be expected to remember how it felt, all those years ago, when they'd been young teachers just starting out and hadn't been able to relate to the older generation in the staff room. I was on my own, sink or swim. And I couldn't help feeling some of them had their money on me sinking.

Part of the reason I'd become a teacher in the first place was because I'd wanted to latch on to that elusive possibility a classroom of open minds seems to offer: I wanted to touch lives. To make a difference. To effect change. But as that first year wore on, my exuberant zeal was displaced by a sobering resignation. I was not moving or shaking anybody. I was not influencing the course of the stars, not even swaying the direction most of my students were headed. I was

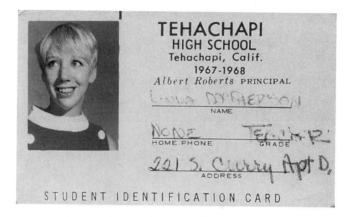

"Yes, indeedy. She's a teacher..." So there.

little else but a role player. Sure, Tehachapi was a lovely place, a lovely school, with lovely people to work with and students to teach. But what, I began to ask myself, was I doing there? What was I *doing?* My teaching consisted of following the curriculum to a T. It was paint-by-numbers. Round pegs in round holes. On the first of January, students will be on page such and such. Your evaluation as teacher will be gauged accordingly. The more creative you try to be, the less likely you are to arrive at this predetermined page. That's what you are, Linda, a voice inside my head started saying: you're a role player. Anyone could walk in off the street and, provided they know how to read, could do this as well as you (maybe even better). You're not helping the situation. You're not touching anybody. You're making absolutely no diff –

And, in my thoughts, I saw myself twenty, thirty years down the road, a teacher like so many of my colleagues, doing their best, year after year, but parrot-like – repeating motions over and over, going round and round, like the drums of Daddy's fertilizer machine, rolling out little pellets, little round balls, all routinely similar, very little difference between them. And not one soul touched.

The crowning blow came when one of my English students, a young man whose inability to read left him terribly depressed about his future, committed suicide. From what the police could construct, he had walked to the freeway on the edge of town and waited for a truck to come down the hill. The driver had no time; the boy stepped into his path, and into oblivion. Just like that. He had been a really nice kid, shy, and worried to the point of death over getting a job without being able to read, but still nice. I knew nothing about dyslexia or other learning disabilities at the time, but somehow I knew he could have been helped. I thought of Buster, and Mr. Brown. There must be ways to get the penny to drop, and I doubted they had anything to do with slavish adherence to a curriculum. Certainly nothing to do with a truck on the freeway to Bakersfield.

By then it was spring. The pear and apple orchards were in flower, the cycle of all growing things intent on another round. And for me, the decision of a contract renewal. It was, the school officials opined, a straightforward decision for me to make, and they expected a prompt response. They couldn't be blamed for not knowing I was in love with Martin.

Before Martin, there was John. Without John, there wouldn't have been Martin. John was in one of my art classes. A jock and a senior, he was big for his age and ran around town with an older set of guys, most of whom were once football heroes in this little town. Martin was one of those guys, and John took it into his head to play matchmaker; I'm sure he thought that more challenging than my art lessons. Linda, there's a guy I think you should meet...

John didn't seem to get it. He'd come up to me after class and start talking about Martin, and each time I'd tell him, in a friendly but teacherly voice, Sorry, John. Not interested.

The night he and Martin turned up on my doorstep, I knew for sure he hadn't gotten it. But I also saw that Martin was gorgeous. So I shot John a halfhearted *how could you?* look, and heard myself inviting them in.

We chatted. Just noncommittal banter, but enough for me to tell that Martin was a nice guy, soft-spoken and seemingly gentle. Enough so that when, a few nights later, the two of them appeared at my apartment again, I invited them in without giving John the look. They kept coming back. During the school day, John worked on me, urging me to keep talking with Martin, and he must have given Martin equal time after hours. Finally, as much to shut John up as anything else, Martin and I agreed to spend an evening together. Not a date, just an exploration – a testing of the waters. A relationship didn't figure in to either of our immediate plans.

But we hadn't figured on becoming friends, either. So there we were, talking in the evenings and hanging out. Just friends. Or was there more to it? I began to resent the evenings John showed up with Martin, and chafed in anticipation of the moment he'd graciously excuse himself and leave us to our private conversation. (Now I knew how Jill must have felt when I'd been buddies with Jeff, her beau, back in Pittsburg.)

Martin and I eventually started dating. Perhaps it was inevitable. We had resisted falling in love as best we could, but our friendship had deepened to the point where we could no longer pretend it didn't amount to much. We were in love, and we finally got around to admitting it.

Martin was a couple years younger than I, one of a family with eight children. On his mother's side, the family was Mexican. His grandfather had ridden with Pancho Villa in the Revolution. His father's ancestors were Basque: peasants, miners, shoemakers, day laborers, sheep herders from the western Pyrenees that separate France and Spain. Years ago, one adventurous soul had made the crossing to America, traversed the breadth of the continent and settled in the Tehachapi hills, perhaps finding solace in the barren landscape and familiar work among the flocks that grazed there. Word made its way home, and others followed. A community of French-speaking shepherds grew up, and a cultural enclave was established. From these Basque ancestors Martin inherited his dark hair and olive skin, his broad frame and easy-going manner – and his curious-sounding last name, Bidabe, which rhymes with *tamale* (though the stressed "a" is hollower, more like the opened-mouth sound tongue-depressing doctors request).

Martin had played football in high school well enough to win an athletic scholarship to Santa Rosa Junior College. Then, in one of the last games of his senior year of high school, he'd blown out his knee. It was his final game. Surgery repaired his knee, but his football days were over. So was his scholarship. But Martin refused to let

July 2, 1968

his dreams evaporate. He went to Santa Rosa anyway. That lasted a year – with a big family to attend to, his parents couldn't afford to keep him there. So Martin had come back home to Tehachapi, back to his cronies. He had found work with the Kern County school district as a driver, transporting students with disabilities from their mountain homes to special schools in the valley, and an opportunity to further his education at Bakersfield College, where he registered for classes in law enforcement. He also found me.

Or rather, John found us.

By the end of my first year teaching at Tehachapi High, I knew two things beyond a shadow of a doubt: that I was in love with Martin Bidabe, and that I did not want to go through another year robotically pegging up holes and feeling like a complete failure, able to execute the curriculum in my sleep, yet unable to inspire a single student.

Martin and I discussed my – or our – situation often and at length. The first part was easy: we decided to get married that summer. The second part wasn't as simple. There was a contract sitting on the desk in my apartment, and pressure mounting from school officials who wanted to know my decision. On the one hand I knew how misplaced and redundant I felt, and on the other I questioned whether I'd allowed myself enough time to give the high school my best shot. Martin helped me see what I actually already knew: no matter how long I stayed there, I was never going to be happy. I might be good at putting pegs in holes, but I myself simply did not *fit*. One year was enough. I would not go back.

We married in July. We had talked about getting married in Tehachapi, to save money. But in the end, I couldn't do it. If nothing else, our union had to be blessed by my family. So we drove home to Kansas, for a small ceremony in Baxter Springs. When it was over, we left. I cried all the way to Colorado. I don't know how Martin put up with me. Finally, finally the truth had hit me: Kansas was no longer my home. By the time we returned to the Golden Hills, though, I was okay again. And then we were back in Tehachapi, adjusting to married life.

I needed something to do, and we needed money, so I took a job at one of the large commercial pear orchards near town. Actually, the job was a lark dreamed up by Martin and Ed Jacobsen, the orchard owner. Ed and his wife were good business people, and a ton of fun besides. Martin had worked for them several summers and was a trusted employee. They loved him, which might explain why Ed figured he could add me to the payroll, inept as I was.

Ed had invented a pear-picking machine, with arms that raised and lowered with hydraulic mechanisms. He paid me to paint this contraption. I got a friend of mine to help me, and we decorated it with bright flowers. It looked pretty far-out by the time we finished, which was fine by Ed.

My biggest job was supervising a picking crew. All men, all Spanish speaking. I was a woman, spoke no Spanish, and had never seen a pear tree up close before in my life. It made no difference. I had something these men didn't: white skin.

All day long the migrant workers labored in the hot sun, slaving their *nalgas* off and laying at my feet the harvest they collected. I held a set of rings for sizing the pears. I tallied the filled boxes as they stacked up and categorized their contents, based on size, either as eatable or for processing. And on Friday afternoons I made the beer run. Pizza and beer, our weekly ritual – for the supervisors only, of course. The men stayed in the fields, sweating to fill another few boxes before the sun robbed them of the chance to make a couple more dimes on the day.

When all the pears were gathered and the trucks had taken them away, the Spanish-speaking men in their torn overalls disappeared

too. On to the next orchard, or the next field. Going anywhere, somewhere. Nowhere. I remembered *The Grapes of Wrath*, and wondered.

Pears never looked or tasted the same again after that.

It wasn't all pears that summer, though. I had fall to think about, and
was checking into positions at other schools within commuting distance. I may not have been cut out for high school teaching, but that
didn't mean I'd totally given up on the profession. I knew I could
easily land a job waitressing, and we'd manage fine. Martin was
making good money, and we had no great financial commitments.
But I wanted meaningful work. In the end, it was Martin's idea that I
look into getting a job at one of the schools where he dropped off
kids each day, the Development Center for Handicapped Minors.
The name had all the pizzazz of a government subcommittee.
Which, though I didn't know it then, in many ways it was. I had the
ridiculous vision of students in hardhats with little glowing miners'
lamps rolling through shiny halls in wheelchairs... The center was
planning to add another class and would need to hire a teacher to
run it. If they hire you, Martin said, you could ride down with me in
the mornings and back up in the afternoon.

Why not? I thought, and arranged an appointment with the
program coordinator at Kern County Superintendent of Schools
headquarters.

You don't know what you're getting into, was the first thing he
said. You'll have to visit first. It's – how should I put it – a very *different* kind of school.

I'd like to see it, I told him.

In September 1968 Bakersfield's Development Center for Handicapped Minors didn't measure up to its elevated name. When Martin
dropped me off at the town fairgrounds for my tour of the center, I
wondered if he'd really brought me to the right place.

He had. The DCHM (everyone opted for the acronym over the mouthful of the name) was nothing but a big old barn. Someone had erected partitions to create two "classrooms" within its cavernous interior. There was one bathroom, for everyone. And a few windows, which let in enough light to make the dust motes glimmer among the exposed rafters overhead and remind me of Grandma's henhouse. It was a drafty place, full of echoes. It had been built, I soon learned, to house exhibits for the annual fair held each fall. When fair time came around, the DCHM moved out. Every scrap of everything worth anything was toted out into trailers and stored, then moved back in after the fair. It was a barn in which to store the program – and its disabled charges – until the building's real use came around. A warehouse for kids.

And there were lots of kids, as many as the handful of staff could cope with, and then a few more besides. When I got over staring at the barn, the kids were the next thing I noticed. They noticed me, too, and looked up with big wide eyes. Some grinned, others stared blankly. There was something odd about many of these children, something I couldn't quite put my finger on. It was in their faces, all so similar. Was it their eyes, or the space between them? I was missing something, I could tell.

Are some of these children related to each other? I asked.

The teacher I addressed turned and looked at me, amazed. A look of incomprehension clouded her face for a moment, then gave way to an unconcealed grin.

Down's syndrome.

Oh.

I'd never heard of it, and wasn't sure I liked the sound of that word – syndrome. It sounded contagious, sort of. I had never been around people with disabilities – handicapped people, as they were then known. It was as though they were from another world, one totally unfamiliar to me. Sure, there had been the young boy in Lowell when I was a kid. I'd walked past his backyard on the way to grade school. The yard was fenced in with chicken wire, and every day when I walked by the little boy was out there playing, running around and around the yard while he flapped his arms and squawked. All day long he stayed in that yard, entertaining himself with his strange noises and weird contortions. He couldn't come to school, not ever. He was mentally retarded – I knew that from what the other kids said about him – and he looked funny. But he could walk and run, and sometimes as I went by he would stop his flapping and come over to the fence and hold on to the wire with both hands, pressing his face into the meshing. He looked so lonely. But he frightened me, he was so different from anyone else I knew. And no one seemed to be able to tell me what made him that way – he was just *different,* they all said, even Mama.

There had been another child, over in Baxter Springs. He was different, too, but luckily for him, so were his parents. Their boy (I learned later) had cerebral palsy. That meant muscle spasms and flailing limbs, and near-incomprehensible speech. But his parents – his father was a doctor at the town hospital – didn't seem to notice. They took their son everywhere with the family, placing him in the back seat where he'd have room to sprawl. When they drove through town, his legs often stuck out the side window, his feet and toes crossed and twisted. He was a bright child, and happy, quick to laugh at a joke, even if his disability prevented him from cracking one himself. Most important of all, he had a family who loved him and was not embarrassed to show it. A family vastly different from the Lowell boy's, and far ahead of their time.

But I hadn't thought of either child in years. Now, looking around the DCHM, I realized how absolutely naïve I was, how I knew zilch about disabilities of any kind – how I'd always taken "being normal" for granted.

My tour didn't take long – there wasn't much to see – but when it was over, I wasn't ready to leave. Here was an entire world I knew nothing about. I was completely intrigued. Far from being put off by my lack of understanding, I found myself wondering if, just maybe, this was the place for me to spend a year. I'd be learning something new and foreign to me. The challenge of it excited me. It reminded me of Mama's sewing machine, the electric Singer she'd saved long and hard to buy and had taken such pride in, the one with lots of novel parts and screws and things that wiggled and moved — the perfect machine for a six-year-old to take apart and put back together on a rainy afternoon. First three screws, carefully unthreaded then put back, for practice. Then more, until I'd taken the whole thing apart. I was just about to start reassembling everything when Mama walked in and threw up her hands. Lawsy! she said, and, Oh, Murder! Linda, she said after she recovered her breath, you will stay in this room until every piece is back together. Do you understand? I understood, all right. Mad as she was, she was going to give me the chance to atone for my ill-advised game, even though the sewing machine was her prize possession. It was the old family rule: you break it, you fix it. Mama stomped out. I felt like the miller's daughter in *Rumpelstiltskin,* facing a mountain of straw to be spun into gold. Only no long-bearded dwarf came to my aid. I was in that room for hours, but I managed to get every screw, bolt, and nut back into its rightful place. All except one, that is — the tiny bobbin screw, which I couldn't find anywhere. Mama had to buy a replacement before the machine ran again, and I was in the doghouse until she did. Secretly I was pretty proud of my feat. It had worked out the way I'd planned (almost), and it had certainly been a challenge.

And now here I was at this barn, thinking how interesting it might be to work here, perhaps even to make a difference in someone's life and be paid for doing it. A job here would pay as well as any other classroom position (I would, after all, be hired as a teacher) and would complement Martin's earnings nicely.

But I was getting ahead of myself. This was still my first day, as a visitor.

And I hadn't encountered Derek Hayes yet...

Derek is one of several children, whom I guess to be about eight- or nine-year-olds, sitting around the classroom table. The afternoon is drawing to a close, and I tell myself it's time to call Martin and go home, but I just can't seem to walk away. These kids, some of them in diapers, with food smeared on their T-shirts — there's something beautiful about them that makes me want to stay.

Then Derek throws up.

He leans forward and vomits chunks of bananas, evidently the only thing he ate for lunch. The banana chunks skitter and slide across the Formica tabletop as Derek retches. His head convulses forward. More bananas. He puts his face on the table, in the bananas. I feel my stomach lurch. Can you hold his head up? someone asks as she darts for rags and a bucket of soapy water. Uh-huh, I say, keeping my teeth together. I'm scared I'll vomit too. I hold Derek's temples as carefully as I can and pull his head off the table. He retches again, and again my stomach lurches. So this is what it's like, I think. This is what happens here. I can do diarrhea; I can clean up diapers. But vomit? Once again Derek retches, and once again my stomach roils. Could I *really* do this?

Finally the mess is cleaned up. I let go of Derek's head, ruffle his hair gently. The afternoon is over. Time for me to meet Martin, to go home, to step outside for some fresh, banana-free air. But first, I need to see the head teacher.

I'll take the job, I say. For a year.

I can do this for a year.

waterloo

By the time I got home the afternoon of my first visit to the DCHM, a choir of singsong voices inside my head had begun nagging. I tried not to, but found myself talking back to them.

Why in the world would you want to do a thing like *that?*

What's *that* supposed to mean?

You know darn well, Linda. A whole year, cleaning up other people's bodily fluids. Why do that to yourself?

Because.

Because what? We want an honest answer.

Because...because of the children. You haven't seen them. I have. (Silence. Some fidgeting.)

That's why I'm doing this, okay?

(A moment's hesitation.) If you say so.

Thank you. I'm going to fix dinner now. You're all excused.

Back at the center, the word was out. *We've got a live one!* Name's Linda Bidabe (that's right, beh-*dah*-bee), she's twenty-three, and — get this — she's got a teaching credential. A real, live teacher.

For my part, I was eager to get started, despite my uncertainties. From what I could tell, here was a chance not only to continue my newly begun career as a teacher but also to delve into the realm of medicine — my true love — for the first time in my life. I would be able to study close up the effects of trauma, disease, and genetic variances. What's more, I thought, these children need me. In Tehachapi, I had been taking up space and air. Now, I had a chance to do something. The best of both worlds, for the scientist in me as well as the humanitarian.

It was late in the year before everything was in place for me to begin, and by then I was ready and eager to get on with the job. Martin dropped me off at the fairgrounds the first morning of December, and I reported for duty.

At the beginning there were four of us there full time: Emma Weldon, Mel Dyess, Georgia Hart, and I, and from my first day on we formed a good team. Mel ran a classroom and shouldered the duties of head teacher, Emma worked with the oldest students, and Georgia and I taught the younger ones. Together with our classroom aides (one each), we worked hard and laughed hard, shared ideas, and commiserated in times of stress. When one of us faced a problem, the others came to the rescue.

Sharing came naturally. With its cathedral-high ceiling and great cavernous spaces, our building did nothing to create an intimate working environment. Six-foot-high partitions (the office cubicle variety) had been used to cordon off our classroom areas, but noise was free to travel up into the rafters and reverberate through the vast hall. Apart from these partitioned areas, the room was left open, and much of our time was spent in this central area. After the concrete walls of Tehachapi High, the DCHM provided an extremely open teaching atmosphere. It was, after all, a warehouse.

The floors were covered with linoleum, which was peeling in places. Furnishings were sparse. There were large wooden cabinets against the walls, for supplies. They were virtually empty. The DCHM had barely been running a full year when I joined the staff – certainly not long enough to have obtained anything worth storing in a cabinet.

In the late sixties, the concept of special education was still a nascent one. Sure, there were classrooms set aside for children who fell into the ambiguous categories of educationally or emotionally disturbed. According to the experts, these kids were basically normal, with minor aberrations – a reading disability, or a propensity for striking out at people; that kind of thing. They might be an inconvenience, but could be accommodated within the school setting without much hassle. On the next rung down the ladder were TMR children. Trainable Mentally Retarded. These were Down's syndrome kids, or kids who'd suffered slight anoxia at birth and sustained permanent brain damage – that kind of thing. Some went to school and benefited from the work of dedicated teachers until they turned eighteen. But many were barred from classrooms simply because they were not toilet trained. That was the rule, and it was understandable enough: if you can't go potty, you can't go to school.

So they stayed home. Or, especially if their disabilities were severe, they were placed in institutions. This child will never know you, a doctor might say to the parents of such a child. She's far better off as a ward of the state. The loving thing to do would be to put her away, where she can get expert help. And the parents would do it, because they loved their child, and because doctors know best.

With each passing year, institutions took in more and more children. By the end of the sixties, they were overrun. Politicians began to take note. Someone crunched the numbers. These institutions, they discovered, were eating up huge swaths of tax dollars. The folks running them were doing the best they could, but it was costing too much, plain and simple. Time to explore alternatives.

Like telling parents to keep their kids at home. And providing programs that would occupy their children during the day so that they, the parents, could remain in the work force (and tax pool).

No state official had any illusions that new programs would improve conditions for the children at stake, but given the circumstances, all agreed that de-institutionalization was the best way forward. They made state funding available to school districts willing to pioneer alternative programs for caring for these children, many of whom had spent their entire lives inside institutions. And so, in Kern County, California, the Development Center for Handicapped Minors program was established.

Of course, I'd had no idea what I was talking about when I had assured the program supervisors I was up to the task of joining the staff. I only knew what I had told the accusing voices in my head – that there was something about these children that made me want to be around them.

I had eight students in my classroom, most of them TMR. Mel, Emma, and Georgia each had about the same number of students. During my first weeks at the DCHM they spent as much time as they could teaching me the ropes, helping me get up to speed. Often, though, I was left to my own devices. And I needed all the devices I could get my hands on. I had students like Jenny Dawson to worry about.

Jenny was four years old when I got her. She was one of my very first students. In many ways, she was no different from the rest of my class, no more or less disabled. But I have never forgotten her. How can you forget a child whose disabilities are the result of abuse and neglect? Prenatal viruses, premature birth, meningitis – these and the like are by far the most common causes of permanent damage. Chromosomal aberrations rank a close second. Only a tiny percentage of the countless children I have loved and worked with have neglect or abuse to blame for their disabilities. And yet, because of the horror, I cannot forget them.

Delicate as a wafer, Jenny was a fine-boned, underdeveloped child. She weighed next to nothing, could not walk (her legs were too weak), and still wore diapers. When she opened her mouth, *ooh-ooh-ooh* sounds came out. She never spoke a word. Her hair was the color of sandbox sand. There was no hair on her temples. She never gave it a chance to grow, because she was a head-banger. If I set her down anywhere near a table or placed her on the floor, she would rock forward and wham her head against the hard surface until her fragile skin yielded and blood splattered freely. Her face was a mesh of scar tissue, and despite our attempts at vigilance, she always seemed to be needing stitches for a new gash. The doctors complained they were running out of healthy facial skin to stitch together. And my heart bled for Jenny.

Jenny's father and grandfather were the same man. He managed to keep both Jenny and her thirteen-year-old mother hidden from the public eye until the day he robbed a gas station, tied up the young attendant, and set fire to him. (He had tried this at home on his dog first, dousing the animal with gasoline and flicking a match onto its back.) When the police found him, he was at home, if it could be called one. It was really a shack. In it they found Jenny's mother, pregnant with a second baby by her father, huddled in a corner. Lying in a pile of filthy rags was the first — two-year-old Jenny, dehydrated and comatose. Her pulse barely fluttered.

The police rushed Jenny to a hospital and placed her poor little mother into state care. Doctors saved Jenny's life, and California's Child Protective Services found her a wonderful foster home. But her brain was damaged, and her emotions scarred beyond telling. She had never before been separated from her mother, the only person who had ever cared for her.

What am I going to do with Jenny? I asked myself constantly during those first weeks. She was in my class, my responsibility, and I couldn't stand to see her hurt herself. But I had nowhere safe to put her, and when she came in each morning, the question was still there — until the day I decided the only way to keep Jenny from banging her head was to keep her on me at all times. On my hip. In my lap. All day, every day. I vowed never, ever to put her down. The only time I would let go of her was when I could hand her to someone else.

The other staff supported me. We carried Jenny together. She and I spent months on end bonded to each other. She leaned her head against my shoulder as we walked through our days, I trying to work with my other students while never neglecting the child on my hip, and she mouthing loud *ooh-ooh-oohs* whenever anything out of the ordinary happened, anything that might be a threat. Weeks went by. My arms ached, and the constant pressure on my hip seemed enough to alter my gait permanently, like polio.

And then she smiled. Jenny *smiled* at me. Her *ooh* sounded more like a baby's coo, the dread in the vowels replaced by a warmth and contentment. It was only for the briefest moment, but it was the sign I had been hoping for.

There were more changes in store. Jenny didn't really eat. She was afraid to. We held and rocked her and bottle-fed her like a newborn. As she showed signs of adjusting to our environment, I tried placing her in a high chair for mealtimes, always sitting right at her side so I could comfort her and prevent her from banging her head if she became frightened. I started with soft food – tuna or peanut butter on Wonderbread. Using only my fingers (spoons were a threat), I eased tiny portions into her mouth.

That was a battle, getting Jenny to eat, but with time she was taking in enough food to allow us to stop bottle-feeding her. I couldn't believe it. This was progress, and it was something I'd been a part of. Granted, it didn't amount to much (at least not in the eyes of anyone beyond the four walls of the DCHM), but it already seemed like more than I'd managed in my year at Tehachapi. Though I tried not to think much about it – there were too many other things needing my attention – I couldn't help thrilling at the realization that, for the first time in my teaching career, I was actually making a difference in someone's life.

Then came the day when, as I went to place a piece of peanut butter sandwich in Jenny's mouth, my attention was distracted by another child and I turned my head. That was a mistake. The next thing I knew, sharp pain ran through my right index finger. I snapped back around in time to see Jenny's head coming up with a mouthful of bread. I was astounded. My thoughts flip-flopped as rapidly as a landed fish between the two alternates *Wow, that hurt!* and *Boy, this is amazing!* Here is a child who fights against every morsel I offer her, whose every nerve is set to register fear and defend against attack, and she's just bitten my finger. Hard. Time to accelerate the feeding program, I thought.

By the end of the year, Jenny was eating real food. We still had to feed her – it would be years before she was able to feed herself – but she was eating, and that was the main thing. And, better still, she was no longer glued to my hip. With practice, she had learned to walk. It wasn't pretty to watch. Her steps were unsteady and her feet splayed out, duck-like, and someone had to walk beside her and hold her arm, because she couldn't catch herself when she tripped. But she could walk, more or less. And that was the main thing. Jenny was enjoying life for the first time. She laughed and cooed. She felt safe. Loved.

And, as my first year on the job came to an end, that was the main thing.

I couldn't leave. I had talked all along about moving on after one year, going who knows where, but when that year was over, I found í couldn't leave Jenny. What would she do without me? I didn't want to see all I had worked for come to nothing. She might not need me to carry her around anymore, but there was no way I could let her down. I had invested so much time (and heartache) in that child, and both of us had grown as a result.

I stayed because of Jenny.

She was the first, but there was always another Jenny. Always someone who needed help and challenged my ability to provide it.

From Jenny I had learned my first important lesson working with children with disabilities. I had been hired, as had the other staff, to run the DCHM as a glorified baby-sitting operation, a safe place for parents to leave their children during working hours. We soon realized, however, that the children in our care had more potential than they were often credited with. Today, it sounds like a hackneyed phrase from *Field of Dreams,* but when the thought first came to me, it rang true: *If you teach them, they will learn.* Wasn't I seeing this reality every day in my classroom, not just with Jenny, but with all the children I was working with? Even in one brief year, each of them had made progress, learned something. It had nothing to do with everyone being on the same page on the same date, or keeping up with a set curriculum, but everything to do with each child moving toward a goal that matched his or her special needs. That was learning. That was teaching.

In those first years at the DCHM, most of my students were ambulatory (Jenny, when she arrived, was an exception). They could already sit, stand, and walk. But that was about the extent of their living skills. When I first took the job, only a handful of students were toilet trained. We teachers spent hours each day dealing with diapers – with only one restroom in the place, shared by some thirty students and the staff. It didn't take a genius to figure out that toilet training was our greatest and most immediate need, not just because of the time factor, but because the future of many of our children depended on it. Many of our Down's syndrome kids could move on to other programs if we could just get them toilet trained – and we had a daunting list of kids waiting to get into our center. Kids sitting at home on backroom floors, waiting.

So I wrote a toilet training program, begged and borrowed potty chairs, and we got to work. And it *did* take work, and patience, and a strong stomach. While we were at it, I thought it wouldn't hurt for us to teach the children to dress and undress themselves too. Panties down, panties up. If a child had an accident, we'd use it as a natural chance to reinforce dressing skills. Occasionally it backfired. One of our students came from parents who had raised twelve girls before they finally had the son they'd prayed for. Number thirteen came with Down's, and ended up in my class. With twelve little mothers to hover over him at home, Junior wasn't expected to do a thing for himself. Before I got him, he'd never changed his clothes himself. As it turned out, he was a quick study. On the bus to school one morning, Junior decided to practice his undressing skills. He stripped, climbed onto the ledge at the back of the bus, right in front of the emergency door window, and lay down, centerfold-style. The bus driver was perplexed when car after car passed her – with passengers pointing and laughing uproariously. Finally she pulled over to check out the source of the commotion. There was Junior, buck naked, waving and smiling sweetly to anyone who happened to glance his way. That was his last ride at the back of the bus.

But we teachers stuck at our endeavors, and worked as a team to get all our students toilet trained. We got good, really good, and so did our students. Well, okay, Buddy Hawkins didn't. But he would, I had no doubt about it. I was teaching, so he was going to learn. Right?

Wrong.

Whereas Jenny was a tiny wisp of a thing, Buddy Hawkins was a chunk. His ears stuck out from his chubby face, and he wore his light brown hair cropped short; with his rounded head and little pot-belly, he reminded me of a VW Beetle with its doors open. Though he could walk and run just fine, his lack of mental acuity was immediately apparent. He'd flap his hands and race in circles, drooling, just like the kid I had seen years before in Lowell. But what Buddy lacked in aptitude, he made up for in attitude. Even when he drooled, he smiled. He was a cheery boy, and his smile was infectious. That is, until his diaper needed attention. At six, Buddy was still not toilet trained.

The Hawkins family lived near Tehachapi, so after I decided to start toilet training Buddy, I went to visit his mother. On the way, I rehearsed what I was going to tell her. I would explain the significance of our toilet training program, outline and reinforce the steps she'd need to take at home to complement our efforts, and help her understand the importance of teamwork in improving the quality of Buddy's daily life.

It took me a while to find the address, because the house was set way back from the main road. Actually it wasn't a house, but a converted boxcar, or half of one box, the sight of which made me draw in my breath. It amazed me that anyone could actually live in such a thing, let alone raise a family.

I parked in the rutted drive and went up to the box. Through the window in the door I could see Buddy's mother seated in an overstuffed recliner facing a glowing TV. It took a full half minute for her to hoist herself out of the chair to answer my knock. Mrs. Hawkins was wondrously obese. Her large frame filled the doorway and blocked my view of the interior behind her. Fat cascaded off her in sloppy, jiggling rolls that not even the pink muumuu under her housecoat could contain. Her hair, dark but streaked with early gray, was done up in pink foam-and-plastic rollers, which snagged in desperate tangles of hair and hung down every which way. She must have had those rollers in for at least three weeks, I guessed. When Mrs. Hawkins opened her mouth to greet me, I hardly took in what she said. I was noticing her missing front teeth. She motioned me into the house.

I stepped through the door and blinked in the half light. Then the odor hit me full on, and I fought the urge to rush back outside again. The smell was so strong, it took me a second to identify it, but when I was forced to breathe a fresh lungful, it was obvious right away. Urine.

We were standing in the front room, with barely enough space for the two of us to maneuver without bumping into each other. A door led into a bedroom crowded with a large double bed and a bunk. Mrs. Hawkins pointed out Buddy's bed. Evidently he and his two sisters shared the room with their parents. Another door opened onto the kitchen, most of which was occupied by a round table no more than four feet across. Breathing as shallowly as possible, I stepped into the kitchen – Mrs. Hawkins was giving me a full tour – and put my hand to my face, both to stop my jaw from dropping open at the sight of the mess and to guard against my gagging stomach. The tabletop was covered in what once had passed for food – crusted vegetables and bits of ketchup-coated meat – and stacked high with empty cans and filthy containers. The floor under and around the table was in no better shape.

Mrs. Hawkins steered me back into the front room and gestured toward her recliner, offering me the only seat in the room. The chair was streaked and dirty, but I perched myself on it and leaned forward, trying to appear casual. She stood in the middle of the room, her squat hands jammed to her broad square hips.

So you're Buddy's teacher.

Yup.

The television, a large color screen, was turned up. Conversation was going to be an effort. Not that it mattered. My rehearsed script had gone out of my head the moment I stepped inside. But I had come on a mission, and I was going to try to salvage something from the situation.

Mrs. Hawkins, I began –

But that's as far as I got. Buddy, who had been playing in the yard behind the boxcar, came bursting into the room, his flapping dance in full swing. He was naked except for a pair of once-white briefs. He stopped in front of the television, transfixed by the images on the screen. I watched a sparkling trickle of yellow descend his leg, and realized he was urinating. Buddy's pee ran off his foot and onto the linoleum floor. It puddled about him, then sidled toward the television and disappeared beneath it, to pool once more in the low corner of the room. Until then I hadn't noticed the way the entire boxcar tilted. I leaned forward as discreetly as I could and caught a glimpse of what must have been years' worth of congealed urine back behind the TV. That explains a lot, I thought to myself, running the back of my hand across my nose.

Mrs. Hawkins didn't even seem to have noticed what Buddy had done. Or maybe she was just too tired to care. I felt suddenly sorry for her and got up to offer her the recliner; she looked uncertain on her feet, as though she wasn't used to being on them for so long at a stretch. She and I traded places. Which is when I noticed for the first time that the back of Buddy's briefs were caked with feces. I looked at his briefs, then recalled the brown spots on the chair where moments before I had been sitting, and into which Buddy's mother was now levering herself with a groan.

I had seen enough.

Thank you for showing me Buddy's home, Mrs. Hawkins.

No trouble, Ma'am. None at all.

Maybe not for you, I thought to myself. But I simply wished her a pleasant afternoon, and showed myself gratefully to the door.

I threw my dress away when I got home. Then I took a shower. Right then, I felt like doing my own head-banging. The shower gave me a place to untangle my thoughts. Was I nuts? Had I really thought I could march up to Buddy Hawkins's house and organize his mother into getting him toilet trained in three days? That had been my plan. But did I know that Mrs. Hawkins lived in a permanent state of despair, her wreck of a box-house crumbling and rotting around her, her eight-year-old daughter the only one in it with enough gumption to see that the other two children got something to eat? Did I know that Mr. Hawkins worked for the sanitation department yet didn't seem to know a thing about hygiene, and next to nothing about how to feed or clothe his family? Did I know – I, who had grown up with a full belly and warm baths – did I know what it was like to be so fully overwhelmed by problems, that basic things like toilet training seemed inconsequential, the least of a long list of worries? No. I knew nothing. I was ignorant of all that.

I shouldn't have been. My visit to the Hawkins home brought back faded childhood memories, tidbits from visits to Tongie. There had been an ancient house at the bottom of Grandma and Grandpa's hill that deserved to be abandoned, or torn down. But the Hazzards lived there, a whole lot of them. Stay away from that place, I was told.

As though their poverty might be contagious, I thought as I soaped down.

In a way, Mr. Hazzard had been Grandpa's saving grace. When times were toughest, he gave him someone to look down on, some- one who was always in worse shape than he was. When a man's run out of self-esteem and is scrounging to get out of the cellar, a fellow a rung or two farther below him makes a great target. Grandma be- rated the Hazzards, too, as did Daddy whenever we came to visit – it was a family tradition. Among other things, I had learned from Grandpa that the Hazzards, disgusting swine that they were, actu- ally let chickens wander into their house. Grandpa, I wanted to say, how would you like it if people said mean things about you? But it wasn't my place to talk back, so I didn't.

Hazzards. Hopkins. Hawkins. Names change, I thought to my- self, but some people stay the same. Their troubles stay the same. And then I remembered Patty and Stinky, and laughed in spite of myself.

They were two tiny piglets, part of a big litter born to our huge sow – the meanest sow in the world. Mama found them. The others were dead, torn to shreds and devoured by their own mother. Mama had put on one of Daddy's greatcoats and gone to the barn to collect the eggs, the way she always did, but instead returned to the house with tears streaming down her cheeks. Mama never cried, so I knew something was terribly wrong. She pulled the two blood-covered piglets out from under the coat and held them out to Allen and me. We rushed to help her, wrapped the piglets in towels on the kitchen counter, and washed the blood from their wounds. One of the piglets was only scratched. The other had been slashed in the groin, and the deep cut was bleeding badly. She was too little even for Mama to stitch together. We doubted she'd live, but we coated her wound with medicated salve, named her Stinky and her sister Patty and, once we'd finished bandaging them up, placed them together in a rag-lined box near the kitchen stove.

Both piglets survived. Thrived, in fact. Allen and I were expert animal nurses, and rose at all hours of the night to urge milk down their throats with eye droppers, and later with baby bottles. Patty and Stinky gained weight with alarming speed. They were our pets, and we made a home for them in the back bathroom.

Daddy, needless to say, found this distressing. He understood our attachment to the animals we had helped to save; it was having them in our house – his house – that he disliked. It's just till they're big enough, we pleaded. Then they can go back to the barn.

Precautions were necessary. Whenever the sound of wheels on gravel told us a vehicle was approaching our farm, Mama called Allen and me to Get the pigs! Get the pigs! We'd shoo them into the back bathroom and keep them still while Mama went out and stalled the visitor until Daddy came and took care of whatever business needed to be transacted. (It was always business on the farm; nobody ever came by just to visit.) Smart things, Patty and Stinky soon learned to skitter for the bathroom as soon as Mama shouted Get the pigs!

Daddy finally put his foot down. We are the McPhersons. We are not the Hazzards. The pigs go out. Even so, he allowed us to make the transition gradually, as much for the pigs' sakes as for ours, and we moved their bed box and food bowls out onto the lawn near the kitchen door, until they adjusted to life outdoors and were ready for the sty. But once a house pig, always a house pig, or so it seemed.

Patty, everyone's favorite, knew Mama had a special soft spot for her, and she took to lying in wait near the door and darting into the kitchen, squealing up at Mama, any time she managed to slip in. It nearly broke Mama's heart to have to chase Patty back outside again. Later, Daddy had her bred and she had her first litter. But she was a hopeless first-time mother and wouldn't let her babies nurse. So Daddy had to corner her in her pen and straddle her, the way he did the day he sliced the old sow with a sickle, and keel her over onto her side so the piglets could get at her. Allen and I watched this operation at some risk – it was painfully hard to keep from busting up laughing, to hear Daddy grunt and the pig curse. But Daddy knew what he was doing, and before long Patty embraced her role as mother, or at least stopped fighting it. She went on to live a happy and productive life on the farm – unlike her sister Stinky, who, unable to reproduce because of the injury to her groin went the way of all flesh.

For a while there, we might have been like the Hazzards, I thought to myself as I toweled off and got into clean clothes. But we weren't anything like Buddy Hawkins's folks. Even our pet pigs had been toilet trained.

Poor Buddy, I thought. We'll just have to keep trying our best.

Say what? Martin asked, looking at me quizzically as I emerged from the bathroom.

Nothing, honey, I said, realizing I must have been thinking out loud.

You're tired.

I was just thinking.

I did a lot of thinking about Angie Phillips too. In a classroom full of flapping arms and constant hubbub, she was a five-year-old oasis of calm. From the start, she was near to my heart. Angie was born with chromosomal aberrations and suffered from a metabolic disorder that left her with a distended stomach and toothpick-thin arms and legs. Though she never went hungry, she looked like one of those starving children on UNICEF calendars. Most noticeable about Angie were the whites of her eyes. Her skin was rich ebony, and the contrast in color was startling. Legally blind, Angie was so cross-eyed her pupils rarely showed. Her eyes were pools of white with dark half-moons facing off across the bridge of her nose. It was a marvel to me how she saw anything at all, but she had just enough vision to allow her to totter slowly about the room, her hands stretched out in front of her, like a firefighter entering a smoke-filled building. And, indeed, life was full of peril for Angie. She was constantly bashing into things, falling down, getting bruised up.

Jenny, my little head-banger, had opened my eyes to the fact that all children can learn, provided a way is found to teach them. Spurred on by the progress she had made, I was enthusiastic about trying to help Angie too. Something just had to be done about her eyes. So I went to the library.

I couldn't have known it then, but I was establishing a pattern that would continue throughout my years in the classroom: homing in on the particular disabilities of a child whose needs seemed to me to be more pressing than those of others in my care, and using all the resources at my disposal in an effort to figure out how to help her. I knew I couldn't help all of my students at one time, but concentrating on the greatest problems would at least keep everyone alive. Or so I hoped.

As part of my research, I visited a local optometrist. The more I explained Angie's problems to him, the more his own eyes lit up. He had, he confided, just read about a program he was sure I'd be interested in. It was eye-muscle coordination that Angie lacked, he explained. The way to fix that, according to the program he'd just read about, was bed jumping. Remember the five little monkeys? he said with a twinkle. Jumping on the bed will exercise Angie's eye muscles, because her natural instinct will be to keep her eyes fixed on a stationary point. Her brain will have to get in on the act and start coordinating with her eyes. There were studies, the optometrist assured me. The incredible benefits of bed jumping were proven fact.

As it turned out, the technique *was* well-documented, even illustrated. The child was to stand on the bed while an adult stood on the floor holding onto the child's arms, which were to be extended at eye level. Then the jumping could begin.

I collected all my research and compiled it in an elaborate and impressive portfolio. Full of excitement, I made an appointment to see Angie's mother at her home. I had worked long hours on this project. Now Mrs. Phillips and I would reap the benefits. Together, shoulder to shoulder, we were going to cure Angie. I could barely contain myself as Mrs. Phillips welcomed me into her house and showed me to the couch. I placed the portfolio squarely across my knees, breathed in, and began.

I'm here to talk to you about Angie's eyes, Mrs. Phillips.

Oh, she said.

Angie's eyes, I repeated, as though she might not have heard me the first time.

Ah, yes, Angie's eyes. Let me tell you about Angie's eyes. They's crossed, right? (I nodded, yes.) Wanna know how come? (Again, I nodded.) Well, I'll tell you how come. I know exactly what happened. When I was carrying Angie her daddy come home one night and popped me upside the head so hard, it crossed Angie's eyes right there inside my belly. She come out with them that way.

I see, I said.

Inside the dark covers of the portfolio on my knees was, among other things, a notebook filled with drawings of eyeballs; explanations of how eyeballs work, how the muscles attached to them coordinate; diagrams illustrating the logic of the exercises I wanted to recommend for Angie. The portfolio stayed closed. I rested my palms on it, spread out my fingers.

Tell me, Mrs. Phillips, what does Angie like to eat?

And, after that:

What does she like to do?

Mrs. Phillips and I chatted amiably for an hour or so before I excused myself.

You know, I said as I prepared to go, let me work on some programs for Angie and get back to you. I'm sure we'll find a way together to help her.

I left the house, and Mrs. Phillips closed the door gently behind me.

That day, I was the one who came away edified. Unbeknownst to her, Mrs. Phillips had taught me a valuable lesson. Mrs. Hawkins, in her way, imparted it the day I went to talk to her about toilet training Buddy, but I had been a little too tough-skinned to absorb it fully then. Now, it was crystal clear: If I was going to set about establishing priorities and goals for the students in my care, I might as well accept that the rest of the world wouldn't rush to fall into line and salute my efforts. I might as well acknowledge that what to me seemed the number-one priority for any particular child might well be a far cry from what that child's parents or guardians interpreted as their chief concern. With each of us coming from a different angle, I couldn't expect others to share my perspective. By the same token, I might as well learn not to take it personally when my well-laid plans erupted in my face. There were no easy solutions, no quick fixes. And this was true of every child in my classroom. I could either embrace that challenge, or fizzle out in frustration. It was, I decided, as it had always been – a simple matter of continuing to give it my best shot. For the sake of all of us.

One thing, however, wore continually on my nerves as the winter weeks passed and spring returned: the barren state of our classroom cupboards. Aside from having doors that could be slammed with a thunderous clap – hours of fun for some of my students – the bulky wooden cupboards that lined our walls served little purpose.

Though Kern County was seen as a trendsetter for being one of the first counties in the state to open development centers, the DCHM program was still viewed with skepticism by some county administrators. With no means of predicting the outcome of "experimental" alternatives to institutionalization, they hoped we would succeed in at least matching current standards and prayed we would not wind up embarrassing the county, or worse. In short, we had yet to prove ourselves.

There was little doubt in our minds that we were stepchildren. Our empty cupboards validated that sense. My allotment of art supplies for the year was five pieces of blue construction paper, five of black, two of yellow, give or take. Number of toys for the kids? None. A couple of old, broken ones, maybe. While other schools had hot lunch programs, we were supposed to be eternally grateful for milk. We were underfunded, understaffed, undereducated. Underlings. We didn't really know what we were doing, but nobody minded – at least someone was trying.

We were doing what we could and smiling and laughing when faced with what we couldn't (tears being the only other alternative), but I was getting just a little tired of playing the hero. Or martyr. When I asked what it would take for our lot to improve, I was informed that there was no budget to pay for any improvements. I didn't know a thing about budgets and, quite frankly, didn't give a damn. My kids were hurting. Maybe there was no money for lunches. But couldn't we at least get them some toys?

I went knocking. First stop: our program supervisor, at the Kern County Superintendent of Schools office. We need toys, I said; some things for the kids to do.

Big mistake. I might as well have been Oliver, asking for more. The program supervisor was indignant: *What! How dare you – who do you think you — ought to be eternally grateful — other places don't even have — you have more than your — should be happy you have a program in the first —*

I left the office with a brushfire in my head. Oliver could go hang himself. It was time for the Little Red Hen to move in and do it herself. I can organize a toy drive as well as the next person, I thought to myself as I stomped to my car.

And so I did.

In the summer of 1969, my first year at the Development Center for Handicapped Minors, I bummed toys off the good people of Tehachapi. It was Christmas in July. We collected more toys than we knew what to do with. Oh, it was wonderful.

Until, back at school, in walked our program supervisor. I opened a cupboard door and proudly revealed the array of toys lined on its shelves. Little did I know the sight of a plastic ambulance could cause cardiac arrest. The program supervisor came very near to having a heart attack right there in the middle of the great linoleum hall.

Where did these toys come from?!

Tehachapi. They were donated, I said.

What! Do you want people thinking our schools can't support themselves —

Here we go again, I thought. Sometimes you just can't win for losing.

Where, then, does all the money go? I asked. There was an edge to my tone. I was exasperated. I never stopped to think that maybe our superintendent had gone out on a limb starting this program in the first place, or to consider that he might well be under fire from higher-ups for taking such a risk. But it would have made no difference to me anyway. My only thought was that these were *my* kids' lives we were talking about.

How much does it take to run this place? I asked the supervisor. I'm not asking for Fort Knox here. Just something, *anything*.

The look on the supervisor's face told me I'd crossed the line. Gone way too far, in fact.

Someone had to bring me back. The supervisor spent two solid hours trying. By means of ranting and raving, screaming to tremulant crescendos while turning amazing shades of crimson and beet.

Sadly, the performance passed me by. I was miles away, oblivious to the dervish whirling in front of me. It was my only defense against laughing out loud.

The program supervisor can't be blamed for not knowing I'm a McPherson, I told myself, or that my family wrote the book on ranting and raving. Which was true: yelling and carrying on doesn't faze me. I am, after all, Mac's daughter. His fizzled-out atomic blond. And Daddy never had any trouble blowing up, or standing his ground either. Back when he was paying his way through the University of Kansas by lifeguarding at a public lake, he'd done more than watch for swimmers in distress. One time a bunch of rowdy guys (drunks, Daddy called them) were out on the lake in a rowboat. They had a girl with them, and one of the fellows started pulling her shirt off. Another of them dropped his trunks and peed into the water. Furious, Daddy swam out to the boat to confront them. The guy at the oars whacked Daddy across the face with one of them, knocking out a couple front teeth and cutting Daddy's lip clean through – and making him wear an upper plate with false teeth for the rest of his life. But that was Daddy. With him, there were clear lines, and heaven help the person who crossed them.

Maybe Daddy and our program supervisor should get together, I thought. Then I had to stifle a grin (cough, cough) and rush to put miles between us again. One time before I was born, back when my brother Allen was still a baby and Daddy was building the atomic bomb, the two of them got on a bus behind an elderly couple. No one was in the driver's seat, so the couple put their tokens in the box. When the driver came onboard, he yelled, Who put tokens in the box? We did, the fragile couple said. Furious, the driver kicked

Mac

everyone off the bus. He shouldn't have. Daddy backed down the steps with Allen in his arms, handed his son to another passenger. The driver was standing by the bus door when Daddy decked him. Everyone cheered as Daddy calmly reclaimed Allen and started walking home. The police caught up with him before he got there. They arrested Daddy, and drove him and Allen to the station. Daddy explained what had happened. The rude driver he had punched evidently had quite a reputation with the police, because when Daddy was done with his story, an officer took him aside and thanked him – someone should have punched that guy's lights out years ago, he said. The police dropped the charges. Daddy rode home a prince.

And now I was his princess, standing calm and collected while the torrent raged wild around me. Eventually the program supervisor's wrath blew itself out, and I was free to resume my day.

The toys I had collected were free to stay in their cupboards, where our children could get at them. Our budget money stayed in Fort Knox.

You can't say I didn't try, I told the crew after our visitor had left. And we all laughed.

Despite our lack of funds, we were growing. And as time passed, more development centers were opening across the county. What began as an attempt to counter the mounting costs of institutionalizing children with disabilities was turning into the most sought-after alternative. The initial idea for the DCHM program – a safe environment for baby-sitting these children – was welcomed by parents who, until now, had been more or less forced into putting their child in an institution. Our waiting list stretched longer and longer. We had no real criteria then for selecting children. We just took the ones we had room for. To the parents of the rest, we said, Sorry, you'll have to wait. I hated those words. They broke hearts every day. But what was I supposed to do about it? I had my hands full with kids like Rusty Lee, Billy, Edgar, and Rene. That is, when my hands weren't already busy holding Jenny.

At fourteen, Rusty Lee Bates was one of our older students. He had pronounced Down's syndrome. I remember the first time his mother came to the center. She walked up to me and, by way of introduction, announced, Ah was raped. Tha's where Rusty Lee came from. Ah want ya ta know, Ah was *raped*.

Okay, I said.

Rusty's mother did her best – there was no doubt she loved her son dearly – but she didn't have much going for her. She sent Rusty to school every day with a plastic bag full of sandwiches, pinto beans on Wonderbread. He'd walk in, swinging his sandwich bag at anything in his path. *Whap whap* went the bread and beans against the walls, *whap whap* on the table. And I would cringe, and wait for the day the bag would burst and splatter us all.

Rusty had tiny feet and a body like Bozo the Clown's. His feet were so tiny because he had learned to walk late; they hadn't had a chance to spread out when he was small. I was always grateful to Rusty's mother for managing to teach him to walk – he was a big boy, and I was glad not to have to shift him around, the way I did some of my other kids.

Before he came to us, Rusty had never been away from his mother. It made him upset to be parted from her, made him swing his bean sandwiches wildly and curl his tongue to utter long train-whistle hoots. *Whooo whooo*, all day long.

Rusty eventually adjusted, but he still got scared any time anything out of the ordinary happened. An open house was out of the ordinary.

I was all dressed up, entertaining parents, doing my best impersonation of a nice little teacher, when Rusty Lee came wobbling over to me, *whooo whooo*, scared to death. He grabbed hold of my skirt, twisted it between his hands – he often twisted things when he was terrified – pulling it up over my head. Any other day, I would have been wearing shorts. Our dress code insisted on skirts, but since most of my day was spent on the floor, I always wore athletic shorts underneath. Not on open house day though. Rusty Lee pulled and twisted my dress higher and tighter, while I tried to calm him down – Rusty Lee, Rusty Lee, Rusty Lee! – and spin myself the opposite direction at the same time. With my skirt wrapped around my head, I pleaded with him to let go. There I was, under-wear and all, in front of the parents of my students. So much for the nice little, prim little teacher.

While Rusty Lee kept us on our toes (literally) during the day, Rene occupied my dreams at night.

Deaf and blind for life as a result of German measles, Rene lived in a night of his own. A silent night. He was as dainty as Rusty Lee was bulky, and so quiet and unobtrusive that he was easily over-looked. In my nightmares, Rene would crawl into one of our big, empty classroom cupboards, and I would forget about him and not send him home at the end of the day.

That certainly wasn't the case with Napoleon. Edgar "General" Hernandez had us all so well organized, we were soon running out of military titles for nicknames. He went variously by General Hernandez, Edgar the Dictator, or Napoleon. I liked Napoleon the best; it had a screwball quality the others lacked.

Napoleon was with me from the beginning, along with his friend Billy Feston. The two came together. I had my suspicions there was a good reason for that – the other teachers had each taken a turn with them in their classrooms, and now it was time for the new girl to do her part. So while Jenny rode around on my hip so as not to be constantly banging her head, and Angie tried to feel her way through the day without crashing into too many tables, Napoleon and Billy ran the show.

Though he was only six years old, it was easy to see that Napoleon was going to grow up to be a very handsome man. He was flawlessly beautiful, his skin a rich olive tone, his hair jet black. On the surface, Billy, also six, had little in common with his friend. Billy was white-skinned, wiry, and had matte-brown hair. But both had brains going a mile a minute. Napoleon marshaled his troops whenever he could, acting out his dictatorial whims. His mouth rarely closed, and his pronouncements were usually curt. A successful morning might include a march around the room to confiscate everyone's scissors (They haven't been good, he would explain). But it was Billy who first discovered that peeing in electrical outlets produced not only a sizzling steam, but also a stench that would force us to evacuate the building. They were smart, those two, which is why I kept them together. With six other children needing my attention, I couldn't afford to worry about what kind of influence they had on each other.

Billy's behavior problems were so severe, in fact, that his parents weren't able to keep him under control. So he lived with a dozen other kids in a foster home.

Edgar's behavior was just as hard to manage, but he lived with his grandmother, who had devoted herself to his care. She had taken him in, she told me, because his mother was a schizophrenic and had a drug problem to boot. I knew what schizophrenic meant, but I didn't have much idea of what, exactly, a "drug problem" was. Drugs were for far-away places, like Haight Ashbury, Woodstock, or Amsterdam.

Now both boys' behavior problems were my problems, and I had to find a way of dealing with them, or at least keeping them sufficiently occupied so that no one got hurt.

The DCHM did not run an academic program – we staff had been hired to keep people alive, not to teach. Yet walking, talking, eating, and toilet training were hardly the issues for my two troublemakers. What they needed, I decided, was some education. A regular classroom environment. I thought back to my university days, dug into my hat of learned tricks, and pulled out – a rabbit.

Well, a couple frogs first. I was going to teach science. Just like any other normal kindergarten. Introducing animals into my classroom would, I reasoned, produce any number of wonderful results. Not only would my children have something to watch and study, but something to take responsibility for.

It was a brilliant plan, and I gloated to myself as I executed it to perfection. I laid out a terrarium with rocks, sand, moss, and grass, and went out to a nearby canal to fish for water weeds and beetles. And a couple frogs. There were no menacing snakes by the canal that day, and I did feel just the slightest bit of pity for the two frogs as I plopped them into their new glass home, a confined space not much bigger than a bushel basket.

Back in the classroom, the frogs did science too. To the delight of my children, especially Edgar and Billy, they mated and spawned – little black poppy seeds in clear Jell-O. The seeds grew darker, like pupils expanding to take in light, and we watched each day as tails and heads took shape, and fed scraps to the parent frogs.

Billy and Edgar were enamored of our terrarium, so much so that I was encouraged to expand our science projects into other areas of the room.

That's when I introduced the rabbit. I knew all about caring for rabbits from my 4-H days, so a classroom bunny seemed just the thing. I put a cage for it in one corner of our room, and the children who were able took turns feeding it and helping to keep its cage clean. Once a day, I would let the rabbit out, and it would hop around the room keeping everybody happy.

I was on to something. My children were responding to the added stimuli, and I wanted to do more. There was still no budget for educational supplies, and the terrarium had come out of my own pocket. Next I wanted a playhouse, but I wasn't going to spend a cent to get one. I drove around town and stopped at department and grocery stores until I'd gathered enough cardboard boxes to suit my purpose. I even went to a carpet store and collected a load of carpet samples. Then I took all my booty back to the DCHM and, one night after the children had gone home, constructed a giant playhouse. When it was finished (it took longer than one night to complete) it had doors and windows, and a tower that the children could stand in and look out from. I reinforced the entire structure so that it wouldn't easily collapse, painted it in hues reminiscent of Knoxville's House of Colors, fashioned petite curtains for the windows from fabric remnants brought from home, and lined the interior floor with carpet samples. It was a masterpiece, and my children knew it. They treated the playhouse with utmost reverence.

In the terrarium, tadpoles hatched and ate what remained of their Jell-O balls. The parent frogs ate some of the tadpoles. We watched, impressed. The tadpoles grew legs, jettisoned their tails. They became frogs. The terrarium was filled with their jumping bodies. It would soon be time for me to take a bucketful of them down to the canal.

Billy saved me the trip. Like the other children, he took his turn at cleaning the tank and feeding the frogs. He didn't like doing it, but I wanted all my children who were able to learn the discipline of following through on a simple task. I had my back turned one morning as he took his turn at terrarium duty, when I heard a soft thud behind me. The sound registered, but I didn't check to see what had caused it; I was busy attending to Jenny. The thud was followed by another, louder. And another, still more forceful. Then by a *splat* loud enough to make me pause to turn my head in time to see Billy grab a frog by its back legs and heave it as hard as he could from the terrarium up to the high ceiling – *smack!* – and I watched it plummet down to the linoleum floor – which accounted for the final *splat*. Billy Feston, you stop that! I shouted, looking for a safe place to deposit Jenny. But Billy wasn't hearing me. He was having way too much fun. And before I could get to him and end the carnage, Edgar had joined in. The two of them pitched frogs skyward with abandon. *Thud* on the ceiling, *splat* on the floor.

The frogs went, those left to save. The terrarium went.

We'll stick to other things, I thought as I scraped the mess off the linoleum. Children can be worse than snakes.

With the frogs gone, the bunny got more attention. My students petted and fed it, and took turns cleaning the hutch. I didn't begrudge the bunny its daily hour of freedom; it was wonderfully well-behaved, and always did its business in its cage. I kept a close eye on the floor, watching for telltale raisins, but never once found any. Which amazed me. A toilet trained rabbit – I must really be doing something right.

Then I noticed that Graham crackers were disappearing from the stash I kept in a cabinet. Those little imps! I thought, and intensified my observations at playtime. I soon picked up an odd pattern. Students were crawling into the playhouse and emerging out the other end with busy little mouths. Aha! I thought, but said nothing. The playhouse was the children's space, their own private space, and I was not about to invade it during classroom hours. Instead I waited until the center was empty, then got down on my hands and knees and investigated. Sure enough, in a corner of the playhouse I found a tidy pile of Graham crackers, carefully broken up into bite-sized pieces. I checked the other corners, and in one of them discovered my bunny wasn't so magical after all: there, as neatly arranged as the cracker pieces, was a pile of rabbit poop. I looked at the poop, then at the crackers, and back at the poop. I remembered the busy little mouths. My hand went to my own. What if – but I let the thought hang. Please, just let it be the Graham crackers.

The rabbit went. The playhouse went. And I went back to the drawing board. I had expected none of this. These were my kids. They weren't supposed to be sneaky, they weren't supposed to be bright enough to organize team efforts. What was wrong with this picture?

Nothing, I eventually decided. This was just my first hands-on lesson in peer interaction — a dramatic illustration of the fact that people learn from each other, good things and bad. My task would be steering them toward positive ends.

Easier said than done. The older he got, the worse Edgar's behavior grew. Billy's, too, did not improve, though at least he had the people at the group home to keep him in check. Edgar, our Napoleon, had only his grandma. He became violent, lashing out at her. One day he picked up a rock and threw it at a neighborhood kid. The rock hit the child's head and gashed it badly. The police came. Napoleon's grandma called me. She was in tears, and at her wits' end. We're going to sit on Edgar, I decided. No two ways about it, we're going to change his behavior.

The next day, I lectured Edgar about consequences. He was seven, nearly eight, and he needed to get some sense in his head. I told him if he kept it up, all his things would be taken away from him, even his grandma, and that he could wind up in jail. I wanted him to understand that some of the things he was doing were outright dangerous, that he could seriously injure someone, or himself. I talked and I talked. Every day I talked to Edgar. Nothing was ever his fault. He struck a kid at the center: That boy over there, he, he, he, he — he made me *mad*.

I wasn't getting through. But I wasn't quitting either. My husband was by now working as a deputy for the Kern County Sheriff's Department. Always spiffy and in full uniform, he could be quite an imposing sight; Martin was a big man. Things were going from bad to worse with Edgar, and Martin was just the guy I needed to help me out. One day when he stopped by the center to take me to lunch, I asked him to do me a favor. I'd told him about my woes with Edgar, and now I wanted him to step into my classroom and be Mr. Hard-Core Policeman. I want you to act mean, I told him. I want you to look scary. This kid has no clue. Okay, Martin said, I'll try.

He walked in, broad shoulders pushed back, boots thudding, his hand on his belt. He walked over to where Edgar was seated at the table and stood over him. Edgar Hernandez! Martin thundered. Edgar gave a jump and whipped around to see this massive law enforcement officer glowering down at him. He hesitated a second, then leaped from his chair and onto the table. He planted his left hand squarely on his hip and, jutting out his right arm, pointed straight at me.

Officer, ar-*rest* that girl!

For all his behavioral complexities, Edgar lacked nothing in flair. But he wasn't at the DCHM to learn; he was there to be *occupied*. And that was my problem – keeping kids like Edgar and Billy occupied. I lay awake at night scheming up things for them to do to stay busy (it beat falling asleep to dream of Rene). I had other students who needed my attention just as much as they did, and it was impossible for me to manage everyone's needs simultaneously. I knew, too, that I took a risk any time I let either of these two rascals out of my sight, even for an instant. When the classroom couldn't hold his attention, Edgar ran away. He'd start by running down to the bathroom and flushing the toilet, once, twice, fifteen thousand times, until I reached him and made him stop. Or he'd range further afield, leaving the building and dashing out across the fairgrounds. And, skirt flapping (shorts showing), I'd tear out the door after him, hollering to Mel or Emma or an aide within earshot to watch my kids, hollering at Edgar to stop in his tracks.

The chalkboard seemed to work best. Both Edgar and Billy loved to draw, and the chalkboard gave them a landscape broad enough to let their imaginations roam, and their muscles flex. They attacked it, scrawling loopy curves and frantic up-down scribbles, jousting for the most real estate. The chalkboard also kept them both in the same place, at the front of the room, where I could keep an eye on them.

It was a dry day in early June. A slow day, everyone subdued by the first waves of summer heat. Edgar was alone at the chalkboard. My back was to him, but I could hear his stick of chalk scraping on the hard surface. When I turned to check on him, my heart leaped into my throat and threatened to catch on my Adam's apple. I gulped. There, in foot-high block letters, was the word MARCH. I couldn't believe my eyes. Edgar, I said as I walked up to him, how did you know to do this? He caught the note of shock in my voice, interpreted it as disapproval.

It was on that wall up there, Teacher, he said adamantly. It was on that wall.

I looked where he was pointing, at the calendar that hung over to the right of the chalkboard. March. That was three months ago.

Flashbulbs exploded inside my head. Boy, are we missing the mark with this kid, I thought. There's got to be a wealth of potential just waiting to be tapped.

I had work to do, and I recruited Dick, Jane, and Spot to help. It was a return to my earliest teaching experiments: *Go, go, go. Go, Dick, go!*

Whenever I could, I made time for Edgar and worked on his reading. It wasn't enough; I had too many things to do, and far too few minutes to allot to his academic development.

With the right program and enough time, Edgar would learn to read quite well. I was convinced of this. But as it was, his behavior grew steadily worse, and I grew increasingly tired of trying to manage it.

For three years Edgar and I shared the classroom. He was Napoleon to my Joan of Arc. Often, I felt outmatched. I was fighting wars on too many fronts to be able to keep up with his constant flank moves. If those three years assured me of anything, it was that there was precious little, maybe even nothing, wrong with Edgar's brain. By the end, he was much bigger than any of the others in my room. Long after he should have moved on to an older class, Napoleon was still with me; no one else would have him. It was high time, I decided, for him to join his peers. Maybe *they* could model good behavior for him.

I pushed the administration into finding a school that would take him, a place where he could start learning academics in earnest. He should have been in second grade, had already missed out on first grade, and there simply was no way I could keep him mentally stimulated. After some prodding, they found a place for him in a TMR class. It wouldn't exactly be an academic environment, but it was better than what we had to offer. I said good-bye to the little general.

But I kept my eye on him all the same. Before long, he was only attending school half days. Behavioral difficulties, they told me. Uh-huh, I said. Next I heard he'd been suspended, then that he'd quit school altogether. And not long after that, they were at my door, begging me to take him back for the summer. You're the only one he'll respond to, they crooned.

I'll take him back, I said. But only for a while – long enough for *you* to find a future for him. Because this young man's future is not about Linda being able to handle things that no one else can. I have other children to worry about too.

Edgar came back. It was a disastrous summer for him. He ran away as often as he could, out to the edge of the fairgrounds, over the fence, into the street.

In the fall, he tried a new place. It didn't work. Finally, they took Edgar to an institution. By then he was eight years old. Just a little guy.

One of my little guys.

My sadness at losing Edgar has never left me. I know he was one of many who should have made it but didn't. Because our time and resources were so limited, because we had so many candidates and so few places for them, because we lacked the know-how to respond to their emotional needs, kids with real potential – kids with names like Edgar Hernandez and Billy Feston – were missing out on the education they deserved. Across the county, across the state and, indeed, the nation, it was the same story: kids with behavioral disorders were being dumped into classrooms for children with mental retardation, where their real problems – their emotions – were never adequately addressed.

One day, I thought, one day there will be programs for the Edgars and Billys of this world. One day my kids with eating disorders, with muscular dystrophy, cerebral palsy, and other severe disabilities, won't have to compete for my time with students who can remember and spell words like MARCH, or pee in outlets to watch the fizzle. One day every child will be in the program he or she deserves.

One day.

The next time I saw Edgar, he was a teenager. The first traces of a mustache darkened his upper lip. He was still beautiful. But his eyes had lost their luster, and their lids drooped. His skin, once bronze, looked sallow. He had been taken out of the institution – it hadn't worked out for him either – and put into a group home for teens. They had found a way to control his behavior problems, sort of. Edgar was so heavily medicated, so drugged, he was little more than a zombie. He scarcely recognized me, nor I him.

The last time I saw Edgar, he was roaming the streets of Bakersfield. Not causing any trouble, just shuffling along the sidewalk, his hands deep in his pockets. Going nowhere.

chapter eight

cradle song

In 1969, my first year at the DCHM, Martin and I still lived in Tehachapi, in the same three-room apartment I had rented when I first moved out to California to begin teaching. To others it might have seemed a cramped fit, but we were in love and to us the place was snug. It was home. Each morning Martin and I rode the forty-some minutes out of the hills and down to the valley floor with a carload of children, whom Martin would drop off at special education facilities throughout Bakersfield after he let me out at the fairgrounds. Then he'd go on about his day, which, at the outset of our marriage, meant law enforcement classes at Bakersfield College, and later, his job with the Sheriff's Department. In the afternoon, Martin made his rounds and reloaded the students and me for our return to high ground. And when his car was empty once again, he came home to me and was mine until the next morning.

This was fine for a year, but after it was clear my foreseeable future was with the DCHM and Martin's with the Sheriff's Department, there seemed little reason to remain in Tehachapi. We moved into the heart of Bakersfield, to an apartment building on 18th Street, across from the park. Two bedrooms, a living room, bath, and a kitchen. A real home.

The extra space soon came in handy. Back in Kansas, my sister
Minta was finishing her senior year at Riverton and was set to
graduate in June with the rest of the Class of '70. Was it really seven
years already since I'd adjusted my mortarboard and tassel and
crossed the stage for my diploma... And now here was Minta, making her own crossing. Only she didn't know where she was going,
she told me.

You could come out here, I said, and get a couple years of community college under your belt before committing to a university.
You could stay with Martin and me, I said.

I'd said enough. She was on her way, glad to be leaving the land
in the middle, to be pushing back the boundaries. Minta moved in
with us. We managed to finagle in-state tuition for her and got her
enrolled at Bakersfield College, where she was soon leading the
school's marching band as a majorette (Gwen, my college roommate, had introduced her to twirling, and she'd been hooked ever
since). The first summer, she was hired at the DCH. We'd dropped
the M for Minors, thanks to the 26th Amendment to the Constitution
of the United States, which President Nixon had just signed. Now
that the voting age was down from twenty-one to eighteen, the
older students at our center could no longer be called minors. We
were now the Development Center for the Handicapped. And we
welcomed Minta as our newest aide.

As soon as one batch of students had mastered toilet training and
moved on to other programs, the next group replaced them. Scuffy
was a new student who came in around the time Minta joined us.
Scuffy's real name was Stephanie, but her mother, Mama Jo, called
her Scuffy, so everyone else did too. She was five years old, and as
floppy as a rag doll. She sprawled on her mat, her arms and legs limp
(there were no wheelchairs for Scuffys then). I've just got to find
some alternatives, Mama Jo told me. Scuffy's grown so big, I can't
carry her around all the time. I need a program that will give her
something to do, and give my back a rest.

A typical day at the fairgrounds.

You've come to the right place, I told her, though inside I wasn't sure how we were going to help her child, and knew I'd probably have to put up a fight to get Scuffy into our program. Scuffy may not have been able to do much with her hands, but she had no difficulty grabbing my heart and soul. We *would* find a way to help her — I was sure of that.

Scuffy had very low muscle tone. She was among the first of many such students I would work with. She could not stand; her skinny legs could not hold her weight. If I held her in a sitting position, she could keep her head up for a while, but then her back would sag, and she'd have to lie down again. Like many of our children's conditions, Scuffy's was undiagnosed. Doctors took occasional guesses, but no one ever came up with a certain cause for her disabilities.

I want to teach her to sit, I decided. I want her off the floor, and not flopping around in a beanbag either. Of course I had no chair for Scuffy, nothing to help hold her in place. So I sent home notes to our students' families, asking if anyone had old car inner tubes. One father, a garage owner, came to school to see me in response to my note. He wore his brown suit (his only suit), and held his felt hat in front of him, his fingers clenched around its brim. A shy man, he did not risk eye contact. He could, he told me, get me as many inner tubes as I wanted. Cars, trucks, tractors — all sizes. I took half a dozen, to start with.

I sat Scuffy in an inflated inner tube, folded her legs under her tailor-fashion. Scuffy soon learned to use her arms to keep her balance. This solution worked for Jenny too. When she sat in an inner tube she couldn't reach the floor, and I didn't have to worry about her head.

In all of this, my sister Minta was a big help to me — another pair of strong arms and sure hands, quick eyes and keen ears. And sometimes, even as we sought to come up with ways to make our children comfortable enough so that they could begin developing life skills, sometimes the most important thing for a child was to have someone there to give her a bear hug and trade smiles.

I smiled when I found out I was going to have a baby, and Martin grinned when I told him.

I cried when, soon after, it was not to be. Martin, not knowing what else to do, put his arm around my shoulder and squeezed me gently. I could tell he felt awful, at a loss for a response.

My second and third miscarriages I kept to myself. I didn't want to burden Martin with them, or with my feelings of inadequacy. I shed private tears and bit my lip so that my pain would remain inside of me. I was not good enough to have a baby. The miscarriages were my fault. And in my insecurity, I decided that if I couldn't carry my child, I could at least carry my loss.

It was early spring, 1971, when Mary called me, at a loss. She had broken up with her boyfriend, the one we'd all assumed she'd wind up marrying. She sounded tiny and far away, her voice floundering on the other end of the line. I miss you, Linda, she said. I miss you and Minta, and Allen. I miss you, too, I told Mary. I could picture her, the only one of us kids left at home, sitting across the dinner table from Daddy, and him telling her to heap her plate, to eat up. She really is all alone, I thought, and could well understand the quaver in her voice. We'd always been together, or at least close enough to stay connected. Now we were miles apart, and Mary was left to fend for herself under Daddy's roof.

She seemed to gain encouragement just from talking to me, so I didn't interrupt her, and let my thoughts duck out for a while and take me back to my childhood, and hers. I remembered afternoons when Mama was gone to the grocery store and Allen and I climbed to the barn roof, to the low place at the back where the corrugated tin dipped down – a perfect place to jump from, down to the spongy ground below. Flying, we called it, and sometimes our friends came over and joined in. Minta (she was five) did too. Which meant three-year-old Mary also had to try; the two were inseparable. We found higher, more daring, launch places. Come on, Mary, hold on to your dolly. You can do it! Just hold on to your dolly and fly. And Mary flew, and landed safely. She giggled, and we helped her fly again. Until she landed wrong and chipped a front tooth, and so of course we had to tell Mama, who was horrified. You could have killed her! Mary is your little sister, and your job is to look after her, not put her life in danger.

Now Mary's life wasn't exactly in danger, but I wasn't exactly looking after her either. And right now she *did* sound like she needed looking after.

I want to come to California, she said. I want to come stay with you for a while.

Mama helped her pack her things and got her on a plane. We had talked beforehand, Mama and I, and she'd made me promise to take good care of my sister. Mary was still Mama's baby, even if she was almost finished with her junior year of high school.

Martin now had all three McPherson girls to contend with around the house, but he was a wonderful sport about it. And just because Mary thought the California sunshine had been ordered especially for her didn't mean I was going to let her loaf around. I got her lined up with correspondence courses so she could complete her school year. When she wasn't occupied with her studies, she came with me to the development center and helped out as a volunteer.

None of us anticipated Mary falling in love again so soon. But then, that was before she met Bobby. They found each other that summer, and when it happened, none of us had any objections.

Bobby was four years old, and one of my students. He got around the classroom by crawling. Unable to talk, he communicated through an assortment of gurgles and coos, smiles and tears. He was a sweet little guy. A twin, Bobby had suffered anoxia inside his mother's womb, and the lack of oxygen had left him with multiple disabilities, both physical and mental.

I put Mary in charge of Bobby. On his own, he took charge of Mary. She was his very special friend, and there was nothing he wouldn't do for her. Secretly, I had been hoping for something like this – it was a pattern I'd seen with other students: give them one-on-one attention and let them form a friendship with their caregiver, then watch both of them blossom beyond expectation. Mary crawled around on the floor with Bobby, urging him on. Under my coaching, she managed to get him up onto his feet, holding his hands while he stood for the first time, rocking unsteadily back and forth, a million-dollar smile lighting his face. Together, they took his first steps. A local magazine ran a feature on the two of them, with Mary's picture on the issue's cover. By summer's end, Bobby was walking independently, a little caution in his steps, but taking them unassisted nonetheless.

Mary too, I felt, was ready to let go of my hand. It was time for her to go home. She would know she was not alone, because we had reconnected.

I compiled an album with pictures of all the DCH kids Mary had come to love, and included the magazine clipping with the write-up about her and Bobby. This was her going-away present. I drove her to the airport to catch her flight home, with Art Garfunkel crooning "Bridge over Troubled Water" through the radio.

She was back at my door within a few weeks. I had been right about one thing: the summer had helped her confidence. Now she had made her decision about where she wanted to be. So Mary stayed with Martin and me through her senior year at Bakersfield High, and when she was finished, she did not return home.

Glad as I was to be helping Mary find her feet, I wanted nothing more than to get back to thinking about my kids and how to help them conquer the immense challenges they faced each day – and to have things running on an even keel once again. It was wishful thinking.

It was wishful thinking because, at the DCH, there never was, never had been, and never would be an even keel. With us, it was always something. Or, in the case of Cecil Woolard, someone.

I first met him at an open house for the families of incoming students. His daughter, Tina, was on my list of new names. I was eager to meet her. Be careful, Linda, I cautioned myself as I looked down at the blue-eyed, blond six-year-old lying at her parents' feet. I could feel my heartstrings tightening to familiar tugs. Tina, woefully disabled and deformed by cerebral palsy, smiled at me as I crouched down to introduce myself. Her bright eyes locked with mine. They flashed with language. Tina, I knew from the start, had a busy little mind. I couldn't help myself: here I was, two minutes into my first encounter with a new kid, and already I loved her as one of my own. There was an unbuffed gem waiting inside her.

Her parents were a different story. I launched into my routine, explaining what Tina's day with us might look like, how I'd be working with them to come up with a program for Tina that best suited her particular needs. I pattered on for a while, then paused to see if I was connecting. Mrs. Woolard nodded, to show she was listening, but said very little. She seemed to hold her breath. When she finally spoke, it was as though she had been storing up the words in the roof of her mouth – her lips parted, and they all tumbled out in a great panting rush. Then her lips resealed, and she ceased to exist once again. Strange, I thought. Very strange.

Why Mrs. Woolard felt intimidated was soon made blatantly clear by her husband. Mr. Woolard did his best to appear detached as I spoke. He slouched his big belly forward so that it sagged over the waistline of his jeans, and mussed his unkempt hair with his rough hands to tout his aloofness. Mr. Woolard reeked. The odor of stale beer, cheap beer, hit me first, and then the stench of his uncleanliness. A rank smell, the kind old mattresses excrete. The beer smell explained his paunch; it was the genuine article – a beer gut. Cecil was an obnoxious man, loud and coarse, as loose with his words as his wife was cramped. I decided to ignore him and direct my explanations toward his wife. We'll start toilet training first thing, I told her, so Tina's going to need some training pants. Please see that she –

Training pants? Mr. Woolard cut me off. What in the *hell* are training pants? He jutted his jaw out when he spoke, working the words through his teeth like laundry through a mangle. He had his hands thrust into the back pockets of his jeans, and his belly jutted out over his big belt buckle. I was going to enlighten him, but Tina's mother pulled at his elbow. Sh, Cecil, they's underpants, like what we wear under our clothes. He twitched his arm away. *I* don't wear none, he said, loud enough to be heard by anyone who cared to listen.

Right from the start I could tell that in Cecil Woolard's mind, he was the axis around which the earth revolved. He showed scant regard for his wife, and less for his daughter. All the more, I was grateful to have Tina in my class. At least during the day I'll know she's getting the love she deserves, I thought.

Tina came to the center on the school bus each morning. From time to time her mother came to school, too, to see how she was getting on. I tried never to let Mrs. Woolard see me looking at her bruises. Mrs. Woolard always had bruises – huge, dark shadows on her arms, neck, and face. I noticed she spoke less haltingly when her husband wasn't around. And when she talked of him, she never uttered his name. Never *Cecil*, or *my husband*. Not *Tina's dad*. Just *he*. He did this, he said that.

Tina Woolard was a child before the days of wheelchair lifts on school buses – before there were wheelchairs for children like her, for that matter. There were no car seats either. Tina rode the bus to and from school each day lying across a bench seat, buckled in by two seatbelts. That is, until the afternoon Cecil stepped outside to meet the bus and, apparently for the first time, took note of how his daughter made the trip. As the shaken driver later reported, Cecil stomped into his shack and stormed back out clutching a shotgun. He boarded the bus, shoved the gun barrel into the driver's face, and threatened to blow her head off *if I ever see that girl laying down again, you hear?*

Cecil never elaborated on how he expected his daughter to be transported, nor did he even wait to see if his threats made an impact. Instead he refused to allow Tina on the bus. He would do things his way, he decided, and haul her back and forth himself in his beat-up truck. And there wasn't a thing I or anyone else could do about it. Except worry.

He stopped by the DCH one morning, out of the blue. He was all spiffed up, his hair combed. Except he still reeked of stale beer. I didn't know it then, but he had come a-courtin'. His mind was made up: Linda Bidabe was his perfect cup of tea. I was courteous, as I tried to be with every parent who dropped in during the day, and happy to see him exhibiting a little interest in his daughter's well-being. Apparently not everyone had been nice to Cecil, for he interpreted my manners as a favorable omen for his designs. His visits became more frequent. Each time, he sought me out. There was always something about himself he wanted me to know.

I'm gonna get paid. I collect a disability. So I'm gonna get paid.

That's nice, Cecil. I'm glad to hear it.

Soon as I get my check, I'm gonna buy you a present.

Oh, no, Cecil. You keep your money. I'm getting paid this week too. Now, let me tell you about Tina's... And I would steer the conversation around (and try to ignore the bile rising in my stomach). Cecil's advances repulsed me, but usually when he stopped by there were other teachers on hand. He was more of an irritation than a threat. Yet as his visits grew ever more frequent and his intentions ever more obvious, I began to feel frightened. When would he knock it off and leave me be?

Cecil came in one day just as we were preparing for a staff meeting. I was alone with the students in my classroom. He had been to the bank to cash his disability check. He had also been drinking. I'd seen him shove a hip flask into his back pocket as he came through the door. Cecil yanked a fistful of bills out of his front pocket and waved them in my face. I was supposed to be impressed. He crinkled a ten dollar bill on top of the stack and stuck it out to me.

Here, take this. It's for you.

I can't, Mr. Woolard. I can't take your money. It's against the law. We get paid, too, you know – they pay me for the job I do here.

Cecil Woolard's feelings were hurt, and his generous mood soured fast. The alcohol wasn't helping anything, I could tell. He glared at me and yelled in my face, demanding I accept his gift. He stepped forward, and I stepped back. He kept yelling, kept coming toward me. I kept backing up until I hit a table and my knees folded under me. Cecil grabbed me by my upper arms as I was using my hands to get up off the table. He was a strong man, and I could do nothing as he pulled me to him, bent his head, and, his fetid breath huffing against my face, forced his lips to mine.

Somehow, I managed to break away. I clawed away from him and ran down the hall. I rushed into the bathroom and vomited. Then I scrubbed my face and hands. I wanted to be rid of him, to purge myself. It would take more than soap.

Cecil started stalking me. He would park his truck outside the center and wait for me to get into my car. Then he would follow me. I guessed he wanted to find out where I lived. I would weave through traffic, take roundabout routes, and try to shake him. Most days, I drove over to the Valley Plaza mall, parked near a door, and darted inside. I wandered from shop to shop, quivering, hoping Cecil would be gone by the time I returned to my car. One day as I got on the highway outside the fairgrounds, I saw his truck in my rearview mirror. He tailgated me into town. So I did what I should have done long before: I drove straight over to the Sheriff's Department and pulled into an open slot along a row of squad cars. Cecil stayed in the street, gunned his engine, and moved on. Evidently he wasn't fond of the law.

Martin came to the center to talk strategy. We sat down with the head teacher and several KCSOS representatives. As we discussed our options I felt reassured to know the situation was being taken seriously. Martin didn't think a restraining order would be very effective. It might even make things worse and infuriate Cecil further – despite what some of my colleagues had tried to tell me about "harmless drunks," none of us wanted to risk anything. I could press assault charges for the kissing incident, but that wouldn't amount to much either and was certain to rile up Cecil. Our best bet, we all agreed, was to be alert, and to see that I was never alone. My classroom had been at the back of the center. Now we combined classrooms in the large, open hall, where I would always have other people around. If Cecil showed up, I could disappear while my friends stepped in to head him off.

In a few short years the DCH had more than outgrown the fairground warehouse, and in September 1971, as Mary began her final year of high school, we packed up and moved to the Greeley Learning Center. With many classrooms and a converted gymnasium, it was a much larger facility, located on the outskirts of Bakersfield. Thanks to an infusion of state money and resources, Greeley was equipped to take in more students, with more staff to attend to them. We were growing, and slowly but surely our status as stepchildren was being reevaluated; we were on our way to becoming a recognized part of the family.

After the move, students and classes were redistributed, but Tina Woolard stayed with me. Cecil stayed too. At Greeley, we implemented the same early-warning system we had developed at the DCH. Anyone who saw Cecil approaching would get a message to me, and see that someone stalled him long enough for me to make myself scarce. We put baffles in his path, to frustrate his efforts at finding me. But Cecil Woolard did not go away. My fear did not go away. It stayed with me through the school day, and into the night, too, sometimes. Sometimes the dream came...

It takes me a long time to find the place, far out in yucca-stalked and cactused wilderness. The grass growing between the ruts in the road swishes under my car as I steer around the last brown bend, and there it is, in front of me: a pathetic carcass of a home, loosely draped in clapboards faded the gray color of weathered bones, and tarpaper showing darkly through gaps laced with cobwebs. I stop, turn off the ignition, set the brake, unlatch the car door (it clicks like the safety on Martin's firearm). Get out. Feet leaden, blood cold.

Mr. Woolard himself comes to the door and ushers me inside. His hand goes for my coat, but I bend around him before he has a chance to take it, or touch me. Mrs. Woolard is in the kitchen, laboring over the stove. She turns as I enter, moves toward me. Her feet – black-socked, bare heels protruding through ratty holes – seem not to touch the floor as, silently, she glides into the front room, where Cecil is showing me to a chair. He is at his most flamboyant, despite his grimy, red flannel shirt and denim jeans. He has me where he wants me, I warn myself, as he folds his arms amiably over his big belly and begins to brag. He puffs up his meager accomplishments into deeds of grandeur completely incongruous with the disastrous reality of his situation. Mrs. Woolard flits past him nervously and takes a frayed wicker-bottomed chair next to mine. She says nothing, only cocks her head like a little gray pigeon, eyes darting, as I pursue my usual tactic for defusing Cecil, steering the conversation around to Tina. She is, after all, why I've come. Home visits, a requisite for all DCH staff, cannot be put off forever, even visits to the Woolard home. I talk the Tina talk while Mrs. Woolard remains mute as the chair on which she sits, and Cecil goes on, full of himself, leering and sprawling. He invites me to stay for dinner, and I, too nervous to refuse, hear myself accepting.

Mrs. Woolard rises from her chair and skitters toward the kitchen. She beckons noiselessly for me to follow her, and I do. Cecil's back is to us, and Mrs. Woolard addresses me for the first time this evening. In her wild-eyed agitation, she whispers, and though I strain I cannot make out what she's trying to tell me. Before I can ask her to repeat it, Cecil comes in and places a firm hand on my shoulder, points me to a chair at the table. The table is bare. No food, no utensils, except for a cutting board.

I turn my head back toward the kitchen, where Mrs. Woolard is removing the roast from the oven. Only, what she slides from the oven is a man's torso, dissected clean through the midriff. I see it in cross section from where I sit. The long arms are folded across the chest, trussed like a turkey. Without a sound, Mrs. Woolard lays a carving knife and fork alongside the torso-roast and turns away from the now-empty oven, back to the table.

With sudden panic, I know beyond all doubt who is next slated for the oven. I have to get away from here! *Run.* But my feet are lead. Behind me is Mrs. Woolard, knife in hand. And before me is Cecil, blocking my escape, his arms still folded, his face still leering. I scream, but no noise comes. The air in my lungs is oven hot, burning, too hot for sound...

When I wake from this recurring nightmare, as I always do before I am either killed or rescued, I am drenched in sweat, and palpitating from the exhaustion of my fears. In the morning, I rise fatigued.

This is ridiculous, I finally decide. I can't keep this up; I've got my kids to worry about. Cecil can't be allowed to terrorize me at night and prey on my thoughts during the day. In need of some reassurance, I go to the policy makers, the ones who say we need to make home visits, and tell them: Go ahead and try to force me, that's one visit I'm never going to make. Not ever. They catch my drift. Before long, the rules on home visits have been modified.

All of that, and I still had Mary's future to worry over. Soon she would graduate from high school and, despite our statements to the contrary, she was concerned about being a burden on Martin and me. Perhaps that's why, when Mary met Ralph and fell in love, she was so quick to marry him – he had a good job, and she wouldn't be beholden to us any longer.

After their wedding, Mary and Ralph decided to stay in Bakersfield. They got an apartment.

They got pregnant.

Mary called me, ecstatic. Then she called Mama. Guess what? I'm going to have a baby!

Mary's excitement was infectious.

A few weeks earlier I had scheduled an appointment with my urologist; I had an infection of my own (my kidneys had given me trouble since I was five). His x-rays revealed nothing unusual. I was scared nonetheless. By the time Mary called, I had my first suspicions that what I'd taken to be a bladder infection was actually another pregnancy. It'll be like the other times, I thought. It'll end the same way. But a month went by, and I did not miscarry. If my sister can do it, maybe I can, too, I thought. Mary's happiness gave me strength.

I told Martin. He grinned from shoulder to shoulder.

I called Mama and Daddy. Guess what? I'm also going to have a baby!

Their excitement was catching, too, though even their support could not allay my fears of failing.

In the months that followed, Mary was my mainstay. Her confidence buoyed me when feelings of doubt tried to encroach on the wonderment I felt at the first stirrings deep inside me. It was her turn to play big sister, to give me a hand up. Together, we were going to make it through. Our babies were both scheduled to arrive the first week of January 1974.

Still, I battled skepticism. Before, my pregnancies had always ended in heartache. It could happen again, I knew, and I braced myself for it, especially when my doctor told me I was dilated to three centimeters. Incompetent cervix, he called it, which naturally made me feel a whole lot better. A trimester passed. Nothing was amiss. At four months, I felt my heart flutter with a little shock of surprise – maybe, just maybe – but remained braced all the same. Martin was a wonderful support, but he was just as scared as I was. Now we began to dare to dream out loud. We talked nightly in pillowed whispers, trying on girls' and boys' names and weaving designs for our future as a family. Eager to get to know the child inside me, I asked my doctor about having amniocentesis. If you do that, Linda, he said, you're going to miscarry. That's all it'll take.

It doesn't take much, I thought.

At six months, my breath caught as I realized my baby was old enough to live, albeit tenuously, outside my womb. How would he/she look? Would she/he be…okay? Normal? Then I thought of my miscarriages and wondered if my body had rejected those pregnancies, as sometimes happens, because of something dreadfully wrong with those potential children.

That's when I got serious and started presenting my case to God. This wasn't anything to do with religion, it was about me and my baby. God, you'd better be listening, I thought as I began my opening arguments: *I have dedicated the last five years – shall we count them together? – five years of my life to working with children with severe disabilities. I know what they go through, I know what their parents go through. And you know I'm not strong enough to handle that. So if you're thinking of giving me a child with a severe disability, think again. You can't do that to me, I won't go along with it. It's not fair for you to even think –*

And on and on.

Seven weeks before my baby was due, I went into labor. Or at least, I thought it was labor; I didn't know what else it could be. But this wasn't right. This was much too early. I wasn't supposed to be feeling this yet.

I remember fear, and mounting panic, as Martin drove me to the hospital.

I am lying on my back on a table in a room with a ceiling of white soundproof tiles. The tiles have little dark pores in them, which seem to open and close as I squint at them. They are soundproof, I know, because this is a place where women go to endure. I notice the ceiling momentarily, but am oblivious to everything else going on around me in the room. There is motion to my right and to my left. Blurred. I am lost inside myself, at the center of my pain. My pain is red. I am bleeding. I am bleeding badly. The room is red. Even the ceiling looks mistily red. Like a hothouse of poinsettias.

Someone is talking at my head. The voice comes through a long tunnel. It drips into my head like an IV.

You are bleeding badly, the voice tells me.

I know this. Yes, I tell the voice.

The voice speaks again, through a drainpipe this time, but the words don't reach me intact. A wave drenches the length of my body, a searing wave that wants to turn me inside out. I lose myself for a moment in the redness of my pain, then pull my head up. *Breathe.* I cannot die. Not now. I will not die. Not now. A fresh wave breaks, crashes hotly through me, followed by countless ripples that tremor and tear and seek to wear me down. I will hold on. I must hold on.

For ten hours, they tell me later, I fight through my labor, one strenuous contraction after the next, with barely room to breathe in between.

The voice at my head belonged to Martin. He was trying to comfort me, to keep me going. The doctors were worried. They kept taking him into the corridor. It doesn't look hopeful, they said. We're trying all we can, but the way it's going, we'll probably lose the baby.

A cesarean was no longer feasible; my baby's head was already lodged in the birth canal. Besides, once the doctors ascertained that the profuse bleeding was coming from behind the baby, who acted as a dam, backing up the blood and building the pressure that created my intense pain, their concern was for my survival more than the child's. Its heartbeat and blood pressure seem stable, they told Martin. Now it's Linda we're worried about.

They stick needles in my arms, start saline drips. And blood. My baby is so small, they decide the best option is to let it be born naturally, and keep pumping blood into me.

There is no voice at my head for the end. I am alone, crossing my Red Sea solo. Martin has been evicted since the real trouble began, and he's pacing out his vigil in the corridor. He is not there when my body finally yields and my firstborn child thrusts from my womb into the white lights and blue chucks of the delivery room. Her name is Tanya.

I catch a glimpse of scrawny arms, hands with long, long fingers. And the most amazing thing is: the fingers are moving. Then she cries – *waaahh* – and with her first sound, the last redness leaves the room. I stay on my back, but my heart lifts from my chest and peers over the doctors' shoulders as they cut Tanya's cord, carry her to the side table, and whisk her off to the ICU. It goes with her down the hallway. I have seen her for only a few seconds, over the rim of her bassinet, long enough to know she has long, long fingers. Fingers that move. What more could a mother ask for?

Tanya Ellen Bidabe was born minutes before midnight, November 23, 1973. I have never felt so tired in my life as I did when it was all over. Nor so awestruck. She was a preemie – weighing in at only five pounds, two ounces – but she was breathing, and the doctors assured me there was nothing wrong with her. Nothing whatsoever. I remembered my arguments with God, and understood now that my baby could have come out green and purple with yellow polka dots; she could have had six arms and three mouths. None of that would have stopped me from loving her. She was my baby, my perfect baby. And I felt ashamed, and thrilled beyond belief all at the same time. I apologized to God several times.

I had to stay put for the night, where I could be monitored and receive more blood transfusions. Martin and I were reunited. His face was a study in relief and pride. After the exertion of labor, the heat had drained from my body and I shivered with cold. Nurses brought hot blankets and tucked them around me. It was early morning by the time the new blood had finished dripping into my veins. By then I had warmed up and was hungrier than I'd ever been before. I devoured a huge breakfast. Then I wanted to see my baby. Not possible, I was told. She was in an incubator down in the neonatal ICU, doing fine, but I couldn't see her just yet. You both need your rest, the nurses told me in their nurses' voices.

My rest could wait, I decided. I was going to Tanya. It was about eight o'clock in the morning when I slipped out of bed and, steadying myself with a hand on the pole of my IV stand, shuffled in slippered feet and nightgown down to the nursery to meet the new love of my life.

I remained in the hospital for a couple more days, regaining enough strength to be allowed home – without Tanya, of course. They might as well not have bothered to release me; I spent as much time as I could with her. She stayed in her incubator, except when they took her out to feed her, or to bake her in a little oven. We don't want her getting jaundiced, the nurses explained.

Tanya cooperated beautifully.

Once home, she slept in a little bassinet right by my side of our bed. For two weeks, I never slept. I dozed off with my hand on her chest, waiting for her to stop breathing. Martin shared my nervousness. Between the two of us, Tanya was never without human contact during those first weeks. Often Martin left the bed at night to scoop her up and carry her to our recliner, where he'd sleep with her curled against his chest.

She was a wonderful sleeper but, being a preemie, needed feeding every two hours, whether she was awake or not. Too tiny to suck aggressively, she would take a couple sips from the bottle teat – *szhupp szhupp* – then lose interest. A tap on the bottom of the bottle was usually enough to get her to sip again, but by the time she'd downed two ounces of formula, it seemed minutes before her next scheduled feed. I didn't care. I was determined to keep Tanya as long as I could.

Tanya did not die. She grew into a healthy, bright, alert baby. No matter how hard I looked, I could discover nothing wrong with her.

It was nearly Christmas. Tanya *is* Christmas, I thought.

But we had obligations. The Sheriff's Department banquet, for instance. I told Martin I didn't think I could go with him, that I needed to stay home and watch over Tanya. His sister Marguerite decided otherwise. She came down from Tehachapi and announced: I am taking care of this baby tonight, and the two of you are going out for the evening. And that was that. I was a nervous wreck, but I trusted Marguerite and left her with my baby, sure the house would burn down while we were away.

We came home. The baby and Marguerite were both fine. That night, for the first time in weeks, I slept like the dead.

Mary's baby arrived December 27. The sun was shining to welcome Minta Lauren to the world. Perhaps it would have reconsidered, had it known that its light now sparkled on infant cousins destined to become two of the greatest terrors known to man. Or woman.

tears

She is the first child on earth. For her the sun rises each morning and paints the day. For her the stars spangle the night sky over the San Joaquin Valley. And I am her mother. I am chosen. A lioness. Nothing will harm my cub.

These are my nighttime thoughts as I fade into the dark, my palm resting on my baby. Even when she's six months old, I won't let her from my side; that way, the darkness can't filch her back to the universe, from where she came. She is mine, I tell myself before I sleep, and anything that wants to do her harm will have to reckon with Mama Lion first. Cecil Woolard, are you listening?

I couldn't help worrying about Cecil – I was still his chosen cup of tea. At Greeley, my protection was by no means guaranteed, and I was afraid to think what he would try if he ever got his hands on me again. These fears for my own safety naturally brought on fears for Tanya.

Relief came from an unexpected source: Mama Jo. Her daughter Scuffy, now seven years old, was still in my class. It was, Mama Jo decided, payback time. She approached me soon after I had returned to work from maternity leave. You've taken good care of my daughter all this time, she said. Now it's my turn to take care of yours.

She meant it too. Like us, Mama Jo and Scuffy lived in town, and now she opened her home to us, and especially to Tanya. On my way to work each morning I dropped her off at Mama Jo's, and returned for her in the afternoon. A self-appointed nanny, Mama Jo cared for Tanya like one of her own. Indeed, as far as she was concerned, Tanya belonged to her. Mama Jo was a mama lion, too, and it gave me comfort knowing my daughter was safe in her care while I faced the uncertainties of each school day.

Since the center's move to Greeley, Cecil Woolard had quit driving Tina to school. At least that whim, it seemed, had worn off. I was greatly relieved.

Then one morning as I drove to work listening to a local news broadcast on the car radio, I came close to swerving off the road when the newscaster announced that Mrs. Woolard, Cecil's wife, had died the night before. According to the reporter, she had fallen down the steps outside the Woolards' shack, broken her neck. DOA at the Kern Medical Center. That's one hell of a story, I thought as I sped for school, panic rising in my throat.

The drivers were pulling their buses up to the school when I arrived. I began looking for Tina, for her driver. No, she said when I managed to find her, Tina hadn't been there when she'd stopped to collect her. She's not on the bus this morning, Linda. Something wrong?

We spread the news as fast as we could. Cecil, that monster, had Tina. I called Martin. By then I was crying so hard I could hardly force out any words. He told me to calm down, that he would get on it.

One of the bus drivers picked up a report from someone in a nearby town who'd spotted Cecil's truck, parked outside a liquor store. Tina was apparently in the truck, sprawled on the floorboards.

I called Martin again. He contacted Child Protective Services, rushed the paperwork through, and rounded up a bunch of his deputies. Then he led them out to Cecil Woolard's shack for a reckoning. They took no chances – no one had forgotten the shotgun

Tawny

incident – and surrounded the shack with weapons of their own. Treed, Cecil came out and surrendered. The CPS agents went into the shack, brought out Tina, and took her away. Martin, my white knight, handled Cecil.

No charges were pressed. Cecil had done nothing illegal – at least nothing that could be pinned on him. But Tina, now in protective custody and a ward of the state, was hidden from him. That was wonderful, but it didn't prevent Cecil from pursuing me. A few days later, he showed up at school, come for me once again. He got as far as the front office, where he met my colleague Eleanor Melvin. *My wife gone and died, you know, so I'm gonna have to get me a new wife now.* Cecil said it as though it explained why he'd come.

Eleanor made sure the message reached me – *Cecil Woolard is on campus!* – and, hero that I was, I jumped into a closet and shut the door. If I can't see him, maybe he can't see me. My own breathing terrified me. For two hours I stayed in that closet. The center was empty when I ventured out. I raced to my car, sure Cecil was waiting to stalk me as he had done before. By the time I reached home, I was shaking uncontrollably – a perfect basket case if ever there was one.

He called on me a few more times, reluctant to give me up as a lost cause. Perhaps it was his frustration at not being able to locate Tina that made him so persistent in trying to pin me down. It was Eleanor who finally outfoxed him. She met him at the door one morning, and decided to put an end to it once and for all. In response to his prying, she told him, straight-faced: *Oh, Linda Bidabe? She's had a baby – she's married, you know – and she doesn't work here anymore. She quit a while ago. Come to think of it, I heard she's moved out of state.* Cecil stared hard at Eleanor, but she didn't waver, didn't even blink. He looked down and walked away.

I never heard from Cecil Woolard again – not until many years later when his obituary surfaced in the local paper.

Mama Jo had been a source of comfort during the Cecil ordeal. Now
that it was over, she became a wellspring of inspiration. With my own
mother half a continent away, I needed someone near at hand whom
I could claim as a mothering mentor. Mama Jo was the perfect, and
natural, choice. Only a few years older than I, she seemed to possess
decades more wisdom. Most important, she was always there to act
as a sounding board – someone to talk to, bounce ideas off of, con-
fide in. Mama Jo took wonderful care of her two daughters – Scuffy
had an older sister, Cissie – and welcomed Tanya as her third, as
though she were the puzzle piece that completed the picture. To her
had been granted, genie-like, the gift of knowing instinctively how
to be a good, involved parent without suffocating her children. I
took mental notes and did my best to learn from her.

It was Mama Jo who suggested that Tanya get involved with Junior Theater. Mama Jo loved the stage and saw it as a wonderful opportunity for children to interact; Cissie was constantly in plays.
Tanya got her first chance at eight months. She played the baby
princess in "Sleeping Beauty." We got her a fancy white christening
gown and made a delicate silver crown for her head. The cast loved
her and cooed over her at every rehearsal, for which she obligingly
behaved her sweetest. Then came the opening performance (which
was also the closing performance, this being Junior Theater): Act I,
scene i, began with Tanya at center stage, in her dainty princessly
cradle. The lights dimmed, darkening the set. And Tanya screamed.
A blood-stopping howl to bring the ladies-in-waiting running and
make the king (a young teenaged boy) bungle his opening lines.
Luckily he redeemed himself by gathering up the screeching bundle
and rocking her in his arms, clucking and smiling at her until she got
over her stage fright and her howls subsided to whimpers, then to
giggles. The show could go on.

Whether it was theater or cookie-making, nose-wiping or hugging, Mama Jo applied the same sage philosophy: finish what you

start, and do it well. Her advice, mother to mother, was, Never over-commit. Don't try to do everything at once. Decide what it is you're most keen on right now, go with that, stick at it and do a good job, then move on. A simple game plan, but one by which worlds could be conquered.

I decided Tanya and I had energy enough to take on two things at once, no more. I would select two activities for her, one geared to physical and one to creative development. She already had a creative outlet – Junior Theater – so that was taken care of. For physical exercise, we started with a gymnastics class for tots, which mostly involved somersaulting and rolling around on vinyl-covered foam mats. These would be our pursuits, and we would do them well.

We. Tanya and I were a team. The time would come soon enough, I knew, when she would need (and probably demand) her own space, but for now she and I were going to be girls together. I wanted her there when I went grocery shopping, not off in someone else's activity. Martin supported me fully. He, too, wanted his daughter to grow up capable of wise choices, able to follow through on her commitments – essential components, we both believed, of a healthy self-image. Later she would be able to choose her athletic and creative endeavors by herself (two at a time). Until that day, though, I would make those choices for her.

By the time most girls her age were going to preschool, Tanya was thriving under Mama Jo's one-on-one attention. Her days were filled with paper, paste, and scissors; air hockey; Carnation instant snacks; naptime; Camp Fire Girls, Bluebirds, and Sweet Adelines. She was getting an education at home as well, but of a different sort.

Back when Tanya was six months old, we had moved from our apartment on 18th Street to a two-story, three-bedroom house on Minor Street. (Living with my two sisters in those close quarters had been a test of our marriage, and now that we could afford the mortgage, both Martin and I were happy to move to a larger dwelling.) Along with the spare bedroom, our new home also had a den and a

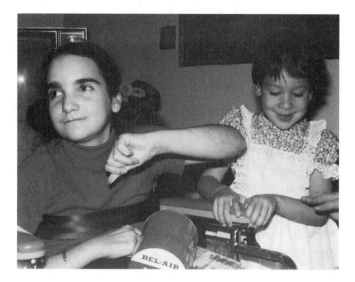

Scuffy, Tanya, and the Junior Theater gang
at Mama Jo's.

living room – plenty of space for guests. And a good thing, too, since more and more frequently I found myself bringing my work home with me.

Tamika was a three-year-old with contractures in her arms and legs so tight that some therapists from California Children Services had said hers was the worst case they'd ever seen. The day Tamika came home with me, the air rasped with swirling dust. We were in the middle of one of the worst dust storms I have ever experienced in Bakersfield, and Tamika's parents couldn't make it to the center to pick her up. The dust was inescapable. It blew in waves across the highway as I drove home, blurring visibility and dragging the traffic down to a timid crawl. The wind hissed at the car's door seals. Dust came up through the dashboard vents and settled in a grainy film. Tamika herself was coated in grime. We got home, and Tanya, my little four-year-old, helped me give Tamika a bath. Tanya climbed into the tub first, and then I hoisted Tamika's twisted body over the side and sat her in front of Tanya, who wrapped her arms around Tamika and held her upright while I scrubbed the dust from her pores. That night, Tamika shared Tanya's bed. We could have had all the extra space in the world, and it wouldn't have mattered – those two would not be separated.

From her earliest years, then, Tanya was accustomed to being around children with disabilities. They were part of my everyday life, so, naturally, they became part of hers. It never occurred to me to discuss it with her; this was simply the way life was going to be. For her part, Tanya was equally at ease playing with children like Tamika as she was with her neighborhood friends Nancy and Dana, with whom she discovered jump roping and hopscotch. She never seemed to notice that some of her friends wore leg braces or couldn't walk at all, that they talked funny or could only gurgle. None of that seemed to make the slightest difference to her. When Tanya started first grade, she asked one of her classmates, Where are your friends who can't walk or talk? To her, this was a straight-

forward question, so she was bewildered by her friend's puzzled
look. Just as I had once thought every family consisted of two parents, a brother, a sister, and a dog, so my daughter thought everyone
had friends like hers.

Tanya grew and developed as I watched, proud to be the very first
mother in the whole wide world. What an exceptional child she was!
So beautiful, so rare.

So normal.

As I watched her — and held her hand through ups and downs
and bumps and bruises, wiped her tears and shared her joys — I
couldn't help thinking of my other kids, my DCH kids. Compared
with Tanya, they were growing up with mammoth obstacles planted
directly in their path. While Tanya grappled with shoelaces and
jacket zippers, her peers in my classroom confronted physical and
mental challenges too great for them to conquer in a lifetime. Yet
they shared one thing in common: despite whatever disabilities hin-
dered them, they were all just kids growing up.

I watched Tanya spend hours at the park, dangling by her knees
from the monkey bars, her untucked shirt falling over her face, muf-
fling her giggles. Later, I sat at an unobtrusive distance as Dana,
Nancy, and Tanya played dress-up in Tanya's spacious bedroom
and sang karaoke to her favorite records before karaoke existed. As
she developed, I saw before my eyes the connection between flexing
muscles and flexing brains. Best of all, I saw my daughter having
fun — growing and learning without ever knowing it.

Even her first steps out of babyhood had started me thinking. All
of a sudden, it seemed clear: that's what they need. That's what my
other kids need, too — the chance to have fun. They're growing up,
but they haven't experienced fun yet. We expect them to lie around on
mats or sit propped up in beanbag chairs; to roll over, lift their heads,
flex their arms and legs, or whatever other exercise we prescribe —

but we're not making it fun. What's the motivation for these kids? Why should they keep trying? What's the goal?

Then I stopped short. What *is* the goal? I wondered.

And I thought back to Tommy. The truth was, I had never stopped thinking about Tommy.

He was there at the fairgrounds during Napoleon's reign. He was there when Billy tested the impact of gravity on frogs. Through it all, he never said a word. Not that anything passed him by. Tommy's eyes tap danced when he was excited, flashing signals of understanding. If he couldn't talk, he sure could smile and laugh – and he did, at all the right times. He never missed a joke. He could communicate, too, if you knew what to look for. He'd look up for "yes," down for "no," and form an "o" with his mouth for "I don't know." But anyone casually walking through our classroom (not that anyone ever *did*) might have been excused for assuming that Tommy was, as one neurologist told me while pointing an index finger at his own head, "just plain retarded." Broken and deformed by muscular dystrophy, Tommy's body lay on a mat in the corner for most of our school day. But, I was convinced, his mind was a million miles away – or close at hand, dashing about the room with the more hyperactive of my students.

One day I caught his bright eyes following several other students playing an impromptu tag game. Without thinking, I leaned down. Oh, Tommy, I said, you wish you could run and play with the others, don't you? His eyes opened wider still, cartoonish, and his hands flapped in excitement. I had understood – finally someone had understood his lifelong dream! My hand flew to my mouth. Horror! Oh no, Tommy, I blurted, I didn't mean –

But the damage was done.

So I went to the hardware store and bought a roll of duct tape. Then I dug around in a supply closet at the center and found a couple aluminum-framed wheeled walkers (the kind geriatrics use to shuffle down hospital hallways) that were no longer in use. This was a gamble, I knew, but I couldn't see any alternative. I had set Tommy up, let him down hard, and now I was going to have to come up with some way to make reparations.

I taped those two walkers together, using broom handles to add rigidity to the structure, and rigged a sling-like cloth saddle tied front and back. An image of Drunken Hinds, Daddy's paraplegic steer, came to mind; I obliterated it.

When I was satisfied my creation wouldn't immediately collapse when leaned on, I wheeled it to my classroom. Tommy, I said, I want to try something. I explained my idea to him, and his eyes grew wider and wider, in total recognition and eager anticipation. There's no guarantee it's going to work, I cautioned, but if you're game, let's give it a shot.

Tommy was more than game. I heaved him into the framework, his legs straddling the saddle so that his feet touched the floor but did not have to bear his full weight – and before I could say anything else to him, he was off like a shot, churning his legs as he raced for the hallway, his arms windmilling wildly, his voice shrieking in glorious crescendos of accomplishment. Tommy Henderson was walking!

Make that running.

In fact, he caught on so quickly and lurched about the room at such alarming speeds, I had to strap an old automobile tire to the back of his jerry-rigged walker to keep it from tipping forward and pitching him onto his chin. Tommy, a kid so easily written off as "retarded," who could only communicate with gargling noises and batted eyelashes, had come to life. He had found his wings – in the shape of some duct-taped, bent aluminum tubing.

Tommy made the move to Greeley with us. He graduated to an older class, beyond my grasp. His walker contraption was scrapped, and he returned to his mat on the floor – back where convention said he belonged. After all, Tommy would never be able to speak for himself, never be able to articulate the ideas flashing behind his bright eyes – indeed, there would be many who would never even concede that he could think for himself. But I had seen otherwise. That day when I had unwittingly committed myself to getting Tommy mobile, he had shown me just how much thinking he was doing. He had shown me how much he wanted to be like the other children – to run, play, have a good time. To be normal. His body might be broken, his mind trapped behind wordless lips, but his spirit dreamed of release. And those eyes, full of language, truly were windows to his soul.

Then there was Rene. Like Tommy, his communications were nonverbal. But whereas Tommy's eyes spoke what his mouth could not, Rene's eyes bulged out, huge and bug-like, and totally useless. Rene was the first student I ever had who suffered from a lack of both hearing and vision. He was also the first one I ever despaired over. How am I supposed to help him? I wondered. What do I teach someone like Rene? German measles had left him so impaired, there was no way he'd learn to do anything – and, as far as I could see, there wasn't anything that would be safe for him to do, even if he could be taught to do it.

Still, we were a "development" center; I had to come up with something for him, if only to stop him from belly-crawling into my dreams, where he hid in classroom cupboards. Maybe if I could get him on his feet, standing at a table, maybe he'd be able to use his hands to feel things placed in front of him. It wasn't much of a brainwave, but it was something to work on, and there wasn't anything to lose.

Rene had never been off the floor of his own volition before. If he went anywhere (and he was usually inclined to remain where I placed him) he wormed across the room, pulling himself with his hands while his body dragged. Now and then he'd get up on his hands and knees, just for a second or two, before returning to the surety of the floor. So naturally the first time I stood him upright and placed his hands on the Formica tabletop, he thought I was nuts.

It wasn't easy convincing him I was on his team; he couldn't hear or see me. I kept at it though. Rene and I practiced standing at the table each day, and I would take his hand and gently guide him down to the floor, the one reference point he had, trying to acquaint him with the space between it and the tabletop. If we can get him to lower himself to the floor, we'll be okay, I thought. Then, maybe, we can start whittling away at the terror Rene has of being upright.

We were doing fine until one afternoon he started lowering himself to the floor and, on his way down, clobbered his head against the lip of the table. I heard his cry and came running over. Rene had a small cut on his forehead, and a rapidly forming goose egg. Worse, his confidence was shattered. He would never trust me, or himself, again, I thought. But once Rene began learning, he did not want to stop. Never mind the bumps and bruises – after he conquered standing, he wanted to get on with the task of exploring his world: a world of edges and rough surfaces, of cool floors and warm windows, of varying shades of black. The shell he had come to me in was cracked open, and he was resolutely chipping his way out.

Tommy warmed my heart and made me smile a thousand times. Rene opened my eyes, taught me never to underestimate a child's will to learn.

At the fairgrounds, Tommy and Rene were two of a handful of exceptions; the majority of my students were able to walk on their own. Now, here at Greeley, things were different. My days of "trainable mentally retarded" students were over. We were an expanded, and expanding, program now, with more students, staff, and space. And money. Kern County, with a flair for the cutting edge (and the foresight to realize that a dollar now could save ten down the road), had come up with a budget that allowed us to grow and equipped us with the resources previously denied us. Consequently, we had restructured. I was assigned the kindergarten class. Ten students, in the back classroom (the one farthest from the door Cecil Woolard might open), and hardly a one of them ambulatory.

What do I do about them? I kept asking myself. What is the goal? The more I thought about it, the more I realized the answer was written on their faces, shining from their eyes. These kids aren't any different than Tommy, I thought. And no different than Tanya, either. Except in some ways: she plays outdoors, runs around, scrapes her knees, while they lie on mats in a sterilized classroom. There's no dirt under their fingernails, no grass stains on their jeans.

I watched my daughter, and my students. The more I observed, the more determined I became to do something about the disparity I was seeing. I had always tried to be a good student, to color inside the lines. Ever since day one I'd been working with students on improving their motor skills. Like the other staff, I stuck to the precepts of the developmental approach, a method rooted in normal child advancements. During the first two years of life, a baby usually learns to crawl, sit, stand, and walk, in that order. This is a normal progression. With children impaired by disabilities, the theory was the same: whether they are six months or six years, get them crawling and sitting, so that they will be ready to stand and, maybe, to walk. Each day I spent time with every student in my class, trying to get one child to hold herself up on all fours, ready for crawling; another to balance himself while sitting cross-legged; another to practice rolling from tummy to back; things like that. I performed these routines religiously. Yet too often progress was so slow it seemed nonexistent, and my students' retention of practiced skills evaporated from one day to the next, so that my faith eroded and I began to question the very basis of the developmental model. What is the point? Why am I doing this?

What is the *goal?*

The truth was, I was impatient. I wanted results — not just for my sake, but for the children's too. I knew enough to know that if I couldn't help them develop some basic skills — soon — their lives were at stake.

Perhaps it was inevitable, then, that I became an apostate. It was time, I decided, to break ranks, time to color outside the lines, to start cracking the code. Time to have some fun. To let my kids be kids.

To get them on their feet.

I started with the ones least restricted by disabilities, the group easiest to teach. Never mind whether they could roll from tummy to back, or balance on all fours. I didn't know a single adult who rolled to work in the morning, nor any four-year-old who crawled across the playground after a ball. My intent was simple: focus on the goal. And the goal, I had decided, was for my floor-bound students to walk. So I pulled them up, held their hands, helped them balance and teeter, coaxed and urged, wheedled and bribed, hugged and cheered. Two years later, half my students were walking, and the other half had made significant improvements.

Toya was a four-year-old in that first pioneer group. Her disabilities were congenital, a heart problem not the least of them. Here, once again, was a child whose eyes – great pools of liquid light – reflected her thoughts while words eluded her. Her family loved her deeply, and I came to love them all too. Through daily efforts (repeated at home as well as in the classroom), we got Toya up on her feet. Our work was rewarded the day she took her first steps, aided by a walker. Life for her would never be the same.

Amazingly, not long after Toya learned to walk, she found her voice as well. It was as though the triumph of movement had lifted a restraining order from her vocal cords; as though freedom of motion had granted her freedom of speech.

Toya wasn't the only one. Other students in the non-ambulatory, nonverbal category discovered words, too, once they'd gained their feet. From then on, the general tempo in my classroom picked up. A chain reaction had been set in motion, and there was no turning back. Once able to move, a child was ready for toilet training, and for any number of independent living skills.

Apart from toilet training, which I now addressed as a matter of course, feeding was the biggest hurdle for my students, who ranged in age from three to five. These were the days before gastrostomies and feeding tubes. Between tongue thrusts and spastic limbs, it could take aeons to get a child to successfully eat even the smallest portion of food – time neither I nor the child's parents could afford. Of course this created great anxiety: If I cannot feed my own child, how can I be a good mother?

So I went to the library (again) and did my homework, culling as much literature on the subject as I could find. Then I started my experiments. I brought in a blender and ladled out pureed food. I concocted swallowing exercises, worked with students on jaw and lip control – anything I thought might result in improvements.

With time and research, I was able to put together a feeding program that really worked. Pleased, I put together a booklet and titled it *How to Get Fed Up with Very Little Help*. It was the first time I'd stopped and set down in words the things I'd learned.

I knew now how to feed my children, but the "very little help" part was a problem. With ten kids in my classroom needing to eat and only my aide, Margie, and I to feed them, we were barely coping. Greeley had resources; it was only a matter of getting to them. There were classrooms full of teenage TMR students, most of whom had Down's syndrome but no difficulty walking or talking. Let's see what we can do about teaching them to feed my students, I suggested.

So we did. And they did. With guidance, those young men and women worked wonders with my students. Together, we fed the masses.

There was one drawback, though, a big one: In the wake of this wave of advances, came a widening gulf between my students who could walk and those who could not. The children on their feet took off running – often quite literally – and progressed to the point where they were ready to leave our program and set out into the world beyond our center. Some later entered the job market, finding work at fast-food places, as custodians, et cetera. For those still on their mats, still slumped in beanbags for hours each day, there was only one direction – down. Without movement, their muscles became hopelessly atrophied. Spines sagged like old willows. Limbs drooped. Sparkling eyes dulled to gray. Each day sapped more strength from the bodies of these children, and over time it seemed that the beanbags that held them were swallowing them – not with the all-at-once violence of a snake downing a frog, but with the fearsome matter-of-factness of a river engorging its banks. Few of them made it to adulthood.

Unsettled, I wondered, Is this as far as it goes? Is this all the difference I can make? I get to help some of my kids, but not all – is that the nature of the beast, the nature of their disabilities, that some just aren't going to make it?

Even as I celebrated the strides we were making with one set of students, I worried about the others: If we could find a way to get them upright and mobile, could we change their fate? Somehow, I was loath to accept that we had reached a plateau and would go no farther. I remembered Tommy, and could not stop dreaming.

Looking back, I remember names and faces. Toya. Becka. Scuffy. Sampson. Shelby. Lisa. And others, too, whose names and faces have blurred across the years. None of them talked and few walked when they first joined my kindergarten class. Two years later, half the students leaving my room were walking, and of those who walked, all – without exception – talked. Every single one of them. Shelby was quiet by nature, but could talk when she wanted to. Becka took her time before starting, but once she began, she was a regular magpie. Toya, too, gained her legs and found her voice. And that bothered me horribly. It was a chicken/egg enigma that I just could not crack: If we got them talking, would they walk? If we got them walking, would they talk? Or, was it all just coincidence? Did we really have any influence on them at all? The ones who didn't walk — were they, as the head-pointing neurologist had said, just plain retarded? So far, our success rate was about fifty-fifty, but I could not believe a cutoff line exists that bars people who walk (or talk) from those who don't. Life isn't like that. Development means a continuum, one thing leading to the next. The only conclusion I could draw was this: If a child is not walking and talking, it's not because she's incapable, but because we're not teaching her properly.

My break with conventional wisdom seemed radical at the time, but the truth of the matter was, I still leaned heavily on the philosophy that backed the developmental model; it was my starting point and my only reference, and though I saw it as flawed, I could come up with few alternatives. Especially with children who weren't improving, the developmental approach at least gave me something to work on with them, kept them busy even as their skills decreased. Yet I never stopped looking for inventive ways to pick the lock to mobility for them too. I wasn't happy with fifty-fifty.

Money, finally, was no longer an issue. With the county pumping funds into special education programs like ours, we could for the first time afford toys and classroom supplies, and things like tumble mats and foam wedges, things we thought could make a difference in the lives of our students. California Child Services was also enjoying a sudden surge in attention and funding, which enabled it to provide us two therapists, one physical, one occupational. Our PT was Jim; our OT, Barbara.

Call us the three musketeers. We were in cahoots right out of the gate. Well, almost. Professionals both of them, Jim and Barbara wanted an explanation of exactly what I was doing back there in the kindergarten room, and how I thought my ideas could possibly improve on decades of research in the field of motor development. But they listened (as true professionals do), and couldn't dispute the results. I can't tell you why, I said, but it's working, at least for some of them. All I know is, the moment I began treating them like kids, and not like patients, they responded.

Soon we were working hand in hand, side by side. We were on the same team, no question about it. Barbara and Jim brought to the Greeley Learning Center the knowledge I lacked. They understood muscular and neurological development; and they gave me explanations and rationales for things I'd only been able to surmise before their arrival. Most important, they brought to their work a love and compassion for children with severe disabilities and – though they never said a word about it – an appreciation for what was driving me.

Five years we shared together. Those years were gifts, perhaps the most important years of education in my life. We talked all the time – Why are you doing that? Wouldn't it be better if...? Their talents as therapists complemented mine as an educator; it was a blend that led us to question things we might otherwise have missed. Margie, my faithful aide, was right there, rowing in rhythm with the rest of us.

And at home, there was Tanya, a very special faithful aide.

Kids with severe disabilities were as common as furniture in our house. Their parents were my friends, and knew they could drop their kids off at our place if they needed a sitter. Tanya could always be counted on to help keep a child occupied. That's how she and Bennie became friends.

Bennie's mom, Ursula, divorced and in her early thirties, juggled the roles of parent and breadwinner. Her son was often with us, and that was fine by Tanya. She was two years old when Bennie – hydrocephalic, with spina bifida, cerebral palsy, and the cutest face you ever saw – came into my class. He was two years older than Tanya, and had an adventuresome personality to match hers. Though his spina bifida had partially paralyzed him on one side, and though he had never stood in his life, he quickly responded to my coaching and learned to bear weight on his legs. When he and Tanya were together, nothing was said between them (Bennie couldn't talk), but they shared an unspoken language. They sat together in front of the TV to watch cartoons and sip apple juice, and

had Saturday night sleepovers, sometimes at our house, sometimes
at Bennie's. They were together so much, in fact, that when he finally decided to try on a few words, one of his first was *bidab-bidab-
bidab-bidab*. No doubt about it, he knew who Tanya was – they
were best buddies.

Tanya was four when her grandfather Martin Bidabe, Sr., a big man
who had given his working years to the Monolith cement factory
tucked back in the Tehachapi hills, became critically ill. It had begun
as lung cancer, but now it had spread to his bones, and he was in
Bakersfield for treatment so often that he eventually moved into our
guestroom. For months on end, Martin Sr. and his wife, Petra,
camped in our home. Adeline, their second oldest, also moved in, to
care for her father. Martin's six other siblings were in and out constantly, and everyone tried to get along. It was a time of wearing
down, and the end was death.

Martin had imagined his father growing old and grandfatherly,
with Tanya there to dote on him. Instead, he was dead at sixty-five.

Half a year later Martin's mother and two of his sisters, Marguerite and Sylvia, were killed in a car crash.

Martin disappeared inside himself. He recoiled from all intense,
loving relationships as from a flame too hot to bear. He would not be
scorched again. Months passed, and though I understood the mag-
nitude of his grief and his reaction to it (I had not forgotten my
grandfather, or Freddie), I felt my shoulders sigh under the extra
burden Martin's absence placed on me. Tanya needed her daddy as
much as I needed my husband. But we had lost him.

Thankfully, Tanya didn't seem to notice any change. She was a
very busy young lady. As much as she loved staying indoors with
Bennie and her other special friends, she also enjoyed being outside
with the girls on our block, spinning double-Dutch ropes and jumping red pepper to the rhythm of their nonsense rhymes, or just

"playing around." One day during the summer she was six, she came in crying. She had fallen and scraped her knee. Tanya was always grazing her knees or stubbing her toes, so I thought nothing of this minor abrasion, just gave her the usual hug, kiss, rubbing alcohol, and Band-Aid treatment. I know it hurts, but be brave and it'll get better fast.

I told Tanya the same thing when, a day or so later, Ursula told me she'd taken Bennie to the hospital. He'll get better fast – probably just a touch of flu. But he had vomited, and his mother was taking no chances – Bennie had been surgically shunted, and dehydration could be deadly. She'd had him admitted, to be on the safe side. In the hospital, he could be hooked to an IV and monitored for symptoms that might create complications. Neither Ursula nor I were particularly worried, but we kept in close contact. It's always nice having someone to talk to when your kid is sick.

At school, we rooted for Bennie to pull through quickly and get back on his feet. He was eight years old now, and had made great progress. Bennie was proud of his achievements, and we were proud of him.

Bennie never made it out of the hospital. The first night of his stay, the IV that assured his hydration was left on too high a setting. His lungs filled with his own fluids, and he drowned.

The next morning, Ursula called and told me through her tears. I rushed to her house, to try to comfort her. But what could I say to a mother who had just lost her child? What was there to do, except share her tears?

For my own daughter, life continued. I told her Bennie was dead, which made her very sad, but at six she had little idea what "dead" meant (she'd been too small to understand when her "Tata" Bidabe died). Other DCH children had died – in those early days of special education, too often death could not be avoided, only postponed – and I had never skirted the subject with Tanya, but she'd never come face to face with it.

Tanya came with me to Bennie's viewing, to say good-bye to her very special friend. We had talked before, because I wanted her to understand, and not be terrified. But as she looked at Bennie, I could picture the little wheels churning in her head. She looked at me, saw my tears, and cried, too, though whether it was for me or for Bennie I couldn't be sure. I knew she didn't like seeing me upset. We were partners in this loss, and it strengthened the bond between us.

Then it was the day before Bennie's funeral, and time for roller-skating. This was Tanya's current athletic endeavor of choice, and she loved it. We drove to the roller rink and entered the din of wheels on wood and children at play. In the changing room, Tanya, eager to join her friends and instructor, was struggling to get into her hot-pink skating dress (her favorite) when I happened to glance at her knee, the one she'd scraped up days before. Where a small scab should have been there was now a red rash, a good inch wide. It ran at least three inches up her thigh, thinning as it went. Tanya had her dress up over her head, wrestling out of it. I took another careful look at that rash, and didn't like what I saw. Tanya, successfully freed from her dress, began climbing into her skating getup. You know what, sweetheart, I said. You're not going skating today. I'm sorry.

We got back in the car, and I drove straight over to the ER. I didn't know what was creeping up my daughter's leg, but I sure wasn't going to wait to find out.

The doctor on duty looked at the rash. She must be terribly allergic to something, I said, wanting to be helpful. I just can't imagine what, though.

That's no allergy, the white-smocked doctor said. That's an infection.

He prescribed an antibiotic, instructed me to see that Tanya remained in bed, absolutely still — You might have to tie her down, he joked — and then we went home.

Bennie

The following morning I attended Bennie's funeral while Mama Jo took care of Tanya. Afterward, I drove to her house. Little white coffins are hard to look at. I was in need of a hug from my daughter. Then, when I put her down again, I checked her leg. The rash was now halfway up her thigh. Instead of subsiding, it had spread like wildfire since earlier that morning.

With the first tastes of panic in my throat, I drove Tanya back to the ER. I've got to know what this is, I told the doctor (a different one this time). He took one look, then asked for the name of our pediatrician. Dr. Polson, I told him. We're admitting her right now, he said, and I'm calling your doctor.

I was scared now. By the time Dr. Polson came over, the rash had spread further. He drew lines around it with a ballpoint pen and, rattling off a formidable string of Latin words ending in *ium*, explained that it was commonly called blood poisoning. Blood poisoning? I'd seen that before — a little red strand, no thicker than toad spawn. This — this was a river sweeping up Tanya's leg. If it gets up to her lymph nodes, Dr. Polson said, pointing his pen at the red band, she could die, or it'll get to her brain and she'll be brain-damaged. This is one of the most serious things that can happen to a child, he finished.

The panic I'd been holding off stepped up and took over. No way was I leaving my baby's side. For the five days it took the medicine and doctors to work their miracle, I left her only long enough to dash home, shower, change my clothes, and dash back again. Martin, too, spent as much time as he could with us. Neither he nor I wanted to believe anything so horrible could happen to our child.

Tanya, good as gold, pulled through. Martin and I could exhale again.

Still, I came away changed. The threat of losing Tanya — a threat that had perhaps been mere hours from reality — fanned the fires of mother love within me, and I saw as never before the thinness of the thread on which life dangles. I also saw for the first time how a parent of a child with severe disabilities watches each day for the inevitable moment when the thread breaks. With renewed determination, I returned to my classroom, vowing to see to it each day that no thread snapped, not if I could help it.

My eyes had been opened in other ways too. During Tanya's stay in the hospital, I witnessed how children with disabilities were cared for in the pediatric ward, and it was not a pretty sight. Some of it was downright cruel, in fact. No one was to be blamed – the staff were doing their best. Ignorance was at the root, I knew. Among the hospitalized children were two with disabilities, which included tongue thrusts that made feeding difficult. When mealtime came and a nurse or aide offered one of these children a bite to eat, the food would not go down. He's not hungry, was the usual conclusion, and the mealtime was over. In reality, the child was starving. His excitement at the sight of food intensified his tongue thrusts, which heightened the danger of aspirating. There in the hospital, I often found myself holding a child I'd never seen before, stroking her head to calm her, and carefully spooning food into her mouth, one morsel at a time. I had put great effort into developing feeding programs to help just such children, but what did it amount to if the information stayed at our center? If people in the medical profession don't have a clue about children with disabilities, what about the rest of society? We've got to get the word out beyond our little bitsy classroom, I thought, or this will never work.

Other things I saw were harder to tackle. There was, for example, the matter of Tanya's IV. She had been started on intravenous antibiotics immediately after being admitted to the hospital, but the IV infiltrated, and her arm swelled up like a water balloon. The nurses inserted a new needle and started over – with the same results. Tanya was wonderfully brave, but this pattern continued over the days she lay in bed, and finally she grew sick of the whole thing. Being plugged into a bag and forced to stay in bed while other children walked around and played wore her down. After several days, when it was time for yet another IV needle, she finally caved in. The nurses approached her bed to do their thing, and Tanya went berserk. I'd never heard her so hysterical before. The nurses, bless their hearts, ordered me out of the room. You'll have to stay in the hall, they said. If she sees you, it'll only make it worse.

If you'll let me hold her, she'll calm down.

No. She'll be much better without you. Step into the hall. Please.

There was no sense arguing. I stepped into the hall, and tried not to beat myself up while Tanya's screams hit the ceiling.

After that, though, I refused to leave her side. If anything happened to Tanya, I would be right there. I had lost faith in the doctors-are-God hypothesis. It didn't matter to me if the medical staff thought they were better at caring for my daughter than I was. They were not all-knowing. Ursula had left her son in the care of professionals, and Bennie was dead. I wasn't going anywhere.

Tanya's hospitalization left me puzzled. Where did the idea come from that a mother's presence would heighten her child's anxiety? It ran so counter to anything I had ever seen with my kids and their parents – it seemed to go against nature itself. I took what lessons I'd learned from Tanya and Bennie's experiences and acted on them where I could, filing them away for future reference where I could not. There is only so much you can do at once, Linda, I cautioned myself, and it's better to do a few things and do them well than take on the world ill-equipped.

At home, Martin and I went on trying to get back together, to fumble our way to a fresh place where our pain couldn't find us. Instead, the distance between us only widened. This was not the way we'd imagined it, not in all our dreams and schemes of a happy home. We carefully constructed a façade that presented a normal Daddy and Mommy to our daughter (and a healthy family to our friends and neighbors), but all the while we were crumbling irreparably.

Tanya was eight when we decided, finally, to quit pretending. It's not your fault, we told her. Daddy and Mommy love you like crazy. We'll always be family. Just now it's going to be different.

How different I did not want to imagine. I had staked my life on our marriage, on building a family with Martin, and now it was gone. The ground beneath my feet had shifted, and I poised for the vast and devastating landslide that seemed to gather beneath me. I was going to fold under the strains of emotion and heartache, yield to their pressures and be interred beneath them, and all would be dark and cellar-dank and cool, and I would not have to think, or act, or deal with myself — just lie back and sleep, sleep in utter blankness.

Only, I had Tanya. She had lost her full-time father; she could not now lose me as well. Hard as it might be, I had to stay awake. For her sake, though it meant torment and self-accusation, I could not abandon myself.

We could go, that much we could do. We did not have to stay and feel the sting of all that swarmed with memories. We could go, and I could begin to model a new life for both of us, to retool for the task of single-parenthood. We could return to the center, to the place where the river arched like a womb-bound child and the umbilical road ran through the flood fields to the house and the people in the house, whose hearts had been broken countless times, and mended just as often. We could return there; I had not forgotten the way home.

We went, Tanya and I.

new leaves

Nothing had changed, and everything had changed. The house, built to withstand the stresses of a family, was as it had been. The farm and garden, too, were as I remembered them. Only, the house was strangely quiet now, the fledglings (all four of us) having long since flapped free of its confines, to begin families of our own. The fields beyond the house seemed to reflect that quiet, as though listening for the whir of returning wings. Mama and Daddy, the nest builders, remained. They welcomed Tanya and me home.

I had returned many times since moving to California, but on those occasions the others had always been there as well. Now, I shunted suitcases into the bedroom where my sisters and I once romped, and padded across wooden floors where in bygone years I *clack-clacked* in Mama's heels. I stopped in front of the living room's wide fireplace, and remembered how Martin had once kept a late-night vigil over the TV's weather channel as it charted tornado warnings. (The rest of us, hardened Kansans, had gone to bed, leaving the weathermen to their speculations. Martin, new to the family and new to the heartland, had stayed awake, to serve and protect.) I was surrounded by memories, and echoes.

But Mama's love surrounded me too. She understood broken hearts.

Daddy, likewise, supported my homecoming, in his own way. *It's such a shame, Linda — we always loved Martin,* he'd said when I arrived. But even he knew how hard I had tried to make my marriage work, and understood that I, too, had always loved Martin. I was home now, and Mama and Daddy were glad for it. Glad, moreover, that I had not returned alone: Tanya was my redemption.

The decision to return had not been automatic. Much as I loved my parents and my childhood home, I had not desired this conclusion. After Martin and I had separated and moved apart, I had tried to hold myself together and think long-term. Tanya and I could get by on my teacher's salary, but with scant room for error. That scared me. If I wanted more money, more assurance, I would need more education. In between teaching and parenting, I sneaked in a few classes at Cal State Bakersfield, working toward a master's degree in special education. I kept ridiculous hours, and ran myself into the ground. The pace was ruining me physically, and emotionally I was in shambles. That was when I requested, and was granted, a year's sabbatical, to return to Kansas and further my studies in special education at my alma mater. I did not tell my colleagues or higher-ups that I was toying with the idea of a career change.

The way I had it figured, I would get my master's in special education, then go on for a Ph.D.; maybe switch fields altogether. New and exciting ventures were opening each week as the first wave of personal computers revolutionized homes and work places, and there were job opportunities galore for creative, forward-thinking types. Then there was my old first love: medicine. It hadn't worked before, but maybe now it would. Maybe now was the time for me to put everything on the line and slog through med school. Or maybe not. Tanya wasn't going for it. I asked her because I knew it had to

be her decision — and she decided she'd rather have a mommy for
the next eight years than a sleep-starved ghost in a white lab coat.
My bank account pointed in the same direction: maybe not. So, it
was going to have to be special ed. Take one year of classes at Pittsburg State, get my degree, be done with it. And afterward, I could
still think about a career change.

But who was going to hold my hand?

Who was going to calm my nerves that first day, after I'd left Tanya
with Grandma and Grandpa and driven the twenty-five familiar
miles to Pittsburg, to have my master's proposal reviewed; after I'd
parked the car and found the main entry and the wide steps leading
up to it. And stopped. Stopped because I was, I realized suddenly, so
small. Smaller than ever before, and terribly frightened besides. And
there was no one to hold my hand and lead me up those broad steps
and into my future. I was alone, and shrinking all the time...

Until I am a little girl again, on my way to music for the first time.
My classmates and I are in a bus, headed for another school, to join
its students for our monthly music lesson. Allen is in the bus, too, at
the back, with his buddies. To get out of Lowell we have to cross the
river, over the old trestle bridge. The bus is too heavy to make it
across the wooden bridge loaded, so the driver pulls over and in-
structs us to get out and walk. The bus goes first, and then everyone
follows. I step onto the bridge, and look down. There are gaps between the boards. The gaps are wide, and I am skinny. I know I am
skinny because Daddy has been telling me for a long time how skinny
I am. If I walk out onto the bridge, I am going to fall through a gap
in the boards and the river will eat me alive. But I have no choice,
unless I want to be left behind, which I don't, so I start to walk. And
for a while I am okay because I concentrate on the back of a girl in
front of me. But then, a third of the way over, I look down again
and see a gap, with rushing water down in the gap. I freeze. I don't
cry, don't make a scene. I just don't know what to do. I look up at the
students ahead of me. Their backs are moving away from me, fast. I

look back down, at the water that will carry me away if I take another step. I stay frozen. And then Allen, my brother, turns back and
sees me, and understands. He walks back, doesn't run, just walks back
and takes my hand in his, unfreezes me and leads me forward a few
steps. Then he lowers my hand and slips his free, tells me so only I
can hear: It'll be okay. We'll get across. Just stay with me, and we'll
walk together. And then we are over the bridge and safely on the
other side, getting back onto the bus, and Allen is back with his buddies. I am myself again, my dignity still intact; and what my brother
did for me that day is something so very important, I have never
forgotten it.

So there on the steps of the university I reach for my brother's
hand, but find instead that it is Teresa Brown who has shown up to
rescue me. Teresa, the young mother of Cha-Cha, a student with
cerebral palsy who joined my class a year ago. Teresa, who works
long, backbreaking hours as a housekeeper and still finds time to be
a mother to her daughter, and to take classes at night. Teresa, who
manages somehow, in spite of everything, to keep smiling, growing.
I think of Teresa, and stop shrinking. I take her hand and walk up
those steps, and I open the door.

As I walk down the shining corridors to the dean's office, Teresa
walks with me. And by the time I reach his door and am ushered in
by his secretary, I am strong enough to be Linda again and to make
my case.

I want to do something different, I explain. I need to be able to
write my own curriculum. I have a reason for what I'm doing. I'll
tell you where the gaps in my education are, and what I need to
know by the end of my year here. This isn't just about a degree; it's
about something I want to do with my life.

He listens to me talk about my work with children with severe disabilities and my urge to understand more about what causes their
problems, so that I will be better equipped to help overcome them. He
listens, and when I am through he tells me, I'm giving you full rein.
You're on to something here, and we'll be happy to work with you.

The courses I selected weren't the easiest ones, but they were the ones I needed – courses like The Gifted Child, because I remembered Tommy, and Edgar, and other children whose disabilities had masked their intelligence. They were the exceptions, but I had seen enough to know we were overlooking something important.

It was while sitting in the Student Union between classes one night that the penny dropped. By then I could pick out a gifted child with my eyes shut – I had absorbed lectures and books on how gifted children act, how to recognize them, and how to funnel their intellect. I was going over my notes when the thought occurred to me for the first time in my life: I had been a gifted child. I had been a gifted child, and I didn't have a clue. What an epiphany! It rattled my head, as though someone were trying to shake sense into me. I felt jarred, dislodged deep inside. Practice breathing, Linda, I told myself. It's okay. In. Out. In. Out.

I sat there, shaken. The self-recrimination and doubt that had clouded my childhood suddenly snapped into focus, like amoebas on a microscope slide. I saw for the first time that things hadn't all been my fault. All those questions I was forever asking – maybe it wasn't because I was born obnoxious and self-obsessed, even if Daddy said I always had to be the center of attention. Maybe it was simple curiosity, driven by a fierce urgency to *know*, to comprehend the complexities of the world around me, and to understand my place in it. Dingdong, Linda, it's time to wake up. This isn't about an ego boost. You just might not be such a rotten person after all. It's not too late – you didn't like yourself much growing up, but you can start now. You can change the way you view your past. You can take off the mask.

That helped. But, frankly, my past was not my chief concern. I had other, more pressing issues weighing on me: the small matter of my shipwrecked marriage, for example.

Some marriages end in explosion. A fuse is lit, a bomb goes off, everything goes up in smoke, comes down in rubble, and that's it. Mine was more like oil spilling from a tanker. It leaked over four years despite attempts to patch the wounded hull, with the end result a slick so large, cleanup attempts seemed pointless. The only thing left was to scuttle the ship.

And, for my part at least, to go down into the depths with it.

No string quartet à la Titanic accompanied my descent, and as I sunk lower I listed to myself the million, trillion things wrong with me, the things that, just maybe, were what broke Martin and me. I was too fat. I was too thin. Too blond, too tall, too flat, too round. Much too talkative. Too invasive. Not sensitive enough. And when I had vomited every negative thing I could think of about myself, I got mad. That's not fair. It's not all my fault. None of it's my fault. It's his fault. And I started a fresh list, his. I catalogued every accusation, every hurt, wrongdoing, or harsh word I had ever borne, even made up a few. When I was done, I was exhausted. My insides hurt. I was drained.

But not yet drowned. This is crazy, you won't get anywhere like this, I told myself as I recouped from the effort of the purge. You're attacking yourself, you're attacking him – but you don't really believe any of it. Say what you like, Linda, but the fact is, it's over. You've got to start from scratch.

That's when I stopped licking my wounds – and mentally clawing out at Martin – and got serious. Enough with the childish garbage, I told myself. If you're really going to start over, you've got to know what you're working with. Make a new list. This time, put down everything you like about yourself, every single positive attribute you can claim possession of, because you're going to be needing them in short order. What do you have going for you?

There were days of agony and incisive soul-searching. Days when, more than anything else, I wanted to stay in bed with my face turned toward the wall and stare cross-eyed at the wallpaper until everything swam away and swept me away. But there were other days, too, when Tanya and her grandfather puttered across the barnyard astride the farm tractor, the tin cap of its exhaust pipe dancing like the lid of a singing kettle; and Mama busied about the kitchen, throwing apple pies together while carrying on a conversation that shined the house until a resinous glow of memories lifted from the floorboards. On those days I felt warm and confident and newly planted.

My courses at Pittsburg State were all evening classes. During the day I kept the books at Mac's Fertilizers, my parents' small fertilizer plant and seed store in Baxter Springs. Daddy had quit his job at Spencer to start the business, and he and Mama had exerted themselves to make it thrive. While I worked, Tanya attended the local elementary school, a few blocks away. I picked her up each afternoon and we shared an hour and a Coke at Luv's or Pizza Hut, connecting before my evening began.

It was, first and foremost, a year for education, in which the greatest (and hardest) lessons were not learned in the university halls. Comprehending the complexities of special education and the needs of students with multiple disabilities demanded concentrated study, but that effort paled in comparison with the strain of picking my way across the minefield of my own apprehensions. Yet once I had begun, I did not look back.

When my list of Things I Have Going for Me reached a satisfactory length, I sat down and asked myself what seemed the next logical question: What do you want to do?

A simple question, perhaps. But each time I repeated it to myself, I came up with a different answer. It was like looking through a kaleidoscope — new turn, new result, same question. What do you

want to do? Now that you've taken back your life; now that your
dreams are no longer entwined with Martin's; now that you're going
to be on your own – *What* do you want to do?

Med school was out. I was a mother, and that was that. A not-so-
well-off mother, trying to carve security for her child. I could head
west again – my job was waiting, and a raise in pay once my degree
was done – and slip back into the familiar milieu. But I had stumbled
into special education almost by accident. Now I stopped to wonder
whether it was really the right field for me. Sure, I loved my kids,
but was I really doing them any good? Over the years there had
been so many little white coffins, and precious little to crow about.
Was it time, I mused, to leave the trail and strike off in a different
direction entirely?

In the end, I modified the question. *What do you want to do?* became *What can you do right now?* I needed to take action. One step at
a time, I could hear Mama Jo saying. Which is why I decided to play
things safe: I would finish my degree, return to Bakersfield and to
the DCH. From there, I told myself, I could always move on. Computers weren't going away. I had time.

I completed my courses, collected my grades, readied for graduation. Curveball: We're sorry, but we forgot to give you the entrance
exam when you started grad school. Please come in this Saturday
and take it – we can't let you graduate until you do. This is great, I
thought. All this work, and you're going to blow it at the last minute.

When it came to surprise tests, I never gave myself a chance (a
childhood thing). The English section would be a cakewalk, I knew,
but the math worried me. When was the last time I'd bumped into
Pythagoras at the DCH?

Happily, I surprised myself...

Classroom achievements aside, it was a landmark year. I had come to Kansas in a time of flood, when storms threatened to erode all that I had once taken for granted. But I had thrust a stick in the ground to gauge the rate of rise, and had willed the water down. I now understood myself better than I ever had before. This, in turn, brought a new relationship between my parents and me. It was a time of undoing fear. With the veil of my own self-loathing gone, I could see Daddy and Mama as never before – with fears of their own, and doubts, and regrets. I was them, and they were me. Each of us imperfect. And I loved them as never before, especially Daddy, who needed it most. I had forgiven him, and myself.

As for Martin... When I said *I do* I was thinking long-term. Forever in the present tense. Till death us do part. No room for *I did*. Love, I have since learned, is a sticky thing, like flypaper. You tack your heart to your sleeve, the right person comes along, and – *bzzz!* – they're stuck with you for always. And you with them. Because once you start loving someone – really, really loving them – there's no stopping it. Pretend you don't care, cover the whole thing over and refuse to have anything more to do with it – it won't help. You can't destroy true love, not all the way. Throw up your arms and walk away, it will go with you. Tear it down and rip it to pieces, it will still be love. Even when every recognizable trace has been done away with, the residue will linger and remind.

I still love Martin. The Martin I met on the doorstep of my Tehachapi apartment. The Martin who played Mr. Hard-Core Policeman for Edgar Hernandez. The Martin who protected me from the Cecil Woolards of this world. The Martin who fell asleep in the living room recliner with our child nuzzled against his bare chest. He is the man I love. That Martin.

Outside my window, vapors danced above the wing and dust skittered across the tarmac as the plane backed away from the gate. The engines' whine gave way to a roar; the wing shuddered like an aspen leaf as its shadow swept across painted runway lines. Tanya and I held hands and climbed into the sky. Behind and beneath: the fields where mice ran among wheat, and crouched panic-clutched before the combine's knife; the river and the lowlands that too often succumbed to its advances; the house and the road, and the people in the house, whom we loved and who loved us in return. Ahead: mountains to cross, and vast, deep canyons – all reduced to shadows and spectrum shades from the air; and then the long, slow descent, holding hands again for landing...

I was back at the Learning Center. The new Harry E. Blair Learning Center, that is. We had outgrown the Greeley facility, which had never been able to shake the feel of being mostly a converted gym, and when Bakersfield's Golden State Junior High closed, the Kern County Superintendent's office took ownership of the downtown building and gave us the keys. Now we had all the space we needed – proper, sensible space. Classrooms.

Some seven years before, in 1975, Congress had passed Public Law 94-142, an Act that forever altered the landscape of special education. *It is the purpose of this Act to assure that all handicapped children have available to them...a free appropriate public education which emphasizes special education and related services designed to meet their unique needs, to assure that the rights of handicapped children and their parents or guardians are protected, to assist States and localities to provide for the education of all handicapped children and to assess and assure the effectiveness of efforts to educate handicapped children.*

Brave new words, balm to the souls of us who had strained under the burden of mass ignorance of (and, in some cases, outright disregard for) the children we worked with every day. Public Law 94-142 – there was authority in the sound of it, and action too. It was our mandate, spelling out our *raison d'être* for any who still questioned the necessity of development centers and other such programs. With it, though, came unforeseen complications. The number of students in our care soared – a good thing, by all accounts, especially as the county continued to back our efforts and anticipate our growth needs. We were a big staff now, able to responsibly manage the new influx. Or so we thought.

Problem was, many of the kids coming to us for "free appropriate public education" were so severely disabled, they required one-on-one professional nursing care. Which, of course, we didn't have. Kids who under the old order had been housed in institutions were now our responsibility, at least during school hours. It was our job to keep them alive – and in too many cases that was no small task. We became expert at feeding through tubes, suctioning, monitoring seizures, administering medication, adjusting braces, doing what we had to do. We had no choice in the matter, but that didn't make the rope we were walking any less precarious, and lives hung in the balance. This was one of the main reasons that had motivated me to study special education at the graduate level.

Tanya and I returned to Bakersfield in September 1982. I was back, thanks to the kids. During my time in Kansas I had given plentiful ear to the voice that for many years had been coaxing me to see the light and to accept that special education was little else but an oxymoron – there was nothing special about what we were doing, and we sure as heck weren't educating anybody. Well, hardly anybody. For, as I was forced to admit, even when the voice's urgings seemed most astute, there were exceptions. It was not all failure; we had our victories, as well – few and far between, but victories nonetheless. And there were the kids. That never changed. They were, after all, what made our work special. They brought me back. I decided I could not walk out on them. Not until the day they walked out with me. For now, I told myself I would try once more to forget the numbers game and content myself with making life more bearable, one child at a time.

They gave me the oldest kids. (Sabbatical had guaranteed me a job on return, but it couldn't give me back my kindergarten class.) Before, I had always worked with younger students, three- to seven-year-olds mostly. The kids who emerged from my classroom could use the toilet, and most were able to feed themselves and had some means of communicating their needs and wishes. I did a decent job, considering the odds, and the kids benefited. Of course once the children passed out of my hands some of my work was squandered, or so it seemed to me. I told myself it was because others didn't understand what needed to be done – or didn't know how to do it – or didn't care – or something. These lesser teachers could not match or sustain the intensity I brought to my task; consequently the same students who had made headway under my careful tutelage declined grossly once beyond my reach. These unspoken accusations couldn't have been farther from the truth, but that was *back then*, and what did I know? I was in for a rude awakening – a very necessary, very rude awakening.

Ten students between the ages of fourteen and twenty-two were assigned to me. Ten students with multiple disabilities, slouched in beanbags or contorted on floor mats. Ten students who, once upon a time, had been sweet, cuddly kids. Then, everyone had been gaga over them. In their helplessness, they had been loved, entertained, cared for with hugs and smiles. Now –

They were teenagers. Boys growing straggly facial hair. Girls menstruating. Body odor. Acne.

– And no one would explain to them what they had done wrong. All these young men and women knew was, they were no longer appreciated, no longer doted on. They were, as some said to their face (these kids couldn't understand anyway, so what was there to worry about?), *stinky*.

They were my new best friends. In short order, I reneged on my former ideas about inept staff. It didn't take an Isaac Newton to see that gravity was these students' worst enemy. A few days in the classroom with them – and an aching back – clarified that point abundantly. My students slumped where I placed them. Toneless, their muscles yielded to the cumulative weight of years of inaction. They were on their way out, with few exceptions. Best days, if there had been best days, were over. All that remained was the process of slipping to the ground, and into the ground. And gravity handled that, for free.

My Tommy had gone this route. I had seen him from time to time during the years after the center's move to Greeley, getting on or off the school bus, or at special events when everyone assembled, but I had made no special effort to keep track of him. Tommy was a young man the day I crossed campus on an errand and entered his classroom. He was in his beanbag, crying. I had to look twice to recognize him.

Tommy was in agony, his legs a mess. His hips, which had borne no weight in years, had dislocated and been pinned in place. The pins were working through his skin. Lack of exercise was exacerbating contractures of his hips and knees. I didn't want to believe this could be the same Tommy who'd squealed with delight and raced down the halls in his jerry-rigged gait trainer, eyes flashing, legs churning. Shocked, I listened to his teacher tell me matter-of-factly that there was talk of severing Tommy's spinal cord. They've tried everything else to manage his pain, he said. I wanted to yell at the injustice of it all. Instead I lifted Tommy out of his beanbag and held him in my lap as we cried together. I rocked him until both of us were exhausted. Then I left him, and took my questions away with me. What *are* we doing?

Tommy died. Of ignorance, I was sure. My ignorance along with everyone else's. This is what happens, I lectured myself, when we don't help these teenagers take care of their bodies. This is what happens to kids who are not able to function without our help and don't get it. This is what happens when we don't keep up the training we start when they are small. It's what happens when we stop asking questions.

I had a classroom of teenagers now, in as bad or worse shape as Tommy had been the last time I saw him alive. The question now was, Would they share his fate?

Not without a fight, I promised myself. It was just a gut feeling, but I felt sure that Tommy's story could have ended differently. I had seen him make great strides before I had lost him in the shuffle, and I remained convinced that had his training continued, he would have made more. If the ragtag gait trainer I'd taped together for Tommy had allowed enough mobility and weight-bearing to improve his overall health, then what might proper equipment and a consistent training program have done for him? There were so many unknowns. So much work undone.

Dirty work, too, day after day. Forget trying to exercise their atrophied muscles – it was all we could do to keep our students dry and clean. None were toilet trained, and even if they had been, it would have been a chore getting them on toilets. At our center, as elsewhere, we changed the diapers of these older students with severe disabilities out in the open, on mats in the classroom. It was the most expedient thing to do. Never mind that they were teenagers, with pubic hair and everything else. This was how it was done, unless you wanted to bust your back. Besides, what did these kids know? It was all the same to them, I was assured.

I was actually getting sick of that song, and it didn't matter to me how popular it was. If our students don't know any different, I thought, it's because we've taught them there's no difference. We've taught them that they're not as valuable as other people. We've taught them their lack of self-respect. We told them they are *less than*, that they don't deserve the same things the rest of us absolutely insist on.

With one bathroom for every two classes, we were better set up than many centers – a far cry from the one-bathroom-for-all scenario of our fairground days. Our bathroom was equipped with a changing table, but there was little space to maneuver a heavy student, and often two people were required to hoist a teenager onto the table. It was a ridiculous task at best. I understood quickly why the bathroom wasn't an option, but I still couldn't sanction the accepted alternative. So we invested in screens. When a student's diaper needed changing, we moved her to a mat and placed the screens around it.

The students now in my care may not have been able to communicate verbally, but the message they gave me, loud and clear, was, We are not imbeciles. Why do you give us rattles to play with? We are not babies. We are teenagers, with thoughts and feelings.

That year, dignity became a watchword for me. I had spent the previous year reclaiming my own, and wanted others to enjoy the same. That was all. I had no idea of the link between dignity and the ability to learn. But it was true: my students came to understand and appreciate the respect I showed them, and it translated into self-respect, which awakened an interest in learning.

But the will to learn was only the first half of the equation. The other was up to me. It served little purpose to stimulate a student's interest in learning unless I had a firm grasp of what, exactly, I wanted to teach him. If I wanted a kid to get anywhere, I had to come up with a road map. I remembered the question I'd put to myself back in Kansas: What is your goal? It seemed appropriate to ask it now, for each of my students, and to tell them: You have a right to be an adult. You have a right to dignity and respect. You have a right to make decisions about your own lives. You have a right to have fun.

The rights, yes – but what about the means? There my ideas bogged down. I knew how to help young children gain mobility and motor skills, but how to help these teens, whose bodies were already so dilapidated that they were, awful as it sounds, on their way out?

What we need, I lamented to myself, is a consistent game plan that goes into effect the day a child arrives here and doesn't quit until they're out the door, ready for life in the real world. Our students need to know what we expect them to have achieved by the time they reach adulthood and move away from our program. The expectations will vary from student to student, but each child will have something to work toward. What they need – what we need – is a goal. And the sooner we set our sights on it, the better.

A year later most of my students were transferred to a newly created "hospital classroom." The perfect place for kids on their way out, I thought bitterly, but I knew there was no other alternative. The classroom had hospital beds and Hoyer lifts. Even so, its staff were tired to the marrow by the end of every day. I turned away, saddened.

I needed a new assignment. Julie Otting-Blaine, our speech and language pathologist, knew this. Our kids who suffered from hearing problems were near and dear to her heart. All too often their disabilities went unaddressed – out of sight, out of mind. More blatant problems – muscle contractions, deformities, eating disorders, glaucoma, and the like – got our attention. Julie introduced me to Gaylord Short, our audiologist, who agreed with her it was high time to see what could be done about these disabilities hidden to the eye. Together, we began an experiment that would last eighteen months.

The first step was to test all students for impaired hearing. Gaylord handled that part, evaluating the ability of every child in the DCH to respond to sound. That done, we selected eleven children who showed the most profound hearing losses. They became my students. We fitted each of them with an auditory trainer. (Like a standard hearing aid, an auditory trainer is molded to the shape of its wearer's ear. Unlike a hearing aid, the trainer has wires connecting the molded part to a small box that is strapped around the user's chest. The box houses a receiver.) I wore a microphone, which transmitted my voice directly to my students' ears. I could set my microphone's frequency so I could speak to individual students or to the entire class.

The purpose of the auditory trainers was to eliminate auditory discrimination. With them my students were only exposed to the sounds we intended them to hear, which at the start were the ones coming from my mouth. From the beginning, I kept my instructions simple, speaking in clear, everyday phrases and tones. My words fell on seemingly deaf ears. Not one child offered any meaningful response to them. Encouraged by Julie and Gaylord, I stuck at it. A year and a half later, all but two of my students had learned to recognize and respond to simple commands. Even when their auditory trainers were removed, they continued to demonstrate understanding of spoken words. The two who did not were both known to us to have actual hearing losses. The rest, we concluded, had simply never learned to interpret sound meaningfully. Perhaps in the very first years of their lives their brains had not been able to handle sound and thus had discounted all noise as meaningless, so that with time these children had learned to block it out altogether. They were not deaf, just profoundly unable to process sound. In only eighteen months of training, these students had made sense of it. To this day, they still use their hearing.

Our success with this group greatly boosted my morale, which had taken a beating after my experience with the older students. More important, it reaffirmed my belief that children would learn if the way to teach was discovered. What started as a vision had given rise to a systematic method of teaching, one whose efficiency could be measured and rated against the children's advancements. Watching the transformation of my kids as they went through auditory training was truly intoxicating. Kids like Michael, who at the beginning sat on the floor, chewed on his hand, screamed, kicked and hurled himself around, smashed his head into solid objects. Sound meant nothing to Michael until we stuck an auditory trainer in his ear and broke down the mystery for him. Once it did, everything about him changed. He began to respond to our voices, and it was as though the shackles of frustration melted away.

Julie and I decided we should take the auditory program to the next step. Our experiment proved we could make sound meaningful as receptive language. Why not go on to include expressive language as well? At that time nearly all our DCH kids were nonverbal. Auditory training could help students interpret sound, but what about their ability to respond to it?

Second only to my love of medicine was my love of language. I had always considered it a great pity that so many of our students would most likely never be able to express themselves in words. Like the other staff, I had studied sign language. Only a handful of our students, though, could sign meaningfully. It didn't make much sense to me: we were spending a lot of time trying to teach a system that wouldn't work in a culture of non-signing people. In a perfect world, we would find ways to teach our students to talk, so that they would be able to communicate with anyone they encountered. Until we reached perfection, we would have to content ourselves with finding other ways to make universal communication possible.

No small task, as it turned out. Julie, ever energetic, suggested we try creating communication boards for some of our students, just to see how they would respond. Fine, I said, and got out my pencils. Finally, I thought as I outlined symbolic people and cups and plates of food, my art major is paying off. We photocopied my drawings, colored them in and cut them out, pasted them to tagboard, and presented the finished products – my first handcrafted communication boards – to my kids. So far so good. Now we had to try to get the kids to understand what the symbols meant; to touch the spoon symbol when they were hungry, the cup when thirsty.

Fat chance. We got nowhere. The kids touched the symbols all right – at complete random. They had been fast to figure out that touching a symbol would draw a reaction from Julie and me. It really didn't seem to matter what our reaction was; they were thrilled just to see us respond.

Julie and I stepped back and took a fresh look. For our next attempt, we collected photos for each child: pictures of their parents, of real-life objects to replace the symbols. Still no luck. Not one student got the point.

More head scratching, and a new idea: If they're not comprehending the correlation between a flat image and a three-dimensional object, why not start with the real thing and work down to symbols from there? Julie agreed it just might work.

We started with cups, since drinking was an important activity. First, though, I had to be sure my kids were physically able to reach the cup placed in front of them. I propped them up at tables on chairs turned backward, so their trunks leaned forward over the chair backs and their arms rested on the tables. When I was sure a child's position enabled him to reach out, I placed a paper cup containing his favorite drink on the table in front of him. During the first sessions, I helped him touch the cup, then gave him a sip. When I was sure he was getting the idea, I waited for him to move his hand toward the cup on his own. It was vital for the student to understand that his action triggered my response; otherwise, nothing would have been learned and we might as well go back to the symbols on the tagboard. Our students caught on quickly, though, and soon Julie and I were busy offering sips to everyone in the room.

Once we were sure they understood the connection between *cup* and *drink*, we switched to empty paper cups. Touch the empty cup, Linda gives you a drink. Next, we cut the top inch off the cups. Then another inch. The cups got shorter, but the drinks kept coming, so the students kept making the connection. I drew small pictures of paper cups and pasted them in the bottoms of the cups we were cutting away. We sliced those cups down until only the bottom circle of paper remained, and still the kids stayed with us. We had arrived back where we'd tried to start: at a symbol.

Time to up the ante. The kids had learned a symbol for *drink* while leaning forward at their particular tables. Now we needed to generalize this learning so that when they sat at a different table (or on the floor, or anywhere else for that matter) *drink* would still mean *drink*. We made buzzer boards – electronic gadgets with big push buttons that triggered wonderfully demanding buzzers – and glued drink symbols to them. Now I trotted around the room like an on-duty Saint Bernard, slaking the thirst of all who called.

I repeated the drill for food. Real food in a real spoon – then an empty spoon, then a photocopied image of a real spoon, and then a reduced image. Soon my kids were hitting the symbols for food or drink at appropriate times, which showed me they weren't just randomly seeking my attention. But *food* and *drink* cover wide categories. Could I find a way to help my kids make specific choices?

I created sub-categories. Now when a child touched the drink symbol, I offered her three options: milk, chocolate milk, and orange juice. We went through the paper cup routine again, until we had white, brown, and orange cup symbols, which the kids touched to select their preferred beverage.

So far, so good. But what did it prove? True, they could hit a symbol that corresponded with one of the three drinks, but did that really mean they were making a conscious decision? To test this, I decided to offer a drink I was sure none of them would like – grape Kool-Aid, without sugar. I tried a swallow myself and charted it just north of poison.

The first time the children tried this purple yuck, they threw their heads away and gave me a look that said, You monster! Excellent, I thought as I wiped the spewed juice from one chin after another. That takes care of that.

It didn't, at least not for most. Over and over again, some of my brightest students reached for the purple symbol, and each time I brought the cup to their lips they gave me the look. They wanted a drink, but they had formed no real connection between the symbol they chose and the fluid they got in return. These kids were responding no differently than factory-farm chickens that learn to push on bars to release feed. The tragedy of it far outweighed the disappointment.

Only later, when I felt brave enough to take stock of the information I had gained through these experiments in communication (I had by now learned the value of keeping accurate records) and sit down to look it over without beating myself up about it, did I start making connections of my own. I found that the children who could not make choices, those who did not comprehend the symbol/real-life connections, were the same ones I'd had the most difficulty propping up at the tables. They were children who had no prior experience in moving their bodies in an intended direction. They were nonverbal, and immobile as well. The children who could roll, wriggle, marine-crawl, or bottom-bump fared much better in communication. They got it.

Bingo!

I was back at Greeley, back in the memories of those early years. I remembered my first kindergarten students, the ones who had found their voices once I helped them find their feet. They had proved to me that the catalyst for meaningful communication is meaningful body movement. It was a pattern I had seen repeat itself consistently over the years. In my excitement over the headway we had seemed to be making with communication, I had somehow lost sight of this.

This, then, was the lesson I took away from that first round of communication training. The work with symbol recognition could and should continue, but unless we addressed at the same time the students' lack of controlled body movement, we would be trekking a long, hard road to nowhere.

Wheelchair vendors made their rounds, and I talked one of them into loaning us a powered wheelchair, thinking I could teach children to operate it and move around unassisted. A few students caught on to the basic idea, but we didn't have a good, safe place for them to practice. Inside the classroom, the other students became prospective bowling pins. Outside, the sidewalks were narrow, with curbs that dropped off several inches. I decided to pare down my group of wheelchair operators. I chose a handful of my brightest students. Even these were not successful, though. They either moved the joystick randomly, seemingly unaware that they were in charge, or they showed no understanding at all of their position in space. The powered wheelchair did little to provide meaningful movement. Certainly, it did not unlock the door to meaningful communication. We got nowhere fast.

Here is a story about truly meaningful communication. It's a story about a boy named Charlie and my eight-year-old Tanya, who's in the thick of her elementary education. It's hard for me to believe she's the same kid who almost died of blood poisoning when she was little. She's still my little girl, though. And sometimes at night I lie awake thinking of all the awful things that just might happen to her, and plotting ways to protect her from the things that lurk in the dark corners of the world.

Tanya wakes up each morning, oblivious to my worries. She waves as she boards the school bus, her backpack strapped on like a parachute. She floats away, carefree.

On afternoons when she's not doing other things, Tanya still likes to visit my classroom, where there are lots of children for her to play with, children who need many smiles (Tanya is a good smiler). One is a tiny boy named Charlie. Charlie is blind – his retinas are detached – and even though he is four, he weighs only fourteen pounds. The first time Tanya meets Charlie, she notices right away how incredibly small and fragile he is. There is a reason for this, but she doesn't know it.

When he was a newborn, Charlie kept throwing his bottle out of his crib. So his parents tied him up. And when Charlie cried because he didn't like having his arms pinned behind him, his father threw him against a wall. Again and again, until Charlie was broken. Nobody ever tried to fix Charlie. One day, Charlie's father threw him against the wall so hard, it knocked Charlie out and his eyes nearly popped from his head. After that, Charlie's parents took him to the hospital. He fell down, they said. But the doctors saw the cracked skull and the detached retinas, the crooked arms and legs (every major bone in his body had by then been broken, but never set), and they knew Charlie didn't just fall down.

The investigators who came to Charlie's house found him in his crib. There was a bottle in the crib, but the milk inside it was too curdled to pass through the nipple. Charlie was almost dead. Charlie went into foster care, and his parents to jail.

A few years later, Charlie is brought to us at the DCH. And even though I am taking care of bigger children, he comes to my room.

Charlie is scared. He's safe in his crib, but a crib is not a happy place for him. Whenever anyone comes close to it, he shakes with fright. He never screams or cries, just shakes all over. We learn to tap Charlie's crib to tell him someone is near, but even so his blind eyes fly open, his jaw clinches, his back arches, and his whole body trembles.

Charlie won't eat. He will die if he doesn't start eating, I am sure. I hold him in my arms and rock him like a baby, until he stops shaking and lies quiet. Then, bit by bit, I dribble crumbs of food into his mouth, rocking him and whispering gently all the while. It takes two hours to feed Charlie properly – more time than I have. I get the school to hire someone just to give Charlie his lunch. Once he is relaxed, he stays calm as long as he's held. But the moment he is set back in his crib, he starts shaking again.

When I can't stand this anymore, I go out and buy a baby carrier, the kind that cuddles the infant in a front pouch, like a joey. Four-year-old Charlie fits inside perfectly. He likes being close to me; it helps him settle down. After a few days, he stops shaking altogether. But fourteen pounds is a lot to lug around all day when there are other children to care for too. So I ask my colleagues to help carry Charlie. If we do this for a few months, I tell them, it might help Charlie stop worrying, and maybe he won't be afraid anymore. Everyone agrees it's worth a shot. So now we all take turns wearing Charlie for an hour or two each day so that he won't have to be on the ground or in his crib, and so someone will always be touching him.

When Tanya comes to visit, she likes to wear Charlie too. Charlie Bear, everyone calls him, because he is cuddly and sweet, like a teddy bear. Charlie Bear can't see Tanya, but he knows she's different from the other, older people who take care of him during the day. Tanya is a special friend. She and Charlie Bear love each other very much.

One day Margie, my aide, breaks the rule. The rule is: Always have at least one hand on Charlie Bear. Otherwise he gets lost in space and starts shaking. But Margie takes her hand away, just for a split second, as she changes his diaper. Charlie Bear puckers up his lower lip. *Waaah!* He bleats like a newborn lamb. Like a tiny baby. I hear it and come running. Margie and I are so excited, we can't help crying, just like Charlie Bear. *He doesn't want Margie to leave him. He doesn't want to be separated from her. He* wants *to be around people!*

Tanya, when she finds out, is excited too. She comes to see Charlie Bear and carries him around the room, hugging him tightly. Fast friends, those two.

In later years, Charlie gets a gastrostomy, to help him get enough food. But eating isn't his only problem. His body had been damaged so badly, it can't keep up with him. Eventually, he outgrows it. Charlie Bear dies. But first he lived. Both Tanya and I know that.

Even now, though many years have passed since he died, Charlie Bear hasn't been forgotten. Do you know what I remember most about him? Tanya asks me. And I think back to the day she ran to me, in tears, to tell me that Charlie Bear had spoken, and to repeat what he had said: *I ubb ooh!* Those three words were the only ones he ever learned to say. But as I remember them, I think: Did he need to learn anything else?

partners

There were highs, like Charlie Bear. Lows, too. It was Tanya who kept me going and carried me through those dry times when lack of progress caused my courage to wilt. As tacky as it may sound, I saw her face in the faces of my students, each of them.

But if I relied on Tanya for inspiration, I counted on her for concrete support as well. The thing about being a special ed teacher and a mother was, there was always another Tamika or Bennie or Charlie who could use a special friend.

The summer of 1982 it was a seven-year-old girl named Christie.

Christie had been enrolled in the Blair Center's program for autistic children that school year. Her teacher was Carrie, who had the classroom directly across the hall from mine. I was busy with my group of hearing-impaired students (Julie and I were in the middle of our experiments) and glad to have Carrie and her class of autistic students as neighbors. At the end of the day Carrie and I often compared notes. During class, she frequently allowed her students into my room, especially at lunchtime, when they helped feed the children too disabled to feed themselves.

Sometimes Christie came into my classroom, too, though only if Carrie came with her. Christie was a doll. I was sure she was the most perfect blond-haired, blue-eyed child I'd ever seen. Unlike the other autistic students, she never spoke. That didn't faze me – I was a master at reading eyes, and I could see she liked me. As we saw more of each other, her eyes told me she loved me. She started to come into my classroom on her own from time to time. For whatever reason, she enjoyed being around me.

As the school year progressed, Christie warmed up. One day she started talking to me. Some of the things she said troubled Carrie and the other teachers working with the autistic students, and they began to pay close attention every time Christie opened her mouth. Bit by bit they pieced together a harrowing picture of Christie's home life. The image was stark, grotesque: Christie's parents were making money off her through prostitution and child pornography.

Based on the things Christie said, Child Protective Services began an investigation. They came to school and interviewed Christie and her teachers. By the end of spring, CPS said they absolutely, positively, had enough evidence to take Christie away from her parents. They took her to a special CPS home.

The experience of being among other children at the Blair Center during the day helped Christie weather the transition to her new home, but even so it was traumatic.

Summer was coming, and the class for autistic children would be switching to an abbreviated schedule, with no afternoon session. Carrie and others worried that Christie would not handle spending the majority of her day at the CPS home; she would miss the routine of our campus. They asked me if I'd be willing to take her on for the summer and have her in my class.

Much as I was eager to do something for Christie, I wasn't sure how I'd manage to keep her occupied in a class of nonverbal, non-ambulatory children with severe disabilities. We knew by now that Christie was really quite bright, and that her condition most likely had nothing to do with mental retardation or autism. Carrie had begun teaching basic academics to her autistic students, and Christie had done very well. I suggested to Carrie that with the needs of the students already in my class there was no way I would be able to coach Christie in academics. We need to get her a tutor, I suggested.

They found a tutor, and I found a place for Christie in my class. That was good, but it still left her with no one her age to play with, and it seemed to me that if she was going to get anywhere socially, she needed to interact with peers. At a staff meeting I raised the idea of bringing Tanya, who was nine, to school to be Christie's buddy. An excellent plan, I was told.

Tanya came with me the next day. We sat her down in the staff room and included her as one of us. If she was going to be Christie's buddy, she would need to understand a few things about her first. Her language, for instance. Christie sometimes uses words that are inappropriate, we told Tanya. She was hurt very badly when she was younger, and it makes her act a bit funny sometimes. Tanya looked at us with an expression that said, Okay, so? She had, after all, been around children her entire life who did not do what all her other friends did. I shouldn't have been surprised by her lack of concern – she left that to me.

Tanya and I soon found out that Christie had a thing for bubble suits, those frilly sunsuits that little girls wear, with string ties at the shoulders. She wanted a sunsuit in the worst way. So I went to JC Penney's and bought eight of them (they cost about two dollars apiece). We kept them at school, and each morning when Christie arrived I let her select one to wear that day.

Christie and Tanya spent their mornings with the class of autistic kids. Their last activity before lunch was swimming. Christie loved to swim. It was afterward, once she was back out of the pool and into her dry bubble suit, that she couldn't cope. A few days into the summer session, Tanya and Christie were walking to my room for lunch following their swim. A bead of water dripped from Christie's wet hair onto her sunsuit. She screamed. *Fuck you, you fuckin' bitch!*

What horrible thing had happened to this child in the past to make her go crazy over a drop of water on her clothing? It certainly wasn't her adoration of sunsuits – other water incidents brought forth similar profanities; and water wasn't the only thing that triggered these tirades. Much as I felt sorry for Christie, I worried for Tanya. Here was this seven-year-old mouth spewing filth, with my daughter in earshot. Tanya's going to be emotionally maimed for life, I thought, and it'll be my fault. But Tanya never even blinked. To her, Christie was just another friend with disabilities. Some of them talked like babies, or bit people, or chewed their own arms, or drooled, but of course that didn't mean Tanya did those things. Likewise, Christie said things no one else ever did (His muscle hurts, she would say, grabbing herself. That man's big muscle hurts…), but Tanya knew that didn't mean she had to repeat them. Indeed, much of what came out of Christie's mouth went right over Tanya's head.

Thank God. One morning Christie just fell apart, raving and screaming at the top of her lungs. She was standing in the middle of my classroom, but her mind was gone, off in some hideous place where kiddie-porn directors whined instructions to their child-stars, to an animal place where childhood was demolished one film frame at a time. Christie recreated her nightmare at full volume, so all the world could hear. Even when she was not shouting, the flashbacks ravaged her brain. Once, on her way to the bathroom, she went into a striptease, looking coyly over her shoulder as she gyrated her pelvis. She turned around and faced me, and said in a voice treacle-sweet and sickly fake, Be nice to the man in the motel, Christie, and he'll give you a new dress.

It was a summer of great difficulty for me, the first time I had to face such horrors. These things really did happen to children. Right here in America, on my own doorstep, this evil existed. Tanya, too, was encountering for the first time some of the worst things that could happen to anyone. We were going through this darkness together. I was still Mama Lion – the instinct to protect still burned strong within me – but Tanya was in this with me. We were a team, doing this together.

Tanya did most of it. She stuck with Christie all summer long. The Skittles awards program, for instance, was her brainchild. Christie, Tanya discovered, loved their bright fruity crunch and would go to great lengths to get them. Especially the "lellow" ones – perhaps because they matched her favorite sunsuit. Tanya spent many evenings at our kitchen table, dumping wholesale-sized boxes of Skittles into bowls and fishing out the yellow ones. She brought a bag of them to school with her each day. When Christie saw water on her sunsuit and managed to control herself even minimally, Tanya rewarded her with a Skittle. A lellow one.

By summer's end, Christie no longer stood up and screamed. Her torments continued, but Tanya's steady friendship and the Skittles' lemony crunch had done more to alleviate her suffering than anyone else had accomplished.

You know, Mom, Tanya told me on the way home one night, Christie and I are different.

Yes, honey. You are.

Tanya is a paradox: I think of her and marvel at how someone so like me in countless ways can be so completely different in others, and still be one person. She is my daughter, my only child, a designation she lamented loudly throughout her girlhood – *Come on, Mom. When are you having another baby?* – and no doubt rues softly still today. She is the fruit of my heart. I love her for being like me, and for being different.

When I left home for college at eighteen, I told my parents, I love you both very much, but I'm never going to do dirt again. Or so I tell people, for a little laugh. The words may not be exact, but it is true that I left determined never to live a farmer's life again – I was fed up with dirt.

So it was with an element of chagrin that I discovered my own daughter, flesh of my flesh, was born with dirt under her fingernails. Tanya, my little dirtaholic. As soon as she was old enough to toddle, she began scavenging, bringing me her findings in a grubby fist – a dead spider, two legs missing; a ball of lint, found in the laundry hamper. Later, it was grass stains on jeans, stubbed toes, and scraped elbows. My daughter, so wonderfully normal. I fed off her energy. On days when she and her cousin Minta Lauren got together, it was all I could do to catch my breath.

Terrors, I have termed those two. Marvelous, good-natured, holy terrors. Call them sisters.

When Minta Lauren was born, my sister Mary and her husband Ralph were living on the coast, but they moved into Bakersfield not long after. For the first few years of their lives, the two cousins lived only minutes apart. Sometimes it was hard to know who belonged where.

One summer afternoon when the girls were three, Minta Lauren was at our house playing with Tanya. I had stopped at a roadside fruit stand earlier that day and bought two large baskets of fresh strawberries. Mary is passionate in her loathing of them (she doesn't even like *pictures* of strawberries), and I had especially picked some up so that Minta Lauren could enjoy at our house what she was denied at hers. During the course of the afternoon, the girls asked for some strawberries from the refrigerator, and I said of course that would be just fine. Taking me at my word, they went into the kitchen, pulled out both those giant baskets, and began a strawberry-eating contest. I walked in just as the last berries were disappearing between stained lips.

Mary came by at the end of the afternoon to collect Minta Lauren. I made no mention of the incident. *Good night, Minta Lauren. Good night, Mary.*

During breakfast the next morning, the phone rang. A voice I decoded as Mary's raged on the other end.

I can't believe you *did* that!

Calm down, Mary. I don't know what you're talking about.

Oh yes you do.

Oh no I don't...

I learn soon enough: Mary and Ralph had gone to bed the night before with Minta Lauren snuggled in between them... Around midnight, her parents deep in slumber, Minta Lauren sits up and vomits strawberries. Nothing escapes – the bedspread, sheets, even the pillowcases take direct hits. The sound of retching wakes Mary, and pitches her face-first into the hated stench of strawberries. Baffled and gagging, she fumbles for the lamp switch, and illuminates the chaos. (Mary, her voice rising to fever pitch down the phone line, recreates the scene in Technicolor, with French subtitles.) Cursing the day I was born, she rises from her bed, pushes her husband toward the couch and her daughter toward the bathroom, yanks off the bedclothes, with the mess folded inside them, and storms out of the house and into the backyard, where she deposits her bundle. Minta Lauren is issued a fresh pair of pj's and relegated to her own bed, Mary takes a long, hot shower while her bedroom airs; and then the night resumes. In the morning, she dons rubber gloves and goes to collect the sheets from the yard, to fork them into the washing machine. But she is not the first to reach them. A neighborhood dog is busily pawing through them. Strawberry puke drips happily from its muzzle. That is when Mary runs inside and calls me. She has lost it completely. (Later, Minta Lauren confirms that her mother had, indeed, lost more than her temper: the sight of the dog licking through the sheets had cost her her breakfast.)

Was it, as I have chosen to think, mere coincidence that within a year Mary and Ralph had pulled up stakes and headed north, to try their luck in the Bay area...

Then came the years when things fell apart. The center could not hold. Martin and I went through dirt of our own, and emerged sullied

Cousins on paper, sisters at heart. Terrors, both of them.

and separate. Tanya proved my mainstay. Inside my heart I clung to her as a sailor clings to a mast in a tempest, even as I tried to hide her from my pain. Because of her, I weathered the storm. When it was over, the two of us headed back to Kansas, for a dry dock...

It is Tanya's first real stay at the flood farm, the first real chance for her to get to know her grandparents, and they her.

Tanya and her Grandpa are like two peas in a pod. Watching the two of them together gives me a strange feeling in the center of my stomach. Here is my daughter, having the time of her life with a man I've never seen before – Grandpa. Daddy? At meals, they hold corn-eating contests, chomping into steaming bowlfuls of fresh-picked ears and stacking the cobs messily around their plates. Grandpa makes the rules: Eat two, you're a dog. Four for a donkey. Six for a cow. First cow wins. Grandpa eats his corn sprinkled with Lawry's seasoned salt. Tanya tries it, and she's converted for life. She's not sure about cheese on apple pie, though, nor about the glass of thick buttermilk Grandpa quaffs each night with his dinner.

Grandpa's knee is giving him trouble. He gets surgery. When he comes home, he moves around the house in a wheelchair for a while. He lets Tanya sit on his lap and ride around with him. His big rough hands look misplaced on the thin wheel rims. When he's able to walk again, he takes Tanya with him on the tractor to bale hay. She perches on his knee, sidesaddle, as the tractor trundles across the wide fields. Sometimes, when he catches her letting the cows out, for instance, Grandpa glowers at her and delivers a stern lecture. Other times, he holds her hand and walks to the concrete-lined swimming pool he built himself, and he and Tanya delight in splashing each other. He's still a master swimmer, and I do not worry for her while they're together.

When Grandpa is busy, there is always Grandma. My Mama, who is thrilled to have a child around the house again, and quietly proud to have an attentive audience of one, someone who will watch her every move from atop the laundry drier. And, indeed,

Grandma's kitchen moves are worth watching. Tanya spends hours observing her cooking. Grandma makes wondrous pies: peach, strawberry, blackberry (gathered from the bushes that clot our headlands), and Tanya's favorite – apple pie with red-hots. Grandma cores and cuts the apples into slivers, which she mounds into the pie shell. She trickles flour and sugar through her fingers, and flecks of butter. Then, with a smile at Tanya, she reaches for her jar of red-hots and tucks a palmful of these zesty cinnamon candies in among the apples before she seals the pastry and puts the pie in the oven. With the leftover pastry she makes "cookies," sprinkled with cinnamon sugar. No one, Tanya says, makes pies like Grandma. And she's right.

Sometimes Grandma gets angry too. She doesn't like it when Tanya wears high-heeled shoes (her own, brought from California) and traipses *click-clack click-clack* from room to room. I know Grandma is worried Grandpa will walk in and fly off the handle at the noise, but I can't help wondering if she's forgotten another little girl, long ago... Grandma bans high heels from the house; they are for outdoor wear only now.

Grandma isn't always home. In fact, much of the day she's behind the counter at Mac's Fertilizers, by the train tracks that run across the back of Baxter Springs. She talks to the farmers that come in to buy seeds or order liquid fertilizers to be spread on their fields. Tanya loves to sit in Grandma's store after school hours and play with the seeds. There are many different kinds, all shapes and sizes, and Grandma says it's okay for her to play with them, so long as she puts them back where she found them and doesn't mix them up.

Tanya and I are glad for our year in Kansas; we each have our reasons. We both spend time sorting, and trying not to mix up, useful seeds. When the year is over and my studies are done, Tanya and I leave the farm and return to Bakersfield. The farm, however, does not leave Tanya. We have not been home long before she starts in on the horse talk.

Mom, she says, I know what I want to do for my next athletic thing.

Sure, honey. What's that?

I want to ride. Horses.

Oh...

When Tanya was eighteen months old, one of my colleagues bought her a daintily painted plastic palomino. Its hoofs were strapped to springs mounted on a metal frame. Tanya learned to pull herself onto its back and bounce up and down, back and forth, as the springs squeaked maddeningly. By the time she was two, she was dragging her horsey to the den each morning to watch *Sesame Street*. Her horsey was her friend, and they spent hours in each other's company, rocking steady. Is that, I wondered, where this fascination began?

Tanya was four when she first placed her foot in a stirrup. Nancy, who lived across the street and was little more than five herself, owned a pony. She invited Tanya down to the stables to ride. I have been kicking myself ever since: it was for me to say yea or nay, and I went with yea.

By the time she turned five, Tanya had ridden in her first show, Walk-Trot, and come away with a blue ribbon. She slept with it on her pillow.

When Martin, Tanya, and I flew to Kansas for a visit to the farm that summer, Tanya was eager to show off her skills. Minta Lauren and her parents had come to the farm too. Daddy owned a couple small ponies, Ginger and Flicka, and Tanya pestered him into bridling and saddling them up. She was champing at the bit, eager to ride. Off to one side stood Minta Lauren, equally agitated, though for other reasons: I don't want to ride! she insisted. She meant it too. Minta Lauren never rode. She left the barnyard trots to Tanya, who by then was hopelessly hooked.

Why couldn't she stick with roller-skating? I asked myself now. She'd been going to the rink for several years and had become quite good at it. Or ice-skating, why not ice-skating? During the fall and winter of our year in Kansas, I'd taken her almost every weekend to the Williams Center in Tulsa, and she'd enjoyed every minute on the ice.

But now she was nine, and it was horses.

I remembered that LaVaun Rogers, a fellow teacher at Blair, had something to do with horses. I asked her where Tanya could take lessons. She laughed and said, At our ranch, of course. Come out any afternoon and my husband, Jim, will be glad to talk to you. That's when I found out that the horsey community of Bakersfield was right down the road from our rented apartment on the outskirts of town.

Jim and LaVaun's Windsong Appaloosa Ranch was only a fifteen-minute drive from our doorstep. Tanya and I paid them a visit. Jim came out of the big ranch house to meet us. He was a tall, rangy man, his features weathered. What little hair he had (he was almost completely bald) was brown. As he walked toward us, Jim was a picture-perfect cowboy.

He was a cowboy on the inside too. In his younger days, Jim had trained horses for the army. When he got out, he returned to school and earned his teaching credential. Horses and kids were his two great loves. In Jim's opinion, one was useless without the other.

Judging him by his appearance and background, I guessed Jim would prefer to teach Western riding. But English jumping was his passion. He believed a person could learn all the important lessons of life on the back of a horse as it cleared fences. Tanya listened, fascinated, as Jim talked to us.

By the time she had announced her wish to make riding her athletic endeavor (I was still sticking to one athletic and one artistic activity at a time), her mind was made up. Certainly once we'd visited the Rogers' ranch, there was nothing I could do to sway her. Besides, if riding was what she wanted – and it was, plainly, what she really, *really* wanted – she could go ahead. She was old enough to choose the activities she took on. And it would only be once a week.

There was one huge obstacle for me to overcome, though: my nose. Eyes, too, to be honest. I have always had allergies, but none worse than my allergy to horsehair. My nose and eyes stream, my ears close up with fluid, I cough and sneeze in spasms.

So on riding days I dropped Tanya off at the ranch, and drove away fast. When the lesson was over I came back for her, by which time she had showered in LaVaun's bathroom, changed her outfit, and stuffed her riding clothes into a garbage bag. I popped the trunk, she put the bag in; and only then did she climb into the seat beside me. Once home, she took the bag from the trunk and marched it straight to the laundry machine, where she washed her clothes while I stayed far away. Upwind.

Before many lessons had passed, she was sitting me down for a heart-to-heart talk across our kitchen table. She had a proposition to make: scrap the artistic endeavor (oil-painting, at the time), and go with two riding afternoons a week. Actually, it wasn't much of a proposition; Tanya had already decided how it was going to be. I recapped, somewhat lamely no doubt, my theory of a well-balanced regimen of active and creative pursuits, but I might as well have been talking to a horse. Or a mule.

My big theory went out the window. She got her two afternoons of riding – *I love you, too, Tanya* – and I got my first of many years' worth of allergy shots.

Casino's Lucky Charm, a.k.a. the ugliest horse in the world. A skinny appaloosa with pink eyes, a mottled pink-gray face, and polka dots all over her body, she was the first jumper Tanya rode. She may not have been the prettiest horse to look at, but when it came to clearing fences in the ring, Lucky was truly a charm. That's why Jim kept her — she was the best teacher for children he had. Tanya took to Lucky right away. She loved that horse, and it in turn responded to her. Before long, they were riding in competitions. Low-key events, mostly, against riders of similar ability, over manageable jumps. In spite of myself, I enjoyed watching her compete (there was usually enough breeze to keep the horsehair at bay). Soon Tanya and Lucky were bringing home ribbons. Blue ones, more and more often.

Next thing I know, she's made the "A" Team.

Nice going, Tawny. What's the "A" Team?

The "A" Team, as it turns out, is for the pros — the girls and boys who are really proficient at their riding, the ones whom Jim thinks have real potential. The show riders.

Instead of two days a week, we ratchet up to five. Then seven. Tanya practically lives at Jim and LaVaun's — which is fine by them. Though they have children of their own, they count Tanya as one of theirs. She and I are family.

And then, just as everything's going so wonderfully for us, July 7, 1983 brings tragedy to Mama and Daddy, to my family. The day begins like any other Thursday, with Daddy driving the thirty-odd miles south to his liquid fertilizer operation in Narcissa, Oklahoma, and Mama tidying the house before heading to the feed store in Baxter Springs. She is there when a neighbor calls: Ethel, your house is on fire!

Both houses, as it turns out. There is an electric line that carries two hundred and twenty volts of current from the attic of the old house out to the barn. The wiring is old, and squirrels have run unchecked through the attic for years. Daddy knows this, and as a precaution usually turns off the breaker for the electric box before he

Tanya and TV Buyer, making it look easy.

leaves in the morning. Usually. Today he forgets. A squirrel makes an errant, deadly scramble. The circuit shorts. Fur sizzles. Fire breaks out.

This they surmise later. The neighbor who telephones Mama has already called the Galena Fire Department. Mama calls the Baxter Springs brigade and heads for the flood farm.

The fire has spread from the attic to the low roof of the carport alongside the new house, and from there to the corner of Mama and Daddy's home. Flames engulf the roof by the time the firemen arrive, and Mama can do nothing but watch.

The blaze makes short work of the entire second floor, with the exception of one bedroom – the one containing heirlooms from Mama's family – which the firemen save. The rest is gutted by the time they have hosed enough water to drown the flames. When it is over, all that is left of the new house, the house that matters, is the cinderblock chimney and basement walls, and the concrete retaining wall, holding back Daddy's hill. The house had withstood floods and escaped tornadoes, but fire gets it this time.

Downcast, Mama and Daddy set about cleaning away the rubble. They give the old house proper burial (if anything good had come from the fire, it had been its destruction). They hire contractors to rebuild the ruined second floor and, as if to give the house renewed confidence, work up plans for a two-car garage on the basement level with a large bonus room overtop. Daddy and Tiger, his beloved pit bull terrier, spend several weeks of nights tenting at the farm; Daddy worries about theft. Mama stays at their store in Baxter Springs, where she lives in a small trailer. Daddy comes to the trailer for his meals, but returns with Tiger to the tent each night, until the screened porch has been redone and he can abandon the tent.

I call often, to offer whatever comfort can be found in words. Mama and Daddy are resilient, dogged. They bend, straighten, and move on again, the river flowing with them.

Two summers on, and Tanya is twelve. She carries the first traces of womanhood with consigned grace, yet remains my little girl (she still loves to curl up on the couch with me). Her love of horses is stronger than ever, and nowhere is she more at home than in the saddle, in the arena. She is a recognized competitor at state jumping trials, and has several trophies to prove it. Now, her hard work and enthusiasm have won her qualification for the World competitions, to be held in Oklahoma City. She is eligible to ride in two events, First and Second Year Green and Open Jumpers. Needless to say, I am not as encouraged by this news as Tanya is. She reads my anxiety, and launches a reverse-psychology campaign: Well, Mom, when we go to World's... (Her inflection beautifully matches my *Well, Tanya, when you go to college* speech.) In her mind, there is no option – she, we, are going. I turn to Jim for advice, but his bias is obvious:

Jim, I say, this is not Hunter Hack, or a flat class, or any of those other events. We're talking Open Jumpers here – professional riders, the highest, broadest fences...

He listens to me, his hand on his chin. Sometimes he nods, sympathetically. Then he breaks the scenario down into bite-sized, panic-free pieces, and shows each of them to me carefully, the way new tack is broached with a fresh horse.

It won't cost you much, Linda. I'll tow Lucky out with the other horses going to World's. Tanya can go with us, and you can fly out and meet us there. It'll be great. And just think of...

I listen to him, my hands on my hips. Sometimes I shake my head, hesitantly.

We talk again the next afternoon. Jim keeps working on me:

The fences she's been taking here in California are far bigger and meaner than the ones they'll have at World's. I'm telling you, Linda, it's a baby course compared to what Tanya's been doing out here.

It took him a few days. Finally:

Your parents live in Kansas, Linda. Oklahoma City might be the only time in their lives they get to see Tanya jump.

You *would* have to go there, I think. He has pushed the one button that actually connects somewhere inside me. I relent, even as my ears ring with the hoofbeats of trepidation.

I fly to Oklahoma City alone. Tanya and three of her rider friends accompany Jim in the four-horse trailer. I have the entire flight to beat myself up.

It doesn't get any bigger than this! is my first reaction to the Oklahoma State Fairgrounds. Row upon row of covered barns, and everywhere horses and trailers and tack-toting trainers and riders. The smell of horses clings to the humid air. The crushed grass underfoot vibrates. I walk among the horses and through the barns. This is not what I had imagined. This is not the show Jim had described as "no big deal" — this is huge. Worse, it's too late to do anything about it; we're here, and Tanya's going to compete.

I find the arena — the monstrous, covered ring where the jumping will be done — and a fresh wave of guilt-laced panic crashes in: My poor little Tanya! She's probably the tiniest, youngest thing ever to compete in Open Jumpers. And I'm going to have to watch her fall and break her neck, or be trampled by some marauding horse, and afterward I'll have a quadriplegic daughter (if I'm lucky and she's not dead) and I'll have to look at her each day and tell myself what a horrible terrible utterly useless irresponsible reckless excuse for a mother —

Hi, Mom!

Tanya has found me. She's higher than a kite. There is confidence and excitement written all over her face, bouncing down her ponytail, and some of it rubs off on me as she wraps me in a hug. My one consolation is that her first jumping event, First and Second Year Green, will not be nearly as bad as Open Jumpers. If Tanya doesn't do well in this first class, I told myself, maybe I can talk her and Jim into pulling her before she gets hurt.

Tanya gets Lucky ready. I make myself as useful as I can, but this is Tanya's realm and she knows what she's doing. Lucky looks perfect, almost handsome with her mane and tail freshly braided and her coat groomed to a high sheen. These are, however, jumping competitions, not dressage events. Together with Jim, who is as confident and excited as Tanya, we make our way with Lucky to the great arena, where she must stand for inspection and be tested for illegal doping. Afterward, Tanya leads Lucky through the tunnel from the main arena that leads into an adjacent warm-up arena (no horse may leave once it's been inspected). She leaves me holding Lucky's lead line while she and Jim go back to walk the course, count strides between fences, and discuss tactics.

Tanya and Jim disappear into the tunnel. Their heads are bobbing; obviously, they have a lot to talk about. I pat Lucky's pink-gray nose. Nice horsey. She pays no attention to me. She is watching Tanya. My Tanya. Her Tanya. Lucky paws the bare ground with a front hoof. She snorts and tugs on the lead line. I try another pat. She tilts back her head and whinnies. Her lips peel back from her teeth as she neighs after Tanya. I watch Lucky's entire body tense in agitation. *Oh, Lord!* Come on, Lucky, we're going for a little walk. I pull gently on the rope in my hand, her head turns, and she follows. Nice horsey, I say again, as I fight to stifle a sneeze. Whatever you do, Linda, I tell myself, do not rile this horse; she could jump clean out of this arena in two seconds flat.

Lucky calms down. Just a touch of nerves, huh buddy? Jumpers, they're a flighty bunch. Tanya and Jim are coming back through the tunnel, with a hint of swagger. I wave, and Lucky, seeing Tanya, starts up neighing again — a nervous neigh, not a happy, *hi-how-are-ya* horse noise. Easy, Lucky. Steady.

She is through with me. She rears back and yanks the lead line from my hands, hits the ground running. The fence separates her from Tanya. Lucky reaches it and leans over, still screaming at Tanya, who is coming toward her at a dead run. I am standing in the middle of the warm-up arena, and all around me are voices: *Horse loose! Horse loose!* And there is nothing for me to crawl under. I stand on ground as bare as my embarrassment.

Tanya has Lucky in hand again, and all is well, my burning face aside. It is time for the competition to begin. I squeeze my darling baby and wish her luck. She stays with Jim and Lucky while I go to take my seat in the arena. Only then do I learn that Open Jumpers is scheduled *before* First and Second Year Green. I stop breathing.

Mama is there. Daddy is not. (He never attends anything, on principle.) Several of my girlhood friends from Baxter Springs have come to support me, as have my sister Minta and her three-year-old son, Gavin. We have seats down near ringside. I sit next to Gavin. He is holding a little stuffed appaloosa, a present for the occasion from his mom. What's your horsey's name? I ask him. Lucky, he says.

Many riders go before Tanya. None perform particularly well. One falls and has to be carried out on a stretcher – a wonderfully encouraging sight, which opens the sluice gates to a fresh flood of accusations: *Where is your* head! *You're such a horrible mother. I can't believe you! By the time this is over your baby will either be disabled or dead – and you're allowing it to happen!*

It is time for Tanya's entrance. *You're too late, Linda.* Maybe, I think, maybe she'll get scared and won't do it. Maybe she'll wheel Lucky around and canter back out the tunnel...

She is in the arena. She does not wheel Lucky around. Featherlight, she posts in her stirrups as Lucky makes the courtesy round before the first approach. Here we go, I tell myself, and realize my teeth are digging deep into my lower lip. I do not unclench them.

Tanya pulls Lucky toward the first fence – and sits down in the saddle. She is supposed to lean forward and raise her bottom off the leather to cue the horse into the jump, but instead she has dropped her stance. Tawny's scared! I think. Lucky thinks so too. She refuses the jump. Tanya pulls her up short, and turns to attack the fence again. *One refusal.* I release my index finger from my right fist. Two more, and she's disqualified. Wouldn't that be a miracle.

Tanya and Lucky canter toward the jump again. Tanya leans forward, comes out of the saddle. *Bogeyman! I'm not going,* Lucky decides. She skids to a halt a brief yard from the jump, Tanya pitches forward but steadies herself with her hands on Lucky's neck. The horse shimmies backward, almost sits down. Tanya tugs the reign, turns Lucky's head. *Two.* My middle finger joins my pointer. Each refusal deducts points; it's mathematically impossible for her to win now. Three's a charm, I say to myself. Let's get home the safe way, Tawny. I'll love you just as much...

She readies for the third approach. Even from across the arena I can see determination in her bearing. There is urgency in the way she brings Lucky around and starts for the fence. A few strides from it she suddenly rises and stands bolt upright in the stirrups, in perfect two-point, moves her reigns to her left hand, cowboy style, and with her right brings her bat down – *whap!* – across Lucky's rear. The bat strikes Lucky just as Tanya lets forth a shrill *up!* And there is the fence straight ahead, and Lucky sees the fence and feels the whap of the bat and hears the will of her rider and says, *Fence! We're going over a fence!* and clears it beautifully, of course. But Tanya does not sit down. She stands in her stirrups and attacks one jump after another. *Up! Up!* I hold my breath and wait for her to fall. But she does not fall, just keeps jumping.

She is turning into the final hurdles, right in front of our seats. These are some of the toughest fences on the course, tricky in-and-outs where every stride counts. The entire audience is on its feet. Everyone screams and yells for the tiny little girl on the big ugly horse who has said to hell with style and form and riding convention and is turning this course into a test of will. I am on my feet too. I am having a heart attack. Tanya is right in front of me now, and I know she will crash. She will crash and fly through the air and land on her head and the helmet will not save her and she will break her neck maybe even die and I deserve to be locked up in jail and I am absolutely having a heart attack. Gavin is screaming in my ear. *Tan-ya! Tan-ya! Tan-ya!* He waves his little stuffed Lucky as she approaches the jump dead ahead – this crazy jump, the worst in-and-out of the course. Tanya looks up, smiles. *I love you, Gavin.* I can't hear her, but I read her lips. Now I know I'm dying. *I love you, Gavin.* How could she be thinking of –

She turns into the final jump. One last *whap.* One final *up!* And then it is over and the grandstand shakes with cries and applause. But I am already out of my seat and down through the tunnel, following Tanya and Lucky back into the warm-up ring, where Jim is waiting. He grabs Lucky and strokes the jitters out of her. I reach them, and Tanya flies from Lucky's back into my arms. She is crying. I have never seen her so white. I hug her in a motherlock from which she will never escape, so that nothing will ever hurt her, and so she will know how overwhelmingly proud I am of her, and how incredibly scared I have been; and also, so we will always be together, and no hurdle will be too big for the two of us to tackle together, even when we both need to cry.

After my arms have said these things, I let them slacken. Tanya pulls her head out of my chest.

I just did it anyway, Mama, she says. I just did it anyway.

Tanya went on to take fifth place in First and Second Year Green. By day's end, she was quite a celebrity. For the two of us, though, the trip to Oklahoma City was special for other reasons as well. It solidified our partnership. Tanya and I had always been a team, but it was as if all the trials we'd come through together now fused us closer than ever before. I was still Mom and she was still my Tawny, but we were partners now who discussed everything and made decisions together. There came a time when Tanya, convinced I was ignoring my own wellbeing, slipped into the mother role. She coaxed me into eating when my appetite had shriveled, packed me off to bed when my bloodshot eyes seemed too ghoulish, and generally coddled me. We both possess a doggedness of character (some might call it a stubborn streak), and we drew strength from our joint determination, even if it occasionally put us at odds with each other. In all things, our unspoken mantra was, Just do it anyway. (And we weren't even Nike partisans.)

It was an attitude thing, a way to face the challenges that came our way, whether at home, at school, or play.

School certainly continued to hold its share of challenges for me. Around the time Tanya was preparing for World's, Julie and I were winding up our experiments in auditory and communication training. Once again we had reached a dead end. It seemed obvious that the children who weren't mobile, the children whom we could not help onto their feet, were going nowhere – in every meaning of the phrase. We could scratch holes in our heads dreaming up new tricks to try, and it still wouldn't amount to a hill of beans. Without motor skills, our students stagnated before our eyes. They lost ground faster than we could shore them up. All too often I headed home in the evening with the sad recognition of having spent another day as a nurse, not a teacher.

On the heels of disappointment, though, came an uplift – in the form of a new physical therapist. Jack was with California Children Services, and had been assigned to the Blair Center. For the first time, we had a physical therapist on staff (Jim and Barbara, our PT and OT at Greeley, had long ago been moved to new assignments).

I shared Jack's belief that it was important for our students who could not bear their own weight to be given the opportunity to stand, so that they would develop (or at least preserve) bone strength. I was still teaching a class of seven- to fourteen-year-olds. Though I agreed on the importance of standing, I shied away from placing my students in the standing devices available to us – rickety,

rundown pieces of equipment that were painful to look at. I could
only imagine how it felt to stand in one of them for any length of
time. Besides, once a student was strapped into a stander, then what?
There was nothing for him to do but *stand*. Or, in some cases, stand
and cry. Jack, I said, you and I don't just stand for the sake of standing. Most of the time we're on our feet, we're doing something.

Aside from inactivity and boredom, it concerned me that these
conventional standers placed children at eye level with their adult
caregivers. That was all well and good for the caregiver, but what
about the child? Didn't she deserve to be on the same eye level as
her upright peers? I believed every child should have the chance to
interact with other children, and not only that: I had learned from
my earlier work teaching children to stand and walk that they responded best when at their natural eye level.

Out of our discussions over the merits of conventional stationary standers, Jack decided we should try mobile standers. We knew
of Eric, a student in Kern County whose mother had collaborated
with a local university to have a mobile stander built for her son.
Eric's stander was essentially a boxy structure into which he could
be strapped, with wheelchair wheels mounted either side so that he
could maneuver himself around. This was what Jack had in mind
when he suggested my students try a mobile stander. I allowed as
how it would be a better option than the dilapidated pieces of equipment we had on hand, especially since a stander like Eric's allowed
the child to be upright at normal height.

The fact that we didn't have any of these mobile standers
around, or that no company we knew of had one on the market,
didn't seem to bother Jack. I can think of a way to get them, he said.

First, though, we needed a model. Another teacher and I pieced
together our first mobile stander using the frame and wheels of an
old wheelchair. It was a crude design: a base platform, low to the
ground, and upright, padded supports against which a child's legs

and trunk could lean and to which he could be strapped. The result was less than satisfactory, but it was a starting point. Jack brought in a local welder, Dean, to see our model. I want the wheels in front of the child, I told him, not like a wheelchair where you have to reach back and pull forward. This thing's got to be easy to get around in, or it's not going to work.

Dean came back a few days later with a prototype. The design was far from polished, but the stander was sturdy, and the large bicycle wheels answered my concerns for easy motion. It would do. We had our first mobile stander, with a promise from Dean of more to come.

I saw its flaws and brainstormed ways to improve it, but as far as my students were concerned, the mobile stander was an out-and-out hit. True, there were children who did not have the muscle tone to stand even with the aid of the stander's straps, but they were the exceptions. The majority of my non-ambulatory students responded quickly and with broad smiles to the unfamiliar freedom the mobile stander provided. Some soon learned to grasp the big wheels and slide their hands to propel themselves forward. Whereas before the floor had been their point of reference, these students could now move around the room at will in the mobile stander. Better still, they could participate with the others in activities at tables or counters.

At least, this was the freedom available to them for twenty to thirty minutes each day, depending. Hefting a teenager in and out of a stander was a two-person job, and there was only so much activity we staff – and our students – could handle. All of us were in the middle of a learning experience.

For a child who has never in her life borne her own weight, standing with the aid of a stander is certainly a great achievement. I was proud of every one of our students and their progress. Those who had learned to move around in the mobile stander were developing arm strength and coordination, as well as self-esteem. But I wasn't satisfied yet. There were other students who simply sagged in the standing devices, without any active involvement.

The way I saw it, teaching kids to stand was not the goal. The goal was independent mobility – for every child in my care, no matter how outlandish this goal might seem. I wanted all my kids to gain their feet, with their full weight on their legs, and to walk unassisted: That was the goal, and I vowed never to lose sight of it. *(Just do it anyway, Linda.)*

My experiences with Tommy, years ago now, remained fresh in my mind. I could still hear his squeals of delight as he lurched his way down our halls in the contraption I'd contrived for him. I could see his arms clutched tight to his chest in excitement as for the first time his feet (tiptoes, actually) pushed against the floor and propelled his body forward. I contrasted these memories with the sight of my kids who couldn't push the big wheels of the mobile stander – and I knew we were coming up short. What we need to develop, I said to Jack, is a walker that can support a non-ambulatory child who isn't bearing his own weight and isn't using his hands. With a walker like that, we could teach a student to move his legs, even if he hasn't yet learned to sit or stand. The majority of our students seemed to learn much faster when their entire bodies were involved in the process, and they seemed to have more control over leg movements than arm movements. I wanted to create a device that would allow them to determine their own direction. It wouldn't just be a walker, it would be a trainer. A gait trainer.

Reenter Dean, the welder. The three of us – Jack, Dean, and I – held heated discussions about what would work. (These were the first of many such arguments. Eventually, our philosophies would diverge to the point of incompatibility, and we would go our separate ways.) I made another contraption similar to the one I had jerry-rigged for Tommy. Jack and Dean hated it. They wanted children completely upright. I wanted them leaning forward so that any

leg movement would propel them in the direction they were looking. I wanted a sling seat so we could teach weight shifting. They
wanted a solid unicycle seat. With that kind of support, I said, the
students will just paddle around, pushing themselves backward. My
whole idea was to get them moving forward so they understood
their own control over movement. When the children realized they
were masters of their own universe, then we could bring them to a
more upright position. In the end, Dean built two walkers: one to his
and Jack's specifications, one to mine. Jack dubbed mine "Linda's
walker." He didn't want his name attached to it. Mine worked. The
mobile standers Jack swore by were an improvement over the old
stationary standers, but the gait trainer, I was sure, held the key to
independent movement.

I was grateful for the equipment we'd come up with, but it held
little interest for me except as a means to move my children toward
the goal of independent mobility. Our students were what was important, not the technology we were creating to assist them. I
dreamed of the day we'd walk together to the scrap yard and leave
our standers and gait trainers, care of the crusher. Some of my kids
might not get within sight of the goal, I knew. For them, though, I
would work to make the equipment they would need as small and as
unobtrusive as possible, so that dignity and self-esteem and the ability to learn could still flourish in the "least restrictive environment."
The key equipment was in place. All we needed was a comprehen-
sive program, to bring all the pieces together.

As 1986 got underway, I began my evaluations. Before we went
any further I had to sit down and process the information I had
gleaned in my fifteen-plus years in special education. I dug out yel-
lowed notes from previous classes and studies, reassessed statistics
and class charts, ransacked files, riffled my brain for shreds of information – anything that would help me put two and two together and
reach a sensible sum. I had long before become an apostate of the
developmental approach. The special ed bible that preached sitting

before standing, crawling before walking had for me lost all credence in the course of my work. Then had followed my agnostic period, when I felt certain there must be some way to help my children, yet had little more than a gut feeling to go on. There had been, too, moments when I teetered on the verge of atheism, so unsure of my ability (or anyone else's) to better the lot of these children hampered by disabilities, that I considered giving up altogether. Yet even then the vision never completely died, the voice was never totally silenced. *If you teach, they will learn… Just do it anyway.* There were signs and wonders: Tommy, Jenny, Scuffy, Charlie Bear, and more. Enough to keep me going. To give me faith. Now, going through the pages of compiled information, I relived the joys and sorrows of more than a decade's work trying to teach children to learn. More clearly than ever before, I saw and knew what I believed.

Throughout my search for clues, the memory of our botched experiment in teaching communication remained raw. I was grateful for it, all the same – it was a red flag waving in our faces. The results were unequivocal, and glaring: Students with any sort of mobility skills at all – crawling, rolling, squirming – had successfully learned to make meaningful choices and interpret symbols. The ones who lacked any ability to move, failed.

What I had no way of knowing then – and what I wanted to find out now – was whether the children who failed were too brain damaged to differentiate, or whether they had simply never learned to choose. I believed they had the brains, and though I couldn't be sure, I thought I was looking at a classic catch-22: Unable to move or communicate, these kids had no chance to prove their cognition. So they were labeled "mentally retarded" and treated as such, which meant everyone's expectations bottomed out, which meant the kids didn't learn, which meant they seemed mentally retarded.

The standard measure of children's mental acuity was the IQ test. Children with severe disabilities who were unable to demonstrate comprehension usually ended up with charts marked IQ BELOW 30. What rot, I thought. How can we be so presumptuous? We're going to write these kids off as essentially brainless, just because they're not able to communicate in a manner meaningful to us "normal" people... We had to come up with a better means of evaluation. Time to say bye-bye to IQ tests. What did they mean, anyway?

What *did* have meaning was rate of learning. Like children everywhere, my students learned by repetition. Perform a task often enough, and it becomes ingrained. I had studied the concept of rate of learning at Pittsburg State, during my master's program. It seemed like the answer to my dilemma of how to quantify in a meaningful manner my students' ability to learn. By charting the number of repetitions required for a child to master a skill, we could measure her rate of learning and thus project her ability to acquire new skills in the future. This evaluation would be far more valuable than an IQ test. We would work with our students to increase their rate of learning, and be able to quantify our progress.

Rate of learning, when I began to apply more thought to it, quantified something else too: our disadvantage against time. I ran the numbers, and didn't want to believe what they told me: Ten students with severe disabilities per class. Between the classroom teacher and her aide, ten hours of instruction were available each day – sixty minutes per student, on average. These students – non-ambulatory, and functioning (according to the developmental model) at a level below a normal one-year-old's – required one-on-one assistance to participate in any activity. Lunch = thirty minutes per student. Diaper changes or toileting = ten minutes. The average student required two diaper changes or toileting sessions each day. That left us with ten minutes – *ten measly minutes!* – a day per student to "teach." And that was on a good day. These numbers were based on "average" students; any student too large to be lifted by one person needed even more instructional time, and many students required specialized help – gastrostomy feeding, periodic suctioning, postural drainage, et cetera. No wonder many of our students seemed to have a hard time learning even the most basic skills...

I ran other numbers too – just to prove a point. According to the developmental approach, we were supposed to analyze the children in our care to determine the skills they had "missed" – the ones other children their age had mastered – and work our way up the list, essentially filling in the blanks. For a student with severe disabilities, we usually didn't have to look much farther than the infant development scale. I got out my pencil (I've liked story problems since grade school). If it takes Davie two thousand trials to acquire a new motor skill (a reasonable average, according to research), and if we're only going to be able to offer him ten thousand practice sessions during the years he's in school (which is pushing it), then by the time Davie leaves, he'll have acquired five new skills. If we focus on teaching him the five skills that he's missed, sequentially, in accordance with the infant development scale, by the time Davie graduates he will have learned to (a) hold a rattle (b) prop himself on his elbows while in a prone position (c) wave bye-bye (d) turn toward sound (e) inspect his fingers.

Or none of the above, I said to myself. Because if it takes Davie two thousand repetitions to learn to maintain head control while being pulled to a sitting position (that's one session a day for six years), we could predict an equal number of repetitions before he'd learn to balance himself while sitting on the floor. At this rate, using the developmental model to designate the skills to be practiced, Davie could be pushing up to a sitting position on the floor by the age of eighteen.

If he's not dead by then, I thought. Lucky for Davie, he only existed on paper.

I turned my thoughts back to the goal, the two-fold goal toward which everything we did should be directed: independent mobility, and meaningful communication.

It starts at the wrong end. That's the main problem with the developmental method, I concluded. If we're serious about moving kids toward the ultimate goal of independence, why don't we look at each child and evaluate what it is, exactly, they need to learn before they can reach that goal? Then we can look for ways to build the necessary rate of learning repetitions into our students' daily activities; we'll buy time that way. There may well be mountains to move, but at least we'll have determined what those mountains are, and where to start chipping away.

I probably should have pushed back my chair at that moment and shrieked *Eureka!* Instead, I began outlining a plan for testing my students' rate of learning. I had a lot of donkeywork ahead of me. Mountains of it, in fact.

stepping out

Revolution, like charity, starts at home. That's why, as I set about flipping conventional special education on its head, my students' parents were the first people I talked to. What, I asked them, do you think is your child's greatest need? What are the things your child is unable to do that limit her activities? I talked with dozens of parents, and listened as if I'd never heard them before. The family activities their children were missing out on were numerous, and basic: things like eating with the family, getting in and out of bed, dressing and grooming, toileting, bathing or showering, communicating, and participating in family recreation. Beyond the home, the list of impossibilities included going to appointments at the dentist or hairdresser, shopping, eating out, attending social events, using public rest rooms, and riding in public transportation or the family car.

Parents weren't the only ones I talked to. I remembered the errant question I'd put to Tommy, though this time, when I used it on my students, I didn't mean it rhetorically. What do you wish you could do? I asked them. They told me, in detail:

I want to turn over on those gym bars, like those girls do on television...

I want to go to that other bathroom — the one where the rest of the kids go...

I want to get on and off the school bus all by myself…

I want to fetch a beer from the refrigerator for my dad…

While parents often seemed mired in the overwhelming feeling that their child was going nowhere, the children had specific goals. There were visions in their heads and hearts. I imagined that my students who couldn't speak shared similar dreams too. I remembered Mama Jo, and went back to the parents with a new question: What activities at home are the most difficult for you? The responses fell within the range I'd already noted, but now we were thinking specific. Now we were able to talk about what, exactly, was most important to tackle first. If you were to pick one achievement you'd like to see your child master, what would it be? What's one thing you'd like to take on, and do well?

The pieces were coming together, one at a time. By the summer of 1986 we were confident enough in our game plan to pitch the idea of a pilot program. It would give us a chance to test our effectiveness at helping students learn mobility skills as part of their everyday activities. Using information we'd gained from our efforts at teaching children to sit, stand, and walk, we'd implement a curriculum built on quantifiable goals, not on what convention considered developmentally "appropriate."

We got the green light for our program. All we needed were kids. There were several non-ambulatory students in my class, but not enough. So I went from room to room. Who'd you like to get rid of for the summer? I asked the other teachers. Who's driving you up the ever-loving walls? Need a break? Okay, let's make a deal.

I got my students, eleven of them, and Jack and I set to work.

And work we did. We didn't waste a single second of the day. Students practiced mobility skills without even realizing what they were doing. When it was time to use the toilet, for instance, we also saw it as time to practice getting up from a sitting position and bearing weight. Time to go to the bus meant time to practice walking in the gait trainer. Everything we did was geared toward making movement a natural part of each child's day. The students understood: the skills they were learning weren't mere exercises – they had meaning for life.

While the children grasped what our intentions were, there were other, more grown-up types, who did not. To them, our program represented a threat. It flew in the face of everything they knew about therapy and what children such as ours should and should not be able to achieve. Moreover, it was a labor-intensive effort that required great commitment, and anyone who wasn't convinced about what we were trying to achieve soon felt overwhelmed. Which, at times, made life quite trying.

Still, the pilot program worked. No one could deny that. By the end of summer, nine of our eleven students could sit unassisted on a regular classroom chair (no straps) for thirty minutes at a stretch – long enough for any classroom activity and for most mealtimes. Nine children could sit unsupported for five minutes on a stool – plenty of time for a caregiver to get a person off a bed, or into a bathtub. Six could bear their full weight on their feet for one minute – a big bonus for toileting. Three could pull themselves to a standing position with assistance. (Ask any therapist who's suffered backache why that one's important.) And five of our students could walk at least five feet, with only a walker or another person aiding them – a crucial skill for getting in and out of small places inaccessible to wheelchairs.

To someone who has never worked with children with severe disabilities, these improvements might seem miniscule. To us, however, they represented giant strides. And we weren't the only ones who thought so.

As the summer neared its end, a group of mothers got together (mothers have a way of ganging together to make things happen) and threw the parent-teacher barbecue at which both Dr. Kelly Blanton, our Superintendent of Schools, and I were thoroughly skewered:

How did you people choose the kids for that program...

My Bobby's always been so much better than Juan. How come he's not in...

My child deserves to be...

And after that was all over, Dr. Blanton wanted an explanation. And after *that*, he said, You've got to expand this.

We doubled the number of students in the program and brought a new teacher on board, Sheron Renfro. Each of us took on a classroom. We were team-teaching from the moment she joined us.

Despite the naysayers, we knew we were on to a winner; too many good things were happening for it to be otherwise. Dr. Blanton knew this too. Linda, he said, you've got to get your work on paper. It won't exist until it's on paper.

He also knew I'd never get any major writing done if I stayed at Blair. I had to get out of Kern County, away from the many commitments that would distract me. Moreover, he understood that I'd need financial backing. He put me on to Bakersfield Rotary West, the chapter to which I applied for a Rotary scholarship. They processed my application and sent me on to their higher-ups at San Luis Obispo.

As Dr. Blanton and his wife, Yvonne, drove me to my interview, they played hardball. Between them, they tried to think up every question the Rotarians might put to me. Together, we hashed out my answers. By the time I sat down in front of the panel of gray-haired men, I felt confident of what I was going to say. But I still knew I didn't have a chance. There were a zillion other people – people with bulging brains and staggeringly brilliant ideas – vying for the same handout I was after. I was nothing but a Kansas farm girl.

Buster Hopkins rescued me. I sat there and told those good people all about my work, but first I told them about Buster Hopkins and the frozen playground in Lowell, an ice age ago. They listened. I told them about the Coca-Cola bottle and said, That's what I'm asking for. Funds for more Coca-Cola bottles, for kids like

Buster. And later they called me and told me they were going to give me a grant.

They didn't know it then, but they were also going to send me to Australia.

It's the only place I'll be able to find the peace and quiet I'll need to write, I told Dr. Blanton. He looked at me knowingly, and smiled. (He'd seen *Crocodile Dundee*, too, I could tell.)

Tanya and I packed up our apartment and our suitcases. It was January 1987, and we were headed to Australia for one year. As our plane cleared the runway at Los Angeles International and began its climb, I looked down on the piers and parking lots and miles of coastline slipping beneath us and out of view. Ahead: open spaces and wide horizons; new worlds, as yet unexplored. I looked out of the window, and felt a chill run through me. I am so small, I thought. I turned away, reached over and put a hand on Tanya's knee. That made the scariness go away. I still felt small, but Tanya was with me. We were partners, and everything was going to work out.

Tanya was twelve when we left for Australia, and I was counting on her every step of the way. If I was going to make it, she'd have to be there for me. She was going to have to be responsible and accountable and all those other *ibles* and *ables* that teenagers love so very much.

The summer before, while I had been in the thick of the pilot program at Blair, Tanya had been enrolled in a special program of her own. I had used all my KCSOS brownie points to get her into an elite program at a local school. This was big guns — computers, science, and music — and everybody in Bakersfield wanted in on it. By rights, I shouldn't have been able to get Tanya in, but I sold my soul and wheedled...

Next thing I know, Tanya is on the phone with her cousin Minta, who now lives upstate in Cobb. Minta wants to visit us for part of the summer. Great idea, says Tanya. Oh, no, says I, that's not going to work. You've got summer school, and I've got to work. It's impossible. And Tanya, who now is wise enough to know when not to press an argument with Mom, says very little. She saves it for the principal of the summer school. I have my cousin coming down for the summer, she tells him, and she's an excellent musician. (I wasn't there; I only know what she confessed later, under torture.)

Tanya makes all the arrangements herself and gets Minta into summer school, into this elite program. I end up with both girls for the summer, and running a pilot program on the side.

When the summer school closes, it's time for us to take Minta home. She and Tanya have decided, however, that they're not interested in me driving them. They want to take Amtrak. And Mary, darn her, thinks, Why not? That's a pretty neat idea. So who was I to say no...

Tanya told me, weeks later, about the "fun" they had on that trip north – about making multiple trips for sodas, forcing passengers to sign autograph books, playing follow-the-leader with a carload of strangers; teasing a little old lady who couldn't find the button to open the sliding door between cars, and getting chewed out roundly in Chinese for giggling at her.

There would be no margin for error in Australia, I knew, no room for shenanigans. If we were going to make it, we were going to have to work together. That's what I told Tanya.

No worries, Mom.

Some nineteen hours after leaving the California coast, we eased out of the sky and down to Australia's eastern rim. Peter, our Australian Rotary sponsor, met us at the Sydney airport. He seemed like a nice-enough guy, even though he talked funny. Once we got our bags and loaded the trunk of his car (the boot, he called it), we headed into town. I went to get into the front passenger seat, and Peter chuckled. Care to drive? he asked. I walked around to the other side of the car and got in. As we joined the traffic, I was glad he was the one behind the wheel – not only were the cars' insides flip-flopped, but everyone was driving on the side of the road that gets you killed back home.

Peter got us safely to our destination – a furnished apartment close to Macquarie University and within walking distance of a shopping center. He handed me the keys. It's your flat, he said. Inside, we found a few groceries and everything we'd need to help us settle in to our new surroundings. The Rotarians wanted to be sure we felt welcome. This is only temporary, Peter cautioned. You'll be moving to another flat before long, but it's still being readied; some furnishings and things need sorting out. You're okay here for a while, but soon we're going to have to ask you to move into a dorm room over at the college for a couple weeks, until we can get you properly situated.

It all sounded fine to us. After all, this trip was supposed to be an adventure.

Tanya and I went out and bought a car. (One similarity between Australia and California we both noticed right away: Without a car, you're sunk.) I, of course, had no experience driving on the left. It was okay as long as we were going straight, but when it came time to make a turn, things got interesting. I flipped on the turn signals, and the wipers started grating across the windscreen. This led me to wonder: if I pull the wheel left, will the car move right? And by the time I convinced myself this was a falsehood, we were past our exit. (Tanya claims it took us twelve hours, at a minimum, to get anywhere in Australia because of my abhorrence of right-hand turns. I don't know; I concentrated on the roads, not my watch. I do know I delegated to her the responsibility of routing our trips in such at way that we eliminated all right-hand turns.)

But I hadn't exactly traveled halfway around the world to test my nerves on the tarmac. There was work to be done, work that was important not only to me, but to my students back home, and to hundreds and thousands of children like them.

With the university's blessing and the Rotary's money, I had come to Sydney to replicate the work I'd been doing in Bakersfield. We'd left the details until my arrival. Now it was time to tend to them.

Macquarie prides itself on being "Australia's Innovative University," and with good reason. At the campus on Balaclava Road, I met with Dr. Meredith Martin, who was in charge of the university's special education research program. She in turn introduced me to their top-flight group of researchers, who welcomed me as one of their own.

I enlisted these elite researchers to help recreate the pilot program we had run in Bakersfield during the summer of 1986. We discussed a variety of ways to conduct my desired research, and finally agreed on some basic methods. We needed some minimal equipment to replicate our program, so we found a man with a machine shop who was willing to work with us. The children who would take part in this re-creation were all residents of what the Aussies called a local hospital. With its wards and on-site school, I (an American) thought of the place as a small institution.

Setting up the project absorbed several months, and I was beginning to worry we wouldn't have enough time left to run the research. But the Australians proved every bit as wonderful in real life as in the movies. They assigned Chris Binns, a New South Wales physiotherapist, to the project, and somehow we managed to get everything rolling. All the while, I heard Dr. Blanton's voice in the back of my head: If it's not on paper, it doesn't exist. And I desperately wanted it to exist.

Tanya, meanwhile, went to school. She wasn't nearly as optimistic about attending school so far from home as I was for her. We had brought her school books and some class assignments along, and I

was prepared to make time each day to home-school my daughter —
if I had to. But my first choice was to immerse her fully in Australian life. Fortunately she complied with my wishes, though with a
grim face. Tanya became a student at Cheltenham Girls School,
which (if its mission statement is to be believed) has since its incep-
tion in 1961 been an institution "committed to providing a variety of
quality learning experiences in a caring, cooperative, and challenging environment."

The environment certainly was nothing to gripe about — Cheltenham is known for the beauty of its campus — and the school was unquestionably challenging. It was over the "caring, cooperative" part
that things got a little fuzzy, at least at the outset. Tanya soon discovered that her new classmates came with a built-in love or loathing of
all things American. By virtue of her natal land she was received
either as a friend for life or, by the same measure, marked for ridicule.
The line ran cleanly down the middle of the student body, like the cut
of a surgeon's knife.

This did have one advantage: it was clear to Tanya early on who
her friends were, and who she could count on to help her untangle
the complexities of year-round school and a seven-day rotating
schedule. But even their enthusiastic warmth could not quash
Tanya's disgust over having to trade jeans and T's for a school uniform. Hideous, was the nicest thing she could bring herself to say
about it. Nor was the ban on makeup and jewelry to her liking.
Prudes, she decided.

But she adapted, and thrived. Loved it, in fact. The short classes
and diverse academic studies, the frequent field trips and numerous
holidays all added up to a school year she would later look back on
as one of her best, ever.

Neither of us spent more time than we had to indoors. We did the
things we needed to do, and then escaped. We were in *Australia*. Our
official flat, when we finally got to it, was located on the northern
edge of Sydney, in North Ryde, a community where houses thinned

out and the bush began. We had only to walk a few steps from our door to put the city behind us. Wildlife, though, didn't mind coming to us, at least not after the birdman who lived one floor down from us taught us a few tricks. Scrap meat from the local butcher's lured kookaburras out of nearby eucalyptus trees and brought them in quantity to our balcony. Other birds too – great, shining cockatoos that screeched their demands, and iridescent lorikeets that grew tame enough to land on Tanya's shoulders.

When Tanya fed the birds, her gaze often wandered from the balcony out over the neighboring fields, to where horses grazed in their paddocks. She held off until we were settled in, then asked me if she could take up riding lessons at the nearest stable.

The owner, after she'd agreed to let Tanya ride, had a surprise coming. At Tanya's first lesson the trainer led a gelding into the paddock. Ever ridden before? she asked Tanya. Yes, she answered. Brilliant, the trainer said. Tanya spent her entire first lesson trotting in a circle, attached to a lunge line... By the time we returned to California, she was training the farm's horses.

Six months into our stay both Tanya and I felt the sharp tugs of homesickness for the first time. It wasn't that we weren't enjoying ourselves; we were, but neither of us had seen, on leaving California, that fine strings remained attached to us, like the strings on marionettes. Luckily, just when the tugging began to intensify, Jim and LaVaun Rogers called from Bakersfield to say they were leaving their ranch and coming for a three-week visit.

Those three weeks were like, well, being back home. Jim and Tanya spent hours riding together, and trekking from one tack shop to another. They bought Driza-Bone oilskin riding jackets (but steered clear of Akubra hats – Tanya was cutting down on that look), and an Australian stock saddle to take home for Lucky.

Jim, predictably enough, was a huge fan of *The Man from Snowy River*. It was midsummer, winter in the southern hemisphere, and Jim roped me into driving all of us south and inland, into the mountains. Into snow country. By now I was accustomed to driving on the wrong side of the road, but the thought of having a furry roo splat on my windscreen made me nervous. In Sydney proper, kangaroos are not a problem, but away from the densely populated areas, they own the road. I put my passengers on roo patrol and admonished anyone who seemed to be enjoying scenery too far from the road edge. We did not make it to Merrijig, Victoria, where *Snowy River* was filmed, but we came close enough, even for Jim.

The good times weren't restricted to the out-of-doors, or the outback, nor to the laughs we shared with our friends from home. In fact, the best part of that year was the sharing of information between two continents a world apart. Until I went to Australia, I hadn't realized how naïve I was. I had assumed special educators were doing the same things the world over. Although the information highway was yet to be paved, the trails had been blazed and research was available to anyone with the desire to dig it out.

What I didn't know was that differences of culture, lifestyles, and even transportation modes could render a program ineffective, even if it worked flawlessly in my hometown. In Bakersfield, for example, we had made concentrated efforts to teach children to stand while having their diapers changed. This was because our children quickly grew too large for the change tables in public restrooms, and once they did, there was no place to change their diapers. As they grew older this problem cut their trips into town shorter and shorter, until finally no one took them anywhere. We knew that if our students could stand up, their diapers could be changed in a restroom stall, where privacy, sanitation, and dignity could be maintained. In the Sydney residential hospital, though, cloth nappies, not disposable diapers, were the norm. Taking off a nappy was no problem, but it took real skill to pin a clean one on and help the child balance at the same time. If the child lay down, it was a much easier operation; and at the hospital there were plenty of private places. So what had been a big deal for us in Bakersfield wasn't exactly the number-one priority here.

At home, we had put great energy into getting kids walking up and down bus steps because the children traveled to and from school each day on minibuses. We wanted them to leave their wheelchairs at home as soon as possible, which meant negotiating steps rather than using the wheelchair lift. The children I worked with in Sydney attended school on the hospital grounds. They didn't need to practice walking up and down steps nearly as much as they needed to learn other skills. What they did need were ways to interact with their peers. They needed to touch each other, to sit side by side, to play together, to socialize without adult intervention. They needed fun, leisure-time activities that didn't require one-on-one adult supervision. The hospital's educators and medical staff provided excellent care. It seemed to me that what these children needed most was self-initiated exploration, independent decision making, and, yes, permission to be naughty – to break the rules.

The one constant was the kids themselves. The children with special needs in Sydney were no different from my beloved children in Bakersfield. They even looked like them.

I was fortunate to have Robin Yates, a special educator working on her master's degree, as part of my research team. Robin was working with Dr. Martin on integrating the first children with severe disabilities into a public school in Sydney. After months of planning and preparation, three little boys, each about nine years old, were introduced to the campus of Orangewood School. These boys were residents of the hospital where we were conducting our research, and all three were part of our program.

The children already attending Orangewood didn't bat an eye when our boys with disabilities joined their ranks. Robin had spoken with the students beforehand and had done an excellent job of prepping them. We put reverse integration to work, inviting kids from other classes into the special education classroom for short periods. Our three then joined their peers for assemblies, and for "little lunch" (Australian for recess) and playground time after big lunch at noon. Even during the short time I was involved in this project, I witnessed the magic. The three boys in gait trainers moved their legs because they wanted to keep up with their friends. They held their heads up because they didn't want to miss anything. They bore weight on their feet during morning assembly because they wanted to stand like all the others.

Near the end of the year I had an opportunity to tour a large hospital north of Sydney, where several thousand adults with disabilities lived in wards on spacious, well-kept grounds. Unlike the small residential hospitals, this setup was more akin to our American concept of a full-scale institution. I visited a ward that housed men and women with severe, complex disabilities. As I entered a wing designed for about twenty people, I took in the pristine cleanliness of the building – shiny, antiseptic, perfectly ordered. It was midmorning. The residents had been dressed and fed. Most of them were in the day room, lying in a neat row of padded troughs by a sunny window. Their bodies were so twisted and deformed, not a single one of them could be placed in a chair. They could only be left lying in their troughs, where they could be occasionally rolled a little to the left or right to vary their position. I was shocked. I knew large institutions existed in the US, but I had never been inside one. To keep myself from overreacting, I began walking down the row of troughs, saying hello to each individual. I wanted to buy a few moments before I had to talk to the staff. *What do I have to offer them?* I thought in panic. *They don't even have chairs, much less equipment for teaching weight-bearing. And what could we do for*

these twisted bodies? How can I help the man in front of me, with
his large body, his legs splayed apart like a frog's, and feet no bigger
than a two-year-old's? Some of the residents smiled as I said hello.
Many didn't respond at all. But as I worked my way down the row, I
felt eyes piercing me. The lady in the shadows at the end of the row,
away from the window, had eyes that danced, eyes like Tommy
Henderson's. As I neared her, she started making happy, guttural
sounds. She was trying to tell me something. I talked to her for several minutes, knowing she understood every word that I said. She
was obviously intelligent, but her mind was trapped in a broken
body and relegated to a life where the highs were pureed foods,
baths, and an occasional visitor like me. In between was endless iso-
lation, loneliness, and never-ending boredom. I wanted to pick her
up and take her with me. I wanted her to live a real life. But of
course there was nothing I could do. I had to leave her body in the
shadows, though I took the memory of her eyes with me. Even now,
years later, whenever I think I am too tired to go on, the eyes of that
woman, whose name I never learned, remind me how different her
life might have been if someone had just made sure her body didn't
become her enemy.

I took many things away with me when Tanya and I boarded the
plane for home in December 1987. The most important things had
little to do with research techniques, and everything to do with real
life. The children I worked with in Australia were just as capable of
learning as our California children. They exhibited as much potential as my Bakersfield students had shown in the early stages of our
program development. But at Orangewood School, the three boys
proved to me just how important it is to have an activity-based curriculum. Learning is not just about practicing skills. Children with
disabilities learn to sit, stand, and walk for the same reason as other
children – because they want to *do* something. The integration experiment at Orangewood also convinced me that peers often make
the best teachers. And those who might be considered behavior

problems sometimes show more patience and dedication in helping children with severe disabilities than their more orderly peers.

I had arrived in Sydney toting a bagful of unrealistic dreams about what I intended to do with my year abroad. I thought I would simply replicate our little pilot project and return home with concrete data to support the concepts we'd already worked out. I would gather research to back the basic theoretical premises of our program. And then I would be done. Little did I know how much the Australian people would teach me, or what an influence my experiences in Sydney would have on the future of our developing program.

My year in Australia solidified my belief that we would not get very far in special education if we did not work as a cohesive team. A team that included parents, educators, medical personnel, equipment manufacturers, and, perhaps most important of all, friends who might have no reason to be involved other than that they cared. Something Dr. Blanton had said to me before I left Bakersfield played over and over in my mind like a refrain during that year: If you serve the children in your classroom, then you will serve the families of those children. And if you serve families, you will serve your community, then your state, and then your country. In this way you will eventually serve the whole world. But it all begins by serving the children in your classroom. These wise words were only just beginning to take on real meaning as our plane taxied to the runway, headed into the sunrise.

We were home for Christmas. After the blazing heat of New South Wales, California in December felt Siberian. But there was plenty of warmth at Jim and LaVaun's, who welcomed us home as family, and as neighbors. In our absence, Jim had bought the house adjacent to his ranch, so that we'd be able to move into it on our return and live right there on the ranch along with them. He made the nicest landlord ever.

He had a present for Tanya lined up, too: a place in the Rose Parade, courtesy of the Exchange Club, which was sponsoring the state's top youth riders to represent their organization on New Year's Day. They're making an exception, Jim announced proudly. Usually riders under sixteen have to be accompanied by adult riders, but not this time. Nothing like getting literally right back in the saddle, I thought. We celebrated the first day of 1988 in Pasadena, amid a wash of color and light and music. And horsehair.

The holidays were over. Big time. Back at the Blair Learning Center, our principal, Dick Towse, had relieved me of my duties as a full-time classroom teacher. Now I was a mentor/teacher, whose priority was to write a curriculum. Or else. Dr. Blanton welcomed me home with a reminder that nothing exists unless it's written down. I want that book in this hand, he said, holding out his right. I want to see it finished.

Writing it shouldn't be such a big deal, I told myself. After all, the tough part was figuring out what works and what doesn't... But I learned soon enough just how hard it would be to say it in words that others could understand.

The starting point for the curriculum, and one of its key components, would be the top-down test, used to assess a student's skills. The results of this test showed us where we needed to concentrate our efforts for that child. Actually, it wasn't just one test. It was a series of sixteen tests, each of which concentrated on a particular mobility skill.

Top-down motor milestone tests, I called them. The thinking behind them went back to the first conversations I'd had with parents, to find out what skills our students were missing. Eating, bathing, dressing, getting in and out of cars – these and other daily activities, I had discovered, all required distinct mobility skills. This led me to analyze activity after activity during our first summer pilot program. I took my findings to Sydney, where I drew on them as I drafted the top-down tests that established the "milestones" on our students' journeys toward mobility.

Now, as I began my first draft of a curriculum that would enable other people to replicate our work, the sixteen skill categories became the first topic I committed to paper:

a. maintains a sitting position
b. moves while sitting
c. stands
d. makes transition from sitting to standing
e. makes transition from standing to sitting
f. pivots while standing
g. walks forward
h. makes transition from standing to walking
i. makes transition from walking to standing
j. walks backward
k. turns while walking
l. walks up steps
m. walks down steps
n. walks on uneven ground
o. walks up slopes
p. walks down slopes

These are the building blocks that allow people to move independently, I thought as I scanned down the list I had typed. For most of us, moving is automatic. When did I last stop to think, *Gee, Linda, you're walking on uneven ground!* or, *Don't look now, but you're climbing a flight of stairs.* No one on earth does that – unless, of course, they've never been able to do these things.

As I wrote, I kept pulling things apart, in search of their key components. I tried to think of it as block play, not atomic science. If you can show someone the pieces to use, they can build a tower that looks like the one in your corner of the universe; and maybe, if everyone builds a tower...

I started with the hardest skills in each category. Take the category *sitting*, for example. The hardest skill for most people is sitting on a flat surface such as a mattress, bathtub, or the floor, because there is nothing to lean against and legs can only be used minimally for balance. The next hardest skill is sitting on the edge of a bed or on a backless stool. Next comes sitting on a chair. I divided *sitting* into seven measurable, sensible levels of achievement. The minimum achievement: *Tolerates being placed in a sitting position...* That, I decided after reviewing my notes and our studies, covers the scope of sitting.

The good thing about working two days a week on the curriculum was that I could spend the other three days with Sheron Renfro, my co-teacher, testing in the classroom the things I was drafting at home on my computer. It sped up the writing process a lot, and helped keep me on task.

As I defined the skills that needed to be tested, I realized I also had to define the parameters. If I wanted people to learn motor skills so they could participate in life activities, I had to decide how long they needed to be able to sit or stand, how far they needed to walk.

I realized, too, that testing was only the beginning. We could use it to establish the point at which a student was entering the program and to determine a child's weakest skill areas. But it did not tell us what to teach. Using the old, conventional method for selecting skills to be taught, teachers would look at a student's test results and start with the earliest skill missed. But I wasn't going to do it that way. I wanted to teach the skills a student needed right now – *today* – for the purpose of *doing* something.

But what? What activity mattered most?

That, again, was a question best answered by parents and students themselves. I thought about these parents, and the obstacles they faced whenever they dared look up long enough to consider their children's futures. I could not know their private pain. Or could I? I knew what a broken heart felt like; I was a mother, and I had been a wife, once. I thought about those black days when my marriage was falling apart, when storms had threatened to ruin me and great waves of confusion had tried to drag me down with their riptide strength; and how, when the winds had whipped themselves out, I had emerged reborn. The thing that had saved me then, I realized, had been having a goal – and focusing on positive ways to move toward it, by building on the things I already had going for me, rather than tormenting myself over my shortcomings. It's always come down to that. If you can't see your way ahead, you're not going to get out of the dark.

The cursor on my Mac's green screen blinked, like a one-eyed cat, waiting. I began to type again. *Step One: Testing.* I had been working on that one for years and felt confident in the validity of it, but so what? If nothing changed after the test, why bother to test?

I keyed in *Step Two,* and stared. Success, I thought, can't exist unless it's defined. *Set goals.* I typed in the two-word command. Yes, and the most important goals are the ones in the heart of the student. The staff should be able to give input and advice, but this life – the future of this life – ultimately belongs to this child, this family. Elisha, for example. Elisha's grandmother would love to take her to family functions. My job is to ask, Why is this hard to do right now? Because I can't get Elisha in and out of the car by myself, her grandmother says. So in step two we define the activity, and set the goal: getting in and out of the car.

The sequence fell into place now; it was all coming together for me. *Step Three: Task-Analyze.* In other words, ask why these activities are hard to do today. When we task-analyzed the skills needed to get in and out of a car and compared these to Elisha's top-down test, we saw that Elisha could help raise herself to standing from her wheelchair but could not lower herself safely to sitting on the car seat. So we circled the "missing" skill – the goal skill – on the top-down test, skill E.4: *Can use legs to lower self to a chair when both hands are held by another person.*

Wow! With the leadership of her grandmother, we had just selected one of the most important skills for Elisha to master. It had
only taken us three steps. But before we could implement change,
we had to solidify our team. Everyone who touched Elisha needed
to know what to do and how to do it. If she was going to reach her
goal, she needed to practice lowering herself to a sitting position
every chance she could get.

Step Four: Measuring Prompts. Elisha needed help to start lowering herself to sitting. Otherwise, she would just plop down without
any control and risk hurting herself. But how much help did she
need? I needed to devise systematic methods for helping people, and
I needed to find a way of measuring the help – the physical
prompts – we offered. This would make us accountable, I thought,
as I tentatively task-analyzed the procedures. I rated the prompts
numerically so we would have a way to crunch numbers when all
was said and done.

Step Five: Reducing Prompts. Now we needed to decide, as a
team, how we would reduce the help as Elisha grew stronger. If we
didn't develop a logical system for taking the help away, Elisha
might spend the rest of her life depending on the help we were giving her now, even if she was capable of doing far more.

Step Six: Teaching the Skills. None of the previous steps meant
anything unless we concentrated on this last step. Step six was the
professional goal. Now we had to decide who was going to be responsible for helping the student practice the skills all through the
day. Since any number of people would be involved, it meant sharing information and making sure each person knew what to do and
how to do it.

For weeks, then months, I played with my blocks, picking up each
one and examining every edge and plane before setting it in place. I
had to make sure I got everything in order and didn't leave any pieces
out. The trials Sheron and I ran at school every step of the way helped
to keep us from barking up wrong trees, and to troubleshoot when we
did. Once I felt certain we were on the right track, I wrote it down.

Don't just sit there, do something... Sheron Renfro helps students bake a cake – and practice sitting skills.

In the back of my mind, always, were the faces of my children and their parents. I dreamed of the day I'd be able to look these parents in the eye and ask, When you think about your child, what goes right through you? What breaks your heart? That, I knew, was the forbidden question, the one nobody dared ask. People who work all day with children with disabilities (and attend their funerals when "their time comes") have plenty of shards in their own hearts; they're not looking for more. Especially since there's nothing they can do – or so they think – to change anything. But I was beginning to realize that there *was* something we could do – and plenty of things we could change. So why not ask that question, and do something about the answer?

When there are no more broken hearts and our children are all marching along merrily, I told myself, we can muster whatever resources we need to go back to step one and set our sights on a new goal for each of them.

And then repeat everything two thousand times until that goal is a reality. Because none of this is easy. It doesn't happen by magic. It's not as if one day little Sammy is lying in fetal position in a beanbag and the next he's hightailing it around the room on his own two feet. It takes time, time, time – and practice – to etch into his mind and muscles the patterns of movement.

At the same time as I was writing the curriculum, I was also making more junky equipment. We now had enough mobile standers and gait trainers for our students to practice unassisted standing and walking, but sitting still required one-on-one assistance. Our children who lacked head control were making the least progress. Over the years I had tried every gimmick I could think of to get children to lift their heads and hold them in midline. The only thing that worked was forearm holders, or prompts, as I termed them. I made these arm prompts out of three-inch diameter PVC pipe sliced down the middle, and stabilized them using half-inch pipe. With something solid to push their forearms against, the children could raise their heads from their chests. As they gained strength, they started to develop trunk control. Then independent sitting skills emerged.

It was through this PVC arm prompt rigmarole that I first met a lady who would make a tremendous difference in my life. Jo Meyer was teaching infants with disabilities on another Kern County campus. She wanted to learn to make pipe chairs, so we spent a few weekends together. During our sessions Jo began talking about writing software for children with disabilities. She and a friend had just started their own company, she said. My eyes lit up, my mouth opened. And then neither one of us could talk fast enough. Here was a chance to make the missing connection between motor skills and communication. I remembered my early attempts at teaching symbolic language. Teach me to program, I pleaded with Jo. Neither one of us needed more to do, but once we'd started dreaming, there was no looking back. Jo and I founded SoftTouch, a software design and production company, and vowed we would never lose sight of the population we wanted to serve.

The summer before Tanya and I traveled to Australia, a cameraman had come to Blair to video our pilot program (I took the tape with me to Australia, as visual proof). At the end of the shoot, Kyle, the cameraman, who was obviously taken with what was going on in our classrooms, looked at the kids in their standers and gait trainers and front-leaning chairs that Dean had welded for us. If you ever want to talk about doing something with this equipment, give me a call, he said. I know people at Rifton. Right, name-dropper, I said to myself, and to Kyle a vague *Sure, okay.* A Bakersfield videographer couldn't seriously have connections with one of the most respected manufacturers of equipment for children with disabilities. I went to

Australia, and came back to write. But one day in late August, in walks Kyle again. Hi, Linda, he says. Hear you've been to Australia, doing good things. You ready to meet people from Rifton yet?

The "people from Rifton" were coming, ready or not, because Kyle had brought them with him. (Like he'd said, he really did have friends.) Whoa! I thought, and braced myself. But Patty and Susan, the two women from Rifton's New York headquarters whom Kyle introduced to me that day, were warmhearted and encouraging as they listened to me explain the rationale behind our work, and openly enthusiastic about our students and their development.

They were the first. Others from Rifton soon flew to Bakersfield on the strength of Patty and Susan's report. As I sat down to review for them our program and the role of equipment in it, I thought how unappealing my explanations must sound. Essentially I was telling a manufacturer: We're an education-based program, not a medical-, therapy-, or equipment-based program. I need equipment that can be dismantled a piece at a time until it's no longer needed. I want you to make equipment that will eventually be of no value to its user. And I want you to tell other people that the best thing they can do is eventually get rid of this equipment... They listened, and looked. They understood what we were trying to do and endorsed our efforts — it was, they explained, the reason they were in the business to begin with. There were details to work out, but I had found my first manufacturer, Rifton Equipment, and moved another huge step closer to taking our message to the streets.

My curriculum was still far from being complete. I spent a couple days each week at home, writing at the computer. The rest of the time I worked with Sheron to test every aspect of the program in the classroom. Nothing came easily, but we stuck at it, and the stack of rough drafts on my desk kept mounting.

By the following summer, though, I was ready for a break. Tanya and I decided to go to Kansas for our vacation. It had been a while since we'd seen my parents, and they were always happy to have us visit. We left Bakersfield on August 7, 1988.

The next morning a close friend called to say Jim had died in the night. LaVaun had tried to wake him, and that's when she'd found out. I had to tell Tanya. We were both devastated. We'd known Jim was sick (heart problems, and the first stages of emphysema, had put him in the hospital for a few days in July), but even LaVaun hadn't known he was in such poor condition. Now his heart had stopped, and LaVaun's was shattered. Jim was fifty-five years old.

We closed our suitcases (we hadn't even unpacked yet) and got back on a plane to Bakersfield, going home to bury Jim and stand by LaVaun. Jim had always kidded that he wanted to die one of two ways: either in his sleep, or being chased by an angry husband. His wish, such as it was, had been rewarded, at the expense of the rest of us.

Linda, can you come to the phone? It's someone from Sacramento on the line.

Who do I know in the capital? I wonder as I head for the staff room phone. Turns out, it's someone who knows me. Kern County Superintendent of Schools hasn't exactly kept mum about our little project, and word has reached the organizers of California's annual Special Education Fall Conference. We've heard all about your work, the person on the phone tells me, and would love for you to come and present a seminar in October. I manage a *Well, sure, of course* and scratch down a few notes – date, time, contact – before I hang up.

I am flabbergasted, and my higher-ups are thrilled too. We've been craving this kind of exposure, and now it's being handed to us.

This isn't even my idea; they're *asking* me to do this. I set to work outlining my presentation. Our KCSOS artist collaborates with me and draws beautiful posters and transparencies, which I'll project onto a screen, and I'll stand there with a long pointy stick and show everyone how it all works and how they can make it work for their students and then we'll all work together so that no one is left behi –

I am dressing you. Tanya is insistent. The jeans, sneakers, and shirts I wear to school each day (and knock about the house in afterward) are, by her standards, yucky. We go shopping for an outfit. She picks out shoes. I'm not spending that much for footwear, I protest. This time, Mom, you are.

Sacramento. The conference center hums with indoor-voiced teachers and administrators from the length of the state. I am ushered to my seminar room, shown how to operate the overhead projector, how to dim the lights, and left to set up my presentation. My nerves are jangled. Breathe, Linda. Breathe. The thought of what I'm about to say to all these people only increases my nervousness, so I try not to think as I place my posters on the easel behind the podium. The word MOVE is stenciled in block letters across the top of each poster. It represents hours of brain-racking. I had wanted our program to have a name, something that would stick in the minds of the people who came to my seminar. Coming up with MOVE had been the easy part; getting the letters (especially the "V") to stand for something meaningful had been harder. In the end, I'd lock in on Mobility Opportunities Via Education. I say it to myself approvingly as I prop up the last poster. It's a good name.

Everything is ready. I sit down to wait for the seats to begin filling.

They don't. No one shows up. I check my schedule, to see if I'm mistaken about the time of my presentation. I am not. Where *is* everyone? The only other people in the room are our people, from Bakersfield. Oh, and three ladies who've wandered in and seem to think they're in the wrong room. Three people have showed up for my seminar. Only three people in the entire state of California care about what we're doing to help children with the most severe, multiple disabilities. *Three!* I am beyond mad. I am losing it. Be careful, Linda, I tell myself. I turn toward my posters, so that no one will see my face. There is that four-letter word: MOVE. Hell, I decide, if these three ladies have bought the ticket, they're going for the ride. I turn to face them, to begin.

I talk to those three as though they are three hundred. I hold nothing back. And they hold on to their seats and come along with me as I show them things they've never heard or dreamed of before. This is MOVE. This is what we do. This is how we do it. These are our children. They are why we do it.

When I am done, I am exhausted. There are questions, and I give answers. When they say thank you, I say you're welcome. Then we go home, all four of us, I back to Bakersfield, they to Los Angeles.

Driving south on the 5, the freeway that makes shortest work of the sweltering San Joaquin Valley, the car tires drone like funereal bagpipes. My discouragement is complete. Nobody cares. Nobody else cares. All our work, all our achievements – and nobody cares. Nobody cares about my kids, or about their progress. It's all ho-hum: so what if they learn a bit, so what if they can do things they've never done before...

By the time I've reached the oil fields on the outskirts of town where dark steel grasshoppers keep up their incessant seesawing, I have resolved to forget the rest of the world, to focus on my job and do the best I can for Kern County, where I know people care. If the rest of the world wants to scratch kids like mine off the list – if nobody's going to listen and nobody's ever going to care – they can go ahead. I'll pretend *they* don't exist either.

A week later there are people on our doorstep. People from LA who want to know what the heck we are doing, because they've heard the three ladies who attended my seminar in Sacramento talk about a program that works miracles for children with all sorts of disabilities. They want to see it with their own eyes, because they're having a hard time believing everything they've heard. They want to see this program in action. This program called MOVE.

moving on

Things more or less erupted after that. Never mind that I had yet to finish drafting the curriculum — we had parents knocking down our doors. Parents who wanted their kids in on what we were doing, *now.* They came from LA, saw MOVE in action, and went home to badger their schools into getting on board. In due time, schools sent delegations to check us out, then called back to arrange in-services. A chain reaction had begun, and there was no way I or anyone else could do a thing about it — which was just how we liked it.

As it had always been since my very first experiences in special education, everything hinged on the parents.

Parents like Kim and John Leonetti, who heard about MOVE from their son's physical therapist and came to investigate. Three-year-old Nicholas suffered from a rare, undiagnosed metabolic disorder. Already, his mother told me, he had been hospitalized numerous times. More than once a priest had read him his last rites. And yet, here he was, with eyes that said he was very much alive. I was keen to see what he could achieve. He could roll over, Kim told me; that was the extent of his mobility skills. He could not speak, though he made sounds and responded when spoken to. I could tell at a glance that he was Kim's sweetheart – and that she would go to any lengths to try to help him.

What would happen if I placed him on that? I asked, pointing to a child-sized plastic chair. He'd fall on the floor, Kim said quickly. He doesn't sit. He doesn't have much sense of balance; his cerebellum is less than half the size it's supposed to be. He'll be okay, I assured her, and explained to Nicholas that I was going to help him sit on a chair. He gave me a look that said, Fine by me, so I placed him onto the chair and held my hands, palms open, a few inches to either side of him, to steady him if he tipped. Nicholas fought against gravity and his weak muscles to keep himself on that chair, and he managed. For several seconds. His parents were speechless, even more so when I told them that I thought with two weeks' work Nicholas would be sitting on his own for half an hour at a stretch.

Two weeks later, Kim and Nicholas were living in a rented apartment a few blocks from Blair, where he was enrolled as a student in the MOVE program. John's work kept him in LA, and for ten long months the Leonettis put their family life on the back burner so that Nicholas would get his chance. He rewarded his parents' sacrifices with hard work and wonderful results. By the time he turned four, his parents were forced to baby-proof their home for the first time in their lives – and they couldn't have been more pleased. It was sheer bliss for them to watch their son wheel himself in his mobile stander across the living room carpet to the TV and swipe a stack of video cassettes onto the floor.

By the time he left us in early February 1991 to return to Los Angeles, where the MOVE program was now being implemented at the Sven Lokrantz School by a dedicated teacher named Lori Adams, Nicholas had not only mastered the ability to sit, but could also walk – and run – with the help of a gait trainer.

Nicholas was one of our ambassadors. While he was still with us news of his progress spread among those who knew him. Diane, a friend of Kim's, brought her five-year-old son, Andrew, who had

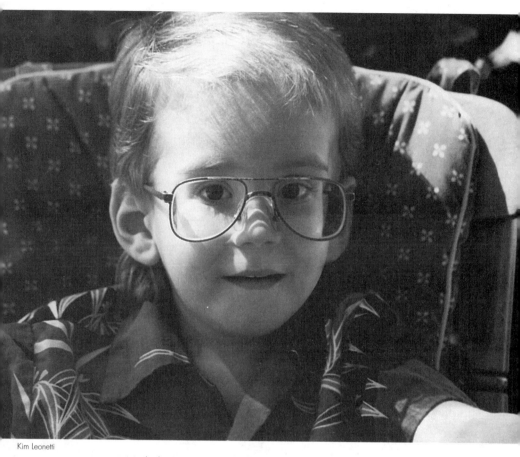

Kim Leonetti

Nicholas Leonetti, MOVE's first poster boy.

CP, to Bakersfield. They stayed for the summer. Soon other parents of children with disabilities were coming to check in on students like Nicholas and Andrew, and to learn what MOVE could do for them. Without any planning on our part, MOVE was taking on a life of its own and gathering momentum, thanks to parents who caught the vision.

It was, Kim later told me, a moral obligation. She and Diane got to talking, and they decided they couldn't just let their boys learn to move and then return home, not without a commitment to passing on the message – and the hope – of MOVE. On the strength of that conviction the two of them founded Friends of MOVE. Their mission: propaganda. They begged friends to give them the names of every physician and therapist they knew, compiled a mailing list, and pumped out a newsletter. They worked hard; it was grassroots and grass stains all the way.

In Bakersfield, we noticed the effects of their efforts, and those of numerous other parents like them – so much so that I had to call Friends of MOVE and suggest, tactfully, that they slow down just a little. There was, after all, a limit to what we could handle – and we were already way over the limit. We had people coming to us from all over California, and from out of state. Our phones rang constantly, with people wanting information, wanting to visit, wanting to know when they could bring their kid to us. There came a day when Dr. Blanton, whose wisdom I have never questioned, pulled me aside and said, Linda, it was never our intention that we become the cerebral palsy capital of the world. What we really need is for you to train other people to run MOVE in their own neighborhoods. The whole world doesn't need to relocate to Bakersfield. And I told him I couldn't agree more; the last thing I wanted to do was to separate families or make hardships for them – MOVE was supposed to be about helping people.

At the behest of several schools in Los Angeles and Tulare counties, I conducted full-scale in-services during the summer of 1990.

The program ran for a few weeks, and when it was over the teachers we had trained went back to their schools. They were among the first to pioneer MOVE outside of Bakersfield.

My curriculum was still not complete. I gave those who came to my in-services copies of the motor-milestone tests and other key program components. This meant many follow-up phone calls to answer numerous questions, but it was the best I could do. The curriculum – the manual that would explain the "how to" and the "why" of MOVE – was still in byte-sized pieces, stored in disc holders on my desk at home. Dr. Blanton kept the screws to me, though. *Nothing exists unless it's on paper.*

Finally, in late 1990, I handed over the last pages and discs of my manuscript to Jim Varley, who, as KCSOS's publicity coordinator, was my editor and project manager. Never mind my sweaty palms – the MOVE curriculum was on its way to a date with a printing press.

Just how badly we needed that finished book was made abundantly clear to me early the next spring, while the curriculum was still at the printer's. Word of MOVE had by this time spread throughout southern California. Now several coastal school districts had banded together and requested a four-day in-service for about fifty people. I didn't relish the idea of four exhausting days in a row (I didn't consider myself a public speaker), but I thought about the children and decided I would just have to brave it out.

The first day was a nightmare. Half of the people in the audience – the back half – sat with their arms folded and either glared at me while I spoke or ignored me and chatted among themselves. The more I said, the madder they got. I told them how hard we had worked in the past and how miserably we had failed. They snickered. Crossed and re-crossed their legs. I told them about my research and how we had spent our time doing exercises that led nowhere. They force-yawned, got up to refill their coffee cups.

The other half of the audience was transfixed. They nodded, leaned forward in their chairs to hear past the chattering in the back rows, and laughed at the jokes I told on myself. They had experienced the same things in their classrooms, so they stayed and listened.

Another thing: the wet hen group had to go to the bathroom an awful lot – in groups of two or three. To gossip, I wondered? Many of them were therapists, though some were educators as well. From what I could gather, the therapists were angry that a mere teacher was treading on their sacred ground. I spent a lot of energy assuring them that the therapist's role was so important, we needed to make therapy a way of life, not just a short session once or twice a week. Some of the educators were mad because they saw the program as extra work. They had enough to do already, thank you very much. I gently suggested they might want to drop anything unnecessary from the daily routine, so their students would have time to practice motor skills throughout the activities of daily living.

Near the end of the first day I really considered walking out. Let them fend for themselves. But Daddy and Mama had taught me important lessons about responsibility and finishing what you start.

The people in the back had appointed ringleaders. Each time I invited questions, these leaders threw questions at me that were obviously designed to cut me down to size. I answered them as honestly as I could. If I didn't have an answer, I said so.

As we wrapped up for the day, I outlined the next morning's schedule. At the back of the room rolling eyes accompanied barely suppressed sighs.

When I saw those eyes start to roll, I felt my blood boil. This wasn't about me and it wasn't about them. It was about children who didn't have choices. I tried to control my voice as I heard myself say: This in-service is supposed to meet your needs, but I don't know what frustrates and worries you. So before you leave I want you to take a sheet of paper and write down every question or comment you have so far. Please be candid and do not sign it. I want to share whatever information I might have that is important to you.

Paper was ripped from notebooks and heads lowered in concentration. The mad group scribbled furiously.

I collected some fifty sheets and took them back to my motel. I worked deep into the night, sorting and making lists. The next morning I announced that we were changing the schedule. I was going to interrupt the in-service to answer every question and reply to every comment the group had submitted. It took most of the day. Often I paused to request suggestions from the audience. *Yes, we have the same problems. This is what we are doing, but it's not the perfect solution. What do you do?*

By the end of four days the anger was gone and the group was enthusiastic. They could see how MOVE could – and would – make a difference. They gave me a standing ovation when I ended the fourth day.

But I was bruised and scarred. I left feeling drained and battle weary. As I worked my way north through the LA freeway system, and up toward the mountains, my throat started to hurt. My head felt hot, my chest was a vise, and I knew I was getting sick.

If I ever have to do this again it will kill me, I thought. So…I just won't do it again. It's over. Let other people carry the banner. I'm just not strong enough to do this.

This self-deprecating litany accompanied me all the way home and stayed in bed with me for several days as I recuperated from one of the nastiest bouts of flu I've ever had.

On my return to work, Beverly Burright, our administrative secretary (she had volunteered to help with MOVE, on top of her many other duties), greeted me with a cheery voice. We have people calling from all over the place wanting in-services, Linda. I'm so proud to be part of this, she said. I looked into her beaming eyes and reminded myself, This isn't about you, Linda. This is about the children.

Later that spring I was slated to go to Atlanta for an in-service (we were making inroads all across the country now). Jim Varley showed up to give me a lift to the airport. He held in his hand a copy of the curriculum, spiral-bound and smelling of fresh ink. Something for you to read on the plane, he said. But I was already flying, soaring with the knowledge that now, finally, we existed. MOVE really, truly existed.

The people at Rifton had never doubted that for a minute. When they committed to manufacturing equipment for MOVE, they committed because they understood the philosophy on which the program is built. They, too, believed in MOVE's ability to improve the quality of life for children with severe disabilities – and not just within the United States either. Fast on the heels of my trip to Atlanta, I conducted an in-service for a school in Midland, Texas. Rifton had sent representatives from England, where their European branch is based, to sit in on the training. And, as it turned out, to present an idea to me.

We want you to come to bring MOVE to England, they said. What would you think if we lined up some events for you?

I was so shocked, I didn't know what I thought. *England*. It was mind-boggling enough for me to be in Texas and to realize MOVE was spreading like wildfire across the continent. All of it was way beyond anything I'd allowed myself to dream of. I'd wanted to do something to help my kids, to make their lives easier and more enjoyable. I had not set out on an international crusade. But England, I could do that. I had always wanted to go to England.

I would love to come, I said.

As it turned out, that was only the first of many visits. The staff of the British schools where I presented in-services organized by Rifton received my ideas with open minds. As elsewhere, of course, there were those who had little use for what I had to tell them, and got quite flustered by it. Such encounters, however, were more than made up for by people like Jenny French, who had spent many dedicated years as a physiotherapist and administrator working with people with severe disabilities, yet was willing to reexamine all she had learned. She wholeheartedly embraced MOVE. Jenny became an outspoken advocate for MOVE in England, and worked together with Rifton to line up appointments for me throughout the country.

It came as no surprise, then, that before long Rifton asked me to cross the English Channel and promote MOVE on the Continent. Requests for in-services were coming from schools in the Netherlands, Germany, France, Spain, and Austria – and that was just the beginning.

Much as it thrilled me to see MOVE accepted and understood by so many people in so many places, I couldn't ignore the fact that I was only one person, trying to manage more than I could handle. If Mama Jo had been with me on my trips to Europe, she would have lectured me about making space and doing things right. But Mama Jo was a million miles away, in a different world, and though I was surrounded by newfound friends who enveloped me with support and enthusiasm, at times I felt overwhelmed, and alone. I missed Tanya. I missed being her mommy. I got tired of staying in Dutch hotels, French pensions, British bed-and-breakfasts. Eventually, I just got tired. In 1994, midway through one whirlwind seven-country tour of European schools, my back decided it was time to go home. My sciatic nerve had a breakdown. Bye-bye Europe.

I was home, and out of commission. Rifton sent people from New York to talk with Dr. Blanton, to discuss how best to proceed. It was obvious to everyone that things couldn't continue at the pace they were going; they could see it was killing me, which had no benefits for any of us. The upshot of it all was the founding of MOVE International, a not-for-profit organization that would shoulder the task of training more professionals and raising funds to sustain continued research. Dr. Larry Reider, the assistant superintendent to Dr. Blanton, was appointed to chair the board of directors. (When Dr. Blanton retired several years later, Dr. Reider replaced him as Kern County's superintendent, but remained our faithful chairman.) MOVE International would put an end to the tag game. I wouldn't have to be the only "it" anymore; we could take turns.

Of course, we weren't alone in our desire to see MOVE succeed. As the program caught on across the country – in more schools than we could keep track of – teachers and therapists used their ingenuity and creative resources to make MOVE work for their particular situation and community. For example, Lori Adams, Nicholas Leonetti's teacher, ran the MOVE program for a school that served Los Angeles's ritzy Bel Air neighborhood. If Lori was sure of one thing it was that she had some pretty powerful parents sending their children to her classroom. She knew, too, that if the MOVE program was going to fly, she needed extra help, not only in the form of equipment, but in people – a therapist and classroom aides – as well. The school's special education budget could not be stretched far enough to provide for these needs. So Lori started talking.

That is how I found myself at a benefit dinner one summer evening at the private residence of Barry Levinson. *The* Barry Levinson, as in the director of *Good Morning, Vietnam* and *Rain Man*. Dustin Hoffman, Carol Burnett, Martin Mull, and a host of other glitterati joined us for dinner, with their check books open.

I came away feeling charmed, and blinking – I had never been so dazzled before. More important, Lori came away with enough loot to buy equipment for her students, and still have some left over to hire the school's first full-time therapist, Larry Sulham. Larry owed his salary to Barry.

Not everyone, though, has access to Barry Levinson's phone number, much less his Rolodex. An hour's drive (in cooperative traffic) away from Lori's classroom, another school's MOVE team was eager to get their show on the road, but were hitting similar snags. Mary Higgins, then the principal of El Camino, a special education school in Pomona, had seen MOVE in action in Bakersfield and very much wanted her students involved. She sent four of her staff to visit us and charged them with the task of bringing the MOVE program to Pomona – not an easy assignment, as they discovered. With classroom teachers already overtaxed, and in some cases cool to MOVE's newfangled approach, their most immediate lack was enough warm bodies to work one-on-one with the students. As the four put it to Mary, We've just got to get some more muscles in here.

Mary listened to what her MOVE team was saying, and puzzled over how best to help them. Every community, she knew, has its resources. Even Pomona, in east LA. Thinking it over, she hit on an idea. A crazy idea, but an idea nonetheless. Mary picked up the phone and called a friend of hers, Sue Thomsen, the principal of a juvenile detention system school.

After she and Sue made all the arrangements, Mary called me. Linda, she said, we have some teenage boys who are volunteering to help with our MOVE program. They're from Camp Afflerbaugh, and I'm wondering if you could come down to give them an in-service.

I'd be thrilled, I replied, imaging what a great camp Afflerbaugh must be. Boy Scouts, maybe?

On the appointed day I drove down to the eastern edge of Los Angeles and entered the parking lot of El Camino School as I had done many times before. Only this time there was a big gray bus hogging most of the parking spaces.

As I entered the school Mary Higgins greeted me. What's the deal with the bus? I asked. In answer, Mary cut her eyes to the wall behind me. I'd like you to meet the young men you'll be training today, she said.

I turned to find twelve teenage boys standing ramrod straight, backs to the wall, eyes forward. Death by firing squad, was my first thought. All had close-cropped hair, and wore blue T-shirts with camp logo and new blue jeans. A man obviously in charge of them stood off to their right.

The next thing I noticed was the gang tattoos on the necks and arms of several of the boys. Slowly the fog lifted and my neurons connected. We had Camp Owens in our county – a jail for naughty boys and girls. Camp Afflerbaugh must be the equivalent of Camp Owens. But I was in east LA, and these were no boys and girls. These guys must be straight from the gangs. Uh-oh.

I had seen television shows about gang members, but as far as I knew I had never touched one. Somehow I had assumed that our paths would never cross; we were, after all, different species. In an attempt to mask my prejudices, I stepped forward and stuck out a hand to the first young man in the lineup. Aren't you nice, Linda, I thought. Look, you're offering to touch a gang member. He'll be so flattered.

The young man hesitated, then extended his own right hand and grasped my finger tips for a quick, rubbery shake. He let go, looked down at his hand, and as if by instinct wiped it on his jeans, to clean it. Panic raced across his face when he realized what he'd done.

It raced across mine, too, when I realized I was going to have to spend an entire afternoon with these aliens and their keeper. But I continued down the row, shaking hand after hand, and as I did, my confidence grew. These young men were as ignorant about me as I was about them. Somehow, we would have to find a common language.

We started in a classroom set up for my lecture. I watched twelve sets of eyes glaze over as I explained the six steps of MOVE, and detailed the important roles that they, as the volunteers, would play. Every head was up, every face turned in my direction. But not one boy made eye contact with me. They all switched into zombie mode the minute my mouth opened. This isn't going to work, I thought.

I stopped my lecture. Come with me, I said. I led the boys to the gym and with the staff's help paired up each of them with an El

Camino student. We sat there on mats and talked about arms and legs and brains. We talked about tendons and contractures. I made the boys feel the tendons at the back of their own knees, then the students'. Which ones have tight tendons? I guided the boys hands as they examined knees. We were touching each other – and nobody was throwing up! I went on to explain how to put children in equipment, what to watch out for. I told them how vital they could be to the lives of these students and how dependent the children would be upon their knowledge. Twelve sets of focused eyes maintained contact with mine without flinching. Soon there were smiles on faces that before had registered little emotion – faces of students and camp inmates. The boys asked questions. We interacted. Communicated. These young children with severe disabilities were the links that brought our worlds together, and for the time we shared at least, we were all the same.

A few months later I drove down to Pomona for another visit. The boys from Camp Afflerbaugh had something special to show me. All the students and volunteers were at work in the gym when I showed up. Four of the camp boys were waiting impatiently for me. As soon as I entered the gym, they moved Carlos, a little five-year-old, to the center of the floor. Carlos's parents had been told that their son would never walk or talk, that he would never recognize them, that he would never recognize anything, for that matter. No one had said any of that to the four teenage boys, though. One of them squatted a few feet in front of Carlos. The other three positioned themselves to his right, left, and rear. They formed his safety net. The boy in back of Carlos lifted him to his feet and, as all four boys counted one, two, three – turned him loose. Carlos stood still for a moment. The boy in front of him held out his hands, grinned, and coaxed Carlos forward. Carlos grinned back, and took a tentative step. Then another. And another. Like a great crab, these boys from warring gangs worked as a team until they had walked Carlos across the entire length of the gym. Together, they had worked a miracle. They taught a little boy to walk. They changed a life.

I stood in awe. How could I ever have imagined these young men as aliens? They were just boys, teenagers, just human beings. Just like me.

Today, the boys from Camp Afflerbaugh are still coming to help out at El Camino. The faces change every few months, but the stories don't. The boys all have a tale to tell, if you get to know them and win their trust, that is. Tales of growing up in the *barrio,* or in the 'hood, of making "bad choices" and hanging with the "wrong crowd," of opting for the action of the streets over the mental strain of the classroom; of dropping out and falling down. Yet when they come to El Camino they discover a set of kids they never knew existed. Kids who, if they could, would tell of being left behind while others grow up, of lying in place while others run on ahead, of having decisions made for them while others choose for themselves; of dropping off, and falling away. The Camp Afflerbaugh boys see these kids, and respond. They form friendships, and work to help their friends succeed. They speak of pride in their work, of achievement and self-esteem, and of feeling good because they know they're doing something to help someone else. After their release the boys often come back to visit – to check on "their" students, and to make sure their Polaroid picture is still on the wall of graduates.

If MOVE has taught me nothing else, it's taught me that everyone has skills, and everyone, if allowed, has dreams. Had I never met the boys from Camp Afflerbaugh, I might have gone through my whole life thinking that gang members are hopeless cases and out of reach, just as the boys might have felt that way about themselves if they hadn't met up with the El Camino kids. Obviously it's not necessary to use incarcerated youth as instructional staff to make the MOVE program work, but El Camino proved that anyone can participate, with some information and training. MOVE is designed so that everyone who touches the life of a person with disabilities can play a role in helping that person become as independent as possible. Not every participant has to possess all the information or physical skills – it takes a team to MOVE.

Education is a lifelong endeavor, and it works best if it is individualized, has personal goals, and a well-defined map for measuring the milestones on the road to success. I wanted so much to apply the MOVE philosophy to the camp boys – *What do you have going for you? What do you wish you could do? What is stopping you? How much help would it take to get you started? How can we reduce that help as you become more independent? Let's make a timeline and measure your progress as you get stronger* – because these young men, like the children they work with, have unique personalities and dreams.

I firmly believe that the day we lose sight of the importance of every single child is the day we lose our right to work with children. It is the child who is all-important – not the revamping of systems; the shifting of mountains, or the leveling of playing fields. What good is MOVE if we use it to push aside a child's dream and, in its stead, impose our own so-called discernment? The business of MOVE is to discover the dream in each child, and to believe in it until it becomes reality. This is a truth I have carried with me since the days of MOVE's infancy, when Jack used a PC and a dot-matrix printer to make a banner, and hung it in my classroom: SOME THINGS HAVE TO BE BELIEVED TO BE SEEN.

Like the majority of the children we worked with, three-year-old Matthew suffered from disabilities that were nobody's fault. A twin, his birth had been traumatic, and he was left with spastic quadriplegia, cerebral palsy. His motor brain damage was severe, and we knew from the first time his mother, Donna, brought him to us that he probably would never be an independent walker. Of course, the idea that he'd ever walk at all, with or without assistance, seemed like a cruel joke to Donna.

She brought Matthew to Blair on the strength of newspaper clippings and pesterings she received from her mother, a Bakersfield resident. Donna and her husband lived down in Ventura County, but they decided it was worth one of them visiting our school, if only to placate their child's grandmother. Lorraine, Matthew's physical therapist, was along that day in February 1991 when Donna brought him to see us.

He was a bright child – one look into his eyes told me that. You're a smart kid, I said as I introduced myself to Matthew, and caught Donna looking at me. It was the look of a parent who has heard countless educators and professionals tell her, in a nice way, that her son will never amount to anything, that since he can't speak, he obviously can't think…

We got Matthew into a gait trainer. He's never really stood before, Donna said. They've told us not to let him stand or walk, because he can't –

She never finished her sentence, because right then and there Matthew took his first steps, without anyone holding him upright.

When it was time to go, Matthew did not want to be taken out of the gait trainer. And Donna didn't want to leave. By summer she and Matthew were back in town, living in the same apartment complex as Kim and Nicholas Leonetti (he was also one of Lorraine's clients) and Diane Simon, who had heard of MOVE from Kim and brought her son Andrew to Bakersfield to check it out. Dorothy Evans, another woman from the LA area, whose grandson Matt attended Blair, had rented rooms there too. The place became a regular MOVE hangout that summer.

In the classroom, we tested Matthew's skills and began the task of teaching him to sit, stand, and walk. Matthew loved being upright, and he especially loved the gait trainer. But he was not interested in learning to walk – he wanted to run. By the end of summer, he was tooling around the classroom and exploring the playground, the gait trainer's saddle and trunk supports bearing what weight his legs couldn't handle. Matthew had progressed so far, in fact, that his parents decided to relocate their family to Bakersfield.

That first year Matthew grew several inches as his bones responded to the task of weight-bearing for the first time in his life. When he first started MOVE his head and hand control were extremely poor. He relied on his eyes for communication, looking up for *yes*, down for *no*. But it didn't take long before his head and trunk control improved, and he was able to sit in a supportive chair.

By the time Matthew was six, he was ready to start kindergarten. His body had made great strides; now it was time for him to flex his mind. There was no question Matthew was bright. His face lit up when someone cracked a joke (often before others got the punch line), and he knew how to express his desires by looking at whatever it was he wanted, then back at the person he wanted to bring it to him. In a regular kindergarten environment, he was able to join the other children for science projects, standing in his mobile stander, and for outdoor activities on the playground, using his gait trainer to keep up with the rest. Or to lead the pack, as he did on special days when the children went to the Rollerama for roller-skating.

Matthew started kindergarten half days, and stayed with us at Blair the other half of the time. As he grew his time in a regular school environment increased, and we saw less and less of him. Then we lost sight of him altogether. That is the way it's meant to be, I thought. We are only a bridge for kids like Matthew. The faster they cross over, the better. Even if it hurts to see them go...

Today Matthew is a high school student, fully integrated in a regular classroom. His fast-paced schedule (a class change every forty-five minutes, just like everyone else) means he's not able to navigate the halls with his gait trainer and has to rely on his wheelchair. But he still spends time each day on his feet, especially during PE, and does his homework while seated in his Rifton Advancement

Cheryl Mestmake[r]

Matthew Stramaglia and his buddies have the run
of the playground.

Chair. With swim therapy three times a week (he has grown too big to continue the horse-riding therapy he enjoyed in his younger years), he keeps himself – and his mother – busy. He is living life on the move, and shows no signs of slowing down.

Cha-Cha had been with me off and on since she entered the DCH as a three-year-old. A frail child with cerebral palsy and developmental delays, she had always been one of my special students. Her mother, Teresa, was near to my heart too (it was she whom I had called to mind to rescue me from my fears, that day on the steps at Pittsburg State). As Cha-Cha grew older I made sure she returned to my class. I wanted her with me, where I could help her. In those first years, though, I often found myself frustrated by how little I could do for her. Even while she was still a small child, her weight buckled her tiny knees and her toneless muscles could not support her head. Cha-Cha's head control – or lack of it – was so bad that when she allowed her head to sag, her ear actually rested on her chest. From the back, it looked like her head was gone. Her spine collapsed as though it were nonexistent, and she scared us to death.

I started her in a front-leaning chair, with forearm prompts for support. This stabilized her enough so she could work at holding her head up, at least for a few seconds. Each day we worked on these positioning exercises, and with time Cha-Cha developed stronger muscles and her head stopped flopping like a rag doll's.

At the age of seven Cha-Cha went through a growth spurt. The more she grew, the weaker she became. She was fast losing the few skills we'd tried to help her develop. Worse, she began refusing food and drink, and her weight was steadily decreasing. Teresa was distraught: she had to listen to people who blamed her for her daughter's decline. At school, however, we had no better luck getting Cha-Cha to eat or drink, and I knew if we didn't act fast we were going to have another (not-so-small) white coffin on our hands.

We put Cha-Cha in a traditional stander, but she let her head drop to the tray and we worried about compromising her breathing. Next, we tried placing her in a device that braced her body from trunk to toes, to improve her posture and support her while she ate and drank. This worked, as long as someone sat in front of her and held her forearms in the same position she used in her front-leaning chair.

By the time we were gearing up to pilot our mobility program in the summer of 1986, Cha-Cha was nine years old. She had grown bigger, and more sluggish. She was an obvious choice for our mobility pilot program. (It wouldn't have mattered what anyone else said anyway – she was my kid.) If nothing else, I thought, maybe we can do something to improve her health.

We got her upright in a mobile stander, and then moving her feet for the first time, in a gait trainer. Though she wasn't bearing her full weight, she responded to the new feeling of independent movement. After a few sessions, her level of activity increased. She seemed to emerge as if from a stupor. At mealtimes she accepted food and drink more willingly. Her health rounded a corner and began to improve. No longer dehydrated, she stopped losing weight.

I could not offer any medical explanation for her sudden turn for the better, but it was obvious that her system had been shutting down under her physical disabilities, and now that she was getting exercise while having fun, her body was giving itself a chance to fight back.

Cha-Cha did more than fight back. She started an offensive of her own, with mobility as her weapon of choice. Over time she learned to walk alone with the aid of the gait trainer, then with only a conventional walker, until she could walk with no support at all other than one hand on the arm of someone walking beside her. Now when Cha-Cha arrived at school, she could step down from the bus herself and be escorted to the entrance under her own steam – an achievement we highlighted in one of our early program

Cha-Cha, listening with all her heart.

videos, *Making Strides*. Right up until her last day of school, she kept practicing her skills and improving on them. The day Cha-Cha left, she was headed in one direction: forward.

Brian had a dream. But when his mother, who worked at a Kern County school, brought him to see us at Blair, he was through with therapy. A seventeen-year-old with cerebral palsy, there was nothing particularly striking about Brian. He had light brown hair and a narrow face, shaved. His thin frame folded into his wheelchair, which his hands were strong enough to propel. He spoke with difficulty, yet not unintelligibly. In short, he was a normal CP teen. He attended public high school and took special classes (Brian was a little learning disabled) but was integrated into regular classes with the other seniors wherever possible. Brian's physical condition made school strenuous, at best. Furthermore, he absolutely refused therapy. It was painful, and boring. He wanted to get on with his life without being poked and prodded, coaxed and cajoled at inconvenient intervals. He'd had to undergo abductor release surgery, a procedure in which the tendons of the legs are lengthened, and his legs had been placed in great, cumbersome casts that held them apart and made him uncomfortable. But the surgery hadn't stopped him from losing more ground, and now his hips were dislocating again. He was going to need more surgery – and he wasn't going to cooperate. That was when his mother, desperate, came to us and literally begged us to do something to keep Brian from having to go through another large surgery. We agreed to let Brian try MOVE for a few weeks. She brought him in, and I gave him his first top-down test, to establish his capabilities. That done, I asked him, What do you wish you could do today that you can't? It was his chance to share his dream, but he let it ride.

Brian told his mom instead. (He was, she explained, too embarrassed to tell me.) He says he wants to be able to stand up and pee like a man, not sitting down like a girl, she said. Well, I told her, I'm glad we're asking these questions, because I sure wouldn't have thought of that one.

We task-analyzed, and Brian started the MOVE program. Back when he was a small child Brian had been able to stand, but he had not been out of his wheelchair in years. With daily practice, though, Brian learned to raise himself from his wheelchair to a standing position, and then to stand unassisted for a minute or two. His knees kinked and he tottered a little on his feet, but he held his ground. He was over five-and-a-half feet tall when standing.

Two months after Brian began MOVE, he and his parents were having dinner together at a local steak house. During the meal, Brian excused himself, wheeled himself into the men's room – not the one with the wheelchair on the door, but the one with the urinals.

Last night, his mother told me the next day, Brian became a man. He came back from that rest room a changed person.

I congratulated Brian in a quiet way, and told him, We still have a few months left before you graduate high school. What else would you like to work on? His eyes lit up as he said, I've been thinking. And what I really want to do is walk across the stage to get my diploma. My first thought: Uh-oh. And then: All right. So he walks with equipment, with his great big gait trainer. So I have to go down and fight about having it on stage. So we put a few people off. Big deal. This is Brian's goal, not theirs.

Except, that wasn't Brian's goal. Oh, no. Where I saw Brian trucking across the stage with the aid of his gait trainer, he envisioned himself walking across the stage. Crossing the stage on his own, *walking*.

Graduation might be only weeks away, but that made no difference to Brian. He wasn't afraid of hard work. We helped him to his feet. His knees wobbled. We held our breath as his body lurched with every precarious step he tried. He fell down. We picked him up, and he kept going. He worked until time was up.

On graduation night Brian was in line with the other seniors. He was in his wheelchair down in front of the auditorium's stage. From my seat alongside his parents back in the audience, I watched him. He was concentrating hard, I could tell. Carefully Brian got up out of his wheelchair. He held his hands out to steady himself. The contractures in his knees kept him from straightening, but he held his balance as, with a hand on the railing and his eyes on his feet, he climbed the stage steps. And then slowly, very slowly, Brian walked across the stage. I was aware of the silence all around me as Brian reached center stage, and (just like we'd practiced) reached out his right hand to shake the administrator's and accept his diploma. Then, very carefully, he shuffled his feet until he was standing with his shoulders squared to the audience. Brian looked out into the crowd, raised his hand, and moved his tassel across his mortarboard. And then the whole place fell apart. Three thousand people rose to their feet, cheering and shrieking for Brian in spontaneous pandemonium.

They understood. They had got it. Every single person in that auditorium knew that Brian had graduated with a real education, one worth more than any transcript or SAT score – an education that would carry him through life. They understood that this was Brian's moment. This was about his pride, about his tough haul. For a moment, they shared a glimpse of his dream.

When the world does that, I reflected later, then I can say, Yes, this is worth it. Yes, we can do this. It helps me put out of mind the cramped ideas of petty spoilsports, like the one who insisted to me that children should not get on their feet until they're ready to walk "normally" – which for my kids, he agreed, meant never. To people like that I can say (at least in my head), Who in the hell do you think you are? And I know Brian will be saying it right along with me.

Of course, I'm waiting for the day I'll never have to ask anyone who the hell they think they are. I dream of the day MOVE will be so common, it will be like Kleenex – taken for granted. No one will think of living a life without it, just as none of us would think of not blowing our nose. Who would just stand there and let the ooze drooze?

One day MOVE will be so common, it will never occur to anyone to think whether a child should try to sit, stand, or walk. It will simply be assumed that sitting, standing, and walking are part of everyday life, for everyone. It will be automatic that we get kids out of wheelchairs – and certainly out of beanbags and off the floor – for at least part of every day. Until then I will allow the child in me to dream, because I know so many children who dream right along with me.

promises kept

The morning comes when I wake to the sounds of Tanya's last-minute packing. She's leaving home, and she seems genuinely excited about it. I think back to the day I left the farm for college, and know how grown up she must be feeling. I know, too, how my mother must have felt. Tawny's going to be fine, I tell myself. Despite my years of sleepless nights, her scars are limited to a few hoofprints on her shins. She doesn't drop out of school, pierce too many body parts, or die in a car crash the night of her senior prom.

Ever since her bug-grubbing days as a three-year-old, Tanya's been marked by dirt: it's one of the universe's little jokes, this mother-daughter combination. For four years of high school, and three more at Bakersfield Junior College, Tanya takes agriculture classes. She earns her associate's degree in animal science, and plans to specialize in bovine reproduction. She's Grandpa's girl, through and through. We are so similar, she and I – and so distinct. Dirt is her choice. Now, as she leaves me, to further her education at Fresno State University, I can't help feeling proud: Tanya's making her own decisions, becoming the woman I always dreamed she'd be.

Then she is gone and, happy as I am for her, I can't deny the half-empty feeling in my stomach. Or the strange sensation of having suddenly aged. I struggle to adjust to the silence of the house, the eerie loudness of the TV in the empty den. I am growing nostalgic, turning into a sap, I admonish myself; yet I can't seem to help it, or to want to. She is gone, and with her a part of me.

The horses are gone too. Tanya hasn't ridden much these last years, not since Jim's death. She tried, as much for his sake as for her enjoyment, but it couldn't last. She had ridden because of him, and loved it thanks to him. When he died, the spark went out. We still went to a few more events – the Rose Parade, again – because Jim had already made the arrangements. I drove the seven-horse rig down to Pasadena (parallel-parked it, too) and walked down the line of horses with a syringe of Ace – nice horsey, nice horsey, nice horsey, *whap!* – tranquilizing every one of those puppies so that by parade time their noses nearly kissed the ground. There were no mishaps that day. But there wasn't much magic either. The magic had belonged to Jim, and he was gone.

Tanya spends three years at Fresno. The bovine reproduction talk falls by the wayside – a lab for a meat science class takes her inside a processing plant, and she is in love. Cattle, pigs, and lambs are led into the lab, but exit in compact little packages. It's the whole process, Tanya explains – it's just fascinating. Uh-huh, Tawnie, I think as I cringe at my memories of butchering days on the farm.

She comes home once or twice a month, and we call each other every day when I'm not on the road. MOVE and SoftTouch keep me busy. I love programming and making characters wiggle and dance on the screen. I love watching the children take control of their own lives by controlling the computer. Life is good. I am happy.

My other baby, MOVE, is growing up too. Rather than promoting the program, I have expended great amounts of energy chasing after it, trying to keep up, just as I have tried to keep up with Tanya. MOVE has swept across the United States, where since 1994 we've trained over ten thousand people in the program's essentials. The curriculum has been translated into ten languages. And as MOVE spreads beyond our borders, I am doing my best to stay abreast of its development. The last thing I want is to be a bottleneck hindering our program's growth.

Even so, when I first meet Hanaa Helmy, an Egyptian determined to bring MOVE to the Middle East, I am unconvinced. Hanaa and her husband spent years in the United States before moving to Kuwait, where she recognized the need for MOVE. Do we really need to spread so far afield? I wonder. That is, until Hanaa sits me down and tells me about the Kuwaiti children she has in mind. They are just like the ones who live in Bakersfield, California. My children. So I make a deal with her. I will funnel information her way if she will arrange its dissemination on her end.

It sounded like a lopsided deal, in my favor. I'd click the mouse, she'd do the donkeywork. I should have known better...

Today, I have dined with intellectuals, and supped with royalty. I have received an honorary fellowship from England's University of Wolverhampton and visited Prince Charles at St. James's Palace to formalize the relationship between MOVE Europe and The Disability Partnership, a charity he presides over. Every year, it seems, MOVE meets new challenges and opportunities. One door closes, ten more open. And I try to keep up, to let go. To be a good mother.

In 1998 Tanya graduates from Fresno State with a bachelor's degree in animal science, and is thrilled to land a job with a specialty meat company. But it takes an advanced course on sausage-making at Iowa State for her to find her truest love. Her company sends her to the weeklong wurstfest, to learn what she can about sausage skins. The first morning, she doesn't get her wakeup call and oversleeps. Embarrassed, she fusses with her hair and waits on the curb outside her hotel for the university shuttle. The van pulls up, and there are good-humored ribbings from the driver about the nature and length of the previous night's party as Tanya buckles up in the first bench seat. There is a man in the passenger's seat beside the driver, but he does not turn around. Not right away. When he does – to acknowledge a joke Tanya's made – he is wearing sunglasses. He affects a snooty *Pardon me* and slides his glasses, librarian-style, down the bridge of his well-made nose. His eyes are magnets – the most beautiful magnets Tanya has ever seen – and she finds herself drawn in by their pull.

Eighteen months later, I have a son-in-law. Tanya Ellen Bidabe marries Gaines Fulghum on October 30, 1999 – and there isn't a thing I can do about it. As Gaines tells me: The first time I saw Tanya, I thought to myself, There you are! I've been looking for you all my life... Luckily for me (and for Gaines, too, I guess), I love him from the start. Thief that he is.

Tanya and Gaines marry in Bakersfield. It is a beautiful, white wedding, with a horse-drawn carriage and wonderful friends from everywhere. Daddy misses the wedding, and that's okay. We all know Daddy won't leave the farm, no matter what. It doesn't matter, not really. We know he loves us. Within the realm of his farm, Daddy loves us.

Everyone else comes and we have a ball, even though I can't hide my nervousness – I'm still waiting for the fatal car crash. Tanya has taken care of every detail. Her wedding goes smoothly, and I am left feeling like a sunning butterfly just out of the cocoon. I have done well; it's my time to fly. But I don't want change. Like Daddy, I want to keep the things I love right next to me, but my loves are moving to Arkansas where Gaines will put his own meat science degree to work.

And then Daddy is ill. Tanya is hardly married, and Daddy is ill. Really ill. We have known about his prostate cancer for almost a year. He's been to see specialists, who've told him that, as a rule, prostrate cancer seldom kills – old age takes over first. Daddy isn't old to us.

He hangs on until Mama gets home from the wedding. Then a tumor wraps around his spinal cord and his legs cannot support him. He is the exception to the rule. Typical Daddy.

Allen calls me. Dad isn't doing well, Linda. We don't really know what to do. We think you need to come home.

He is a shadow in pajamas, this big man whose square-cut jaw now anchors canvas-colored cheeks. *Hi, Daddy. It's good to see you.*

We do what we can to make him comfortable. The cancer won't let him pee. I arrange for a catheter. His back bothers him. We plump his pillows. He says thank you, though the pain shows on his face.

Daddy has changed. It's been five years since Mary moved back to Kansas to help care for him, and time has worked wonders. Time brought Mary home. She wanted to be close to Mama and Daddy once again; and her new husband, Paul, wanted a shot at a farmer's life. They live in Lowell, a few blocks from our school (it's a nursing home now) and minutes from the flood farm. It's still Daddy's farm, and Paul is wise enough to know this, even as he gets on about the task of keeping it running. *What'll it be today, Mac?* For Daddy, there is time for thought. For steps back and long looks. For regrets. Time to try on new words. *I'm sorry. I love you.* They are five years for slowing down and winding down. For binding up and stitching back together the fabric of family, patching the fraying of the years. Mary is our leader in this, pulling us all together. Nothing has changed, and everything has changed.

I notice other changes too. The deepened sag of the old barn's roof. The hollow places between the ribs that show through the yellow bristle-haired coat of Fuzzy, Daddy's favorite mongrel. The thin cracks in the concrete sides of the swimming pool. (Paul says he's been meaning to patch them, but hasn't gotten around to it yet.) The farm has aged. The river, though, is as it has always been. The same brown water, swirling as though in troubled sleep, sweeping by. The river, somnambulant, unchanged in its bed.

Daddy cannot sleep. He drifts off, wakes in a sweat, wants a drink. He is in the master bedroom – the one he shared with Mama for an eternity. It's a big room with a second bed moved in because of Daddy's illness. Mama rises to tend to him. The long nights wear her down. I'll take a turn, I tell her, and we trade beds. She goes to the guest room. Thank goodness.

Two o'clock. His waking wakes me. He doesn't say anything, just lies awake. You okay, Dad? I ask. What time is it? he wants to know. I tell him. Then we talk for a while. He is snared in memories, regrets clinging to them. He speaks of raising us, and how he'd do things differently if given a second chance. I'm sorry, he tells me. He is sorry for many things. I tell him I wish I'd been less scared for Tanya. I wish I had just enjoyed her more. She is a wonderful person, I say, and he agrees.

He remembers Two Bits, the stray that followed Mary home, like a little lamb, and that Grandpa had named, on first sighting: That dog isn't worth two bits... In the middle of the night, Daddy and I talk about Two Bits, about how he was the smartest dog we ever had. How he could catch wasps between his teeth and never once get stung. How he climbed trees, just for the heck of it. And how he'd sit by the edge of our pond, still as a stone, and wait for minnows to swim by, to snap up and gobble down. We remember the day Two Bits saved the life of a child who fibbed to us about his swimming prowess. We remember how smart he was (the dog) for swimming to the boy in distress when no one else had noticed, and for letting the child cling to his fur while he paddled to safety. And we remember Two Bit's last afternoon, chasing butterflies out in a hay field Daddy was mowing. Neither saw the other until it was too late – the sickle bar bit into Two Bit's back legs and sliced through bone. Daddy shut off the tractor in the field and raced for the house. He ran back, cradling his shotgun, and with tears in his eyes laid its barrel against Two Bit's head and squeezed the trigger. We remember our tears for Two Bits, and add a few more, in memoriam. You didn't do it on purpose, I tell him. It wasn't your fault.

Like so many other things. How do I tell him? How do I bring him to realize that he is my Daddy, for always?

It is the first hours of a new day, still too early for the first strip of gray light to leak under the window blinds. We lie in our separate wakefulness. I'm sorry for some of the things I did when I was younger, he says again, and I wonder from the way he says it if he is speaking to me or to the darkness. I know, Daddy, I tell him. I think all parents wish they'd done some things differently. And I speak whatever words I can find, knowing they are trite, yet glad nonetheless to be saying them. *It doesn't matter. You were a good dad. You did your best. We're all alive. We're all okay. Our kids are turning out okay. You've done a good job. It doesn't matter. I love you, Daddy.*

I am part of him. And I want to tell him that he is part of me, that we are not so different. I have my fears, too, and they are not unlike his own. As my father's breathing steadies into sleep and, finally, fills the room with a measured pulse, I brood into my own secret places.

Buster is there, waiting for me. Buster, who is a grown man now, married, and at home in a world more stable than my own. I am linked to him for always, through a painted Coca-Cola bottle, and through my childhood fears of Daddy.

It happened at the beginning of third grade, when the memory of the pie-box supper still soured my mouth like a canker sore. Mama took me to Baxter Springs, to the store where we could get all the things on the school's list for new third graders. I was excited – this year I would have real textbooks, not just the exercise sheets and notebooks that I had toted to class each day of my first two years of education. Real hardbound books. New ones, most of them. We paid cash, and went home. I sat at the kitchen table, eager to thumb through fresh pages and record my name in the front of my books. I picked my math book off the top of the stack. It wasn't new, but almost. The cover was still clean and shiny, and the corners didn't curve in; that's why I'd picked it from the pile at the store. I flipped open the cover, my pen at the ready. There was no mistaking the printed letters under Student's Name: BUSTER HOPKINS. Plain as day. I stared, to be sure, then eased the book shut quietly and sneaked it to the bottom of the stack. Maybe it will just go away, I thought as bile rose up in my throat. But when I finished with my other books, it was still there. And my terror had not subsided. *What if Daddy picks it up and looks inside!* Mama, I whispered – and showed her. I'll take care of it, she said. And the book was gone. Mama got me another one. I didn't care about the corners anymore. Mama saved me, for the price of a secret.

Across the room, Daddy is deep in sleep. Drowning in it, I think. No. Not my daddy. He is too strong, too powerful a swimmer. Daddy is the river, I decide. He has always been our river – at times choleric and unpredictable, yet strong and deep and quick to move on. I study the brown water of Daddy's river, with fear as its surface tension, and catch my own reflection. Love connects us, love and fear.

It is the hour when, as a girl, I would often wake before my sisters and lie with the covers tight around my shoulders, feigning sleep until Mama or Daddy came in and hollered for us to get out of bed. After nights when my nightmares were at their worst, I counted on this time of grace for reparation. It allowed time for the blood to drain from dreams of Daddy slaughtering cows, for the balance of color to be restored to the world. Sometimes, I dreamed of Two Bits, of his eyes, at the end. There was also the rabbit I had killed. Its mother, one of my 4-H does, had chewed off all its legs. There was no way it could survive, and I couldn't stand to watch its pain. I filled a bucket with water and held the little pink ball under until its twitching stopped. When I lifted it out, it lay slack and damp in my hand, water trickling off its rubbery skin and between my fingers. Its blood stayed on my hands.

These are the memories that cut into me like shards of broken bottle glass as my father lies dying. I do not know why. They are not thoughts I carry with me on normal days. But these are not normal days, and so I am left to ponder such things as, Could I have saved that rabbit? Could I have stitched its wounds the way Mama sewed up Patty and Stinky? Maybe, just maybe, it might have healed, and I could have built some sort of motorized bunny-mobile, like Daddy's contraption for Drunken Hinds. Maybe I didn't try hard enough. Maybe I was too afraid.

There is light on the floor beneath the window now, a thin line of watery gray light. Snake light. It's eighteen years ago, but it comes slithering back. We were at the farm, Tanya and I, trying to start again from the ground up; but first to dig ourselves out from the wreckage of my collapsed marriage. It was summer, and oppressively hot. Mosquitoes clung in ambush to the screen door, and inside the TV scrolled its storm-watch warnings. Outdoors the snakes slid from ponds and ditches and made themselves bold. They slunk onto flat rocks to soak up the warmth, or shimmied through the long weeds that choked the dusty roadsides. They were everywhere. Inside of me, even. I ventured out with Tanya, for a walk away from ourselves. It was no use. The snakes were there before us. One in particular, a five-foot-long, oily mud snake, its musk like skunk cabbage lifting from the damp gash of ground where it lulled. On an impulse, I reached among the hedge brush and found a forked branch dead enough to break when I pulled it down. I snapped the forks short. Then I reached back into the bushes again and found a branch for Tanya, with some heft to it. I pronged my forked stick into the mud just behind the head of the snake and pressed it home.

The snake came alive and thrashed vigorously, but I had it pinned. Go, Tanya, go! I urged as she raised her stick and took aim at the snake's head. I cheered her on as, blow by blow, she bashed its poor little single-digit neurons to death. *She will not be afraid. She will know she is bigger than snakes, and stronger, and in control. And she will not be afraid. Not like me. This is for her. For both of us.* When we were done, its reptilian body still wriggled. Mud already had begun to dry on its yellow underbelly. I caught the snake up with my forked stick and pitched it into the bushes. It snagged and hung swinging. I took Tanya's hand and walked away. I, Dorothy Linda McPherson Bidabe, who had nightmares about butchering cows, had killed something on purpose. And I am still ashamed.

I have to leave. There is no way around it. For months my trip to Kuwait has been in the offing. MOVE is indeed international – there are schools using our curriculum in Canada, Mexico, South America, Europe, Pakistan, Russia, Israel, Japan, New Zealand, Australia, the Netherlands, and perhaps other places we're not even aware of – and now Kuwait wants to start a program. There will be meetings with oil sheiks and emirs, whose nod will open or close coffers, and with children and families whose faces I have never seen but whose stories I have heard a thousand times. This is one trip I cannot cancel. Too much is at stake, for too many people. *I have to go, Daddy. I'm sorry, but I have to leave. I'll come back. I promise.* Don't you worry about me, he says. I'm so proud of what you're doing. I'm proud of you, Linda.

He waits to die until I am back in the United States. I am sure of it. My plane gets into Bakersfield on Friday, the day after Thanksgiving 1999. The next day he lets go.

The family rallies around Mama, strong for her. We pass around memories like cookie platters and serve Coca-Cola to the friends who stop by to pay their respects and remember Mac. He will be missed, they tell us with well-meant ceremony. Among ourselves, we laugh and joke and remember the best of times. Cry, too, in between.

And then it is over. He is cremated, as was his wish. His ashes will be interred in the cemetery on the edge of Lowell, not far from Buster Hopkin's childhood home. First, though, we take his urn to Allen and Shari's house for a family wake. It sits at the center of their dining room table. Daddy in a jar. Small enough to be a bomb, or a womb.

We are all there: Allen and Shari and their girls, Pam, Kim, and Meagan; Minta and Gavin; Mary and Paul and Minta Lauren; Tanya and Gaines; Mama and me. We mix drinks – strip-and-go-nakeds, Daddy's favorite – and toast his memory. I am surprised at our laughter, how much of it there is, and how freely it comes. We are standing in a sort of unintentional horseshoe, with Daddy included in our arc. Tanya raises her glass and asks for our attention. I'm not sure when we'll be together again like this, she begins, so Gaines and I have an announcement to make. She tries to go on, but her voice cracks and she stops to collect herself. We wait for her. This isn't like Tanya, I think. She's always been comfortable in the spotlight. Mary tries to help: What, you're pregnant? It's a joke. Tanya nods. Yes.

Gaines and I are at her side now, hugging her as she speaks. *It's early still, but we didn't want to wait to tell everyone. The doctor picked up its heartbeat the day Grandpa died. You understand, don't you?*

Nathan Allen Fulghum is born July 22, 2000. I am there when his perfect little body emerges from Tanya. I am there to see the look on Tanya's face the first time she holds her son to her. He is the first child on earth, and she is his mother. Gaines and I face each other, in awe.

He will learn to ride, Tanya says, to sit straight in the saddle. I'll be a good mom, she tells me. I've had a great teacher...

Beginnings and endings are nothing new. For me, though, it seems beginnings outnumber endings these days, and I'm glad for that. I have a lot left to learn, a lot of work still to do. MOVE has taken off beyond my wildest imaginings, and each new week brings word of some fresh development. Where will it end? I wonder – and hope it never does.

Still, in spite of everything, there are days when my other life niggles at my consciousness and tries to bait me into mind games of *what if*. Thankfully, I've learned to count on Mama's voice to rescue me: If you'd gone to med school, Linda, you'd probably be just another doctor worrying about malpractice insurance, or working your tail off for an HMO. And all of this would never have happened.

She means the work my heart has given itself to, and the progress we've made. But I mean, also, the link between us, between the generations of people I love: dirt-farmers, home-makers, heart-breakers, fear-tamers. I mean Scuffy and Edgar, Rene and Jenny, Tommy and Charlie Bear – all of them, every last one of my children. It is this – all of this – that gives me purpose and keeps me going. This is my life.

So far.

the author

Linda Bidabe (M.S., Pittsburg State University, Kansas, 1981) has done postgraduate work at the University of Tennessee, California State University, and Macquarie University (Sydney), and has earned international acclaim for her groundbreaking work in the field of special education, particularly in founding and developing MOVE. A Division Administrator for California's Kern County Superintendent of Schools, she is an Honorary Fellow of the University of Wolverhampton, England, and a regular speaker at educational conferences around the world. Linda lives in Bakersfield, California.

To learn more about the MOVE program and how you can become involved, visit *www.move-international.org* or contact one of the following addresses:

MOVE International
1300 17th Street
City Centre
Bakersfield CA 93301
(Tel.) 1-800-397-6683

MOVE International
University of Wolverhampton
Gorway Road
Walsall WS1 3BD
United Kingdom

acknowledgments

My appreciation goes to all the parents and children I have worked with, who have taught me far more than I ever taught them; to my wonderful family and friends in Kansas; and to my co-author, Chris Voll, who helped me tell our story. I'm also grateful to the harrumphers who, over the years, made me stop and explain the philosophy of MOVE "one more time" – because still today, some things have to be believed to be seen.

Thanks also to Karel and Berta Bobath, the founders of Neuro-Developmental Treatment (NDT); to Nancie Finnie, author of *Handling the Young Child with Cerebral Palsy at Home;* to Dick Towse, the former principal, and the entire staff at the Harry E. Blair Learning Center, where MOVE was conceived; to the MOVE International and Site Trainers; to the people at the Kern County Superintendent of Schools Office, and to Drs. Kelly Blanton and Larry Reider, two superintendents with vision; to David Schreuder, Administrative Director of MOVE International USA; to Sheron Renfro, MOVE Program Specialist; to Peter Holland, CEO of England's Disability Partnership; to Jo Meyer, my partner in creating SoftTouch software. These remarkable people have dedicated themselves to providing unprecedented possibilities for all individuals with disabilities.